Praise for

12

TOM BRADY AND HIS BATTLE FOR REDEMPTION

"Casey Sherman and Dave Wedge's *12* delivers what the title promises...First-timers to the absurdity of the endlessly baffling Deflategate investigation should be able to follow it easily. That was no small feat in real time. Sherman and Wedge steer readers through it all without leaving anything essential out or dumbing things down."   —David Steele, *Washington Post*

"An astute history...The authors' balanced treatment of the quarterback is refreshing, making this a welcome addition to many a football fan's library."   —*Publishers Weekly*

"Authors Casey Sherman and Dave Wedge lay bare an incredible tale laced with hatred, deceit, mistrust, and petty grievances...For any football fan, *12* is an interesting and revealing look at the NFL and one of its premier players. For the New England fan, it is an oh-so-sweet tale of revenge and resurrection of the reputation of one of the greatest players to ever grace a football field...*12* takes us places in this amazing Patriots' story where we've never been before."   —Dave Kindy, *Providence Journal*

"Giving readers a close look into Tom Brady, his marriage to Gisele, and his bounce back after Deflategate, this book explores the relationship between the NFL and its players through dozens of exclusive interviews, including with Brady himself."

—Today.com

"Just how Brady attempted to defend himself in court and his redemptive return to lead the Patriots to a Super Bowl triumph is retold in detail in *12,* the book title that bears Brady's jersey number."

—Ross Atkin, *Christian Science Monitor*

"A shocking new tell-all."   —Melissa Roberto, *Radar Online*

"Expect sports-talk radio to be buzzing over this one."   —*Booklist*

"This is the Deflategate book that needed to be written… There is plenty for the average NFL fan to enjoy."

—Jeff Berckes, *Windy City Gridiron*

12

12

TOM BRADY AND HIS BATTLE FOR REDEMPTION

CASEY SHERMAN and DAVE WEDGE

BACK BAY BOOKS

Little, Brown and Company

New York Boston London

Back Bay Books / Little, Brown and Company
Hachette Book Group
1290 Avenue of the Americas, New York, NY 10104
littlebrown.com

Originally published in hardcover by Little, Brown and Company, July 2018
First Back Bay paperback edition, September 2020

Back Bay Books is an imprint of Little, Brown and Company, a division of Hachette Book Group, Inc. The Back Bay Books name and logo are trademarks of Hachette Book Group, Inc.

The publisher is not responsible for websites (or their content) that are not owned by the publisher.

The Hachette Speakers Bureau provides a wide range of authors for speaking events. To find out more, go to hachettespeakersbureau.com or call (866) 376-6591.

ISBN 978-0-316-41638-2 (hc) / 978-0-316-41642-9 (pb)
LCCN 2018939664

Printing 2, 2021

LSC-C

Printed in the United States of America

For Kristin. You have my love for always.
And for my uncle Jim Sherman, one of the greatest
sportsmen I've ever known.
                                      —*Casey Sherman*

For Dad. Thank you for making me love football, the
fall, and snow games.
                                      —*Dave Wedge*

CONTENTS

Part IV

Part V

PREFACE TO THE PAPERBACK EDITION

Gillette Stadium. January 4, 2020.

A blanket of drizzle and fog swallowed Gillette Stadium in the final moments of the New England Patriots' shocking playoff loss to the upstart Tennessee Titans. Pinned inside his end zone and trailing by one point with only fourteen seconds to play, forty-two-year-old quarterback Tom Brady took the shotgun snap from his backup center Ted Karras, faded back over the team's painted "Flying Elvis" logo, and scanned the field quickly for an open receiver. He eyed wideout Mohamed Sanu Sr. and tried to force it into tight coverage by Titans safety Tramaine Brock. The ball bounced off Sanu and into the waiting arms of defensive back Logan Ryan, a former Brady teammate, who galloped untouched across the goal line for the deciding score.

Brady unbuckled his chin strap in disgust and marched off the field feeling both deflated and defeated. Glancing up through the mist and rain at the concrete towers at the far end of the field, he could barely make out the six giant championship banners that had marked his career in Foxboro. The evening's weather was eerily similar to the conditions that Brady had masterfully overcome five years before when he demolished the Indianapolis Colts on this same field to secure a trip to the Super Bowl against the Seattle Seahawks. He'd win that game and go on to collect two more championship rings, giving him six altogether and ending any discussion about who was the greatest player to ever play the position.

Despite the wet weather, fans remained standing by their seats, craning their necks to catch a glimpse of the superstar quarterback, a real life version of the mythical Roy Hobbs wearing the team's uniform perhaps for the last time, and likely thinking to themselves, *There goes Tom Brady, the best there ever was.*

Having just experienced the cruelest curtain call, a pick six on the final play of the season, Brady would be making no rallying cry to his teammates about reloading for a seventh championship run next year. In Brady's mind, he knew he was done. This inevitability had been creeping into his head since that Colts game in 2015 when his coach had first betrayed him.

Farther downfield, wearing a scowl under a navy blue hoodie drenched with rain and sweat, Bill Belichick stared at his aging quarterback and wished he could turn back the clock, not to any special milestone in Brady's storied career but to the moment when his own power was usurped and his hand was forced to deal his young signal caller Jimmy Garoppolo to the San Francisco 49ers. Had he stood up to his boss, owner Bob Kraft, then, the coach felt that he would have been in a better position to take his team deeper into the playoffs in 2020.

Belichick took the call from San Francisco's first-year general manager John Lynch just before the trade deadline in late October 2017. The coach's phone had been buzzing all season long as NFL executives were hungry to get their hands on Garoppolo, the young quarterback whom Belichick had plucked from Eastern Illinois University three years before in the second round of the

2014 NFL draft. The coach's plan was for Garoppolo to serve as an apprentice under Brady before ultimately replacing him as the Patriots' starting quarterback. John Lynch contacted Belichick at his office at Gillette Stadium following the team's 21–3 win over the LA Chargers. Lynch, a former star defensive back with the Tampa Bay Buccaneers, was as aggressive in his role as general manager as he had been as a player. After a quick hello, he asked Belichick if he was interested in trading Tom Brady's promising young backup.

"Well, would you be interested in Brady instead?" Belichick responded.

Lynch was stunned. Tom Brady was fresh off his MVP performance in the comeback win against the Atlanta Falcons in Super Bowl LI and showed no sign of slowing down even at the age of forty. For Lynch, this could be the deal of a lifetime. He'd dreamed of the idea of bringing Brady, a Bay Area native, home to finish out his legendary career, but it was just that—a dream.

Now Belichick was putting an offer on the table. It was an offer that Lynch couldn't refuse.

While other GMs were still talking about Brady's historic performance in the fourth quarter against the Falcons, Belichick focused his attention on the first three quarters of that classic game when his aging quarterback made uncharacteristic mistakes, moving slowly in the pocket and overthrowing his receivers. The Patriots' coach studied the game film during the offseason long after the confetti was swept away from the team's victory parade. Sure, Brady had miraculously summoned the will to fight back and win that game, but could he be counted on to do it again approaching age forty-one?

No, thought Belichick. The time to move on from the quarterback legend was right now.

"Let me call you back," he told Lynch.

The coach wasted no time. He marched toward Bob Kraft's

office, where he found him seated behind his large, unkempt desk. On the opposite side stood the owner's son Jonathan, his wiry arms folded across his narrow chest. The younger Kraft was dressed in a shirt and tie with a pair of wire-rimmed glasses pinching the bridge of his nose. Jonathan could be mistaken for your local CPA, while his father, in sharp contrast, wore silk pants and sneakers, looking more and more like his friend Elton John than one of the most powerful owners in professional sports. But together both father and son had built a vast empire and owed much of their success to their former sixth-round draft pick out of the University of Michigan.

Belichick, the most unsentimental of coaches, had jettisoned popular players before, including many of those who had formed the foundation of the first half of the Patriots dynasty such as NFL Hall of Famer Ty Law, defensive end Willie McGinest, and legendary kicker Adam Vinatieri. But even Belichick knew this situation was very different. There would be no statue erected at the gates of Gillette Stadium for those other players. There is no doubt that one day, Tom Brady's bronze likeness will stand sentry in Foxboro as a glorious reminder of the greatest championship run in pro football history.

Belichick sat down with the Krafts and methodically walked them through the possible trade. As the head of football operations, he always had final say over which player to move and which player to bring in. The coach focused on Brady's advanced age and the deterioration (to his mind) of the quarterback's skills. Possibly he even cited history during his sales pitch and pointed out the situation in San Francisco when the 49ers had let Joe Montana go in favor of the younger Steve Young. As difficult as that deal had been at the time, it resulted in another Super Bowl win for the 49ers under Young, who would go on to have a Hall of Fame career of his own.

Jonathan Kraft remained silent while Belichick spoke. Normally he'd chime in first to question or offer support for the coach's decision. But this move would have to be approved by Bob Kraft himself. Like a Roman emperor, the owner could give a thumbs-up or thumbs-down, thus sealing the fate of his franchise for years to come. Kraft had worked diligently to repair his own fractured relationship with Brady, whom he loved like a son. His heart leaned toward keeping TB12 in New England for the rest of his career. His head also agreed. Tom Brady filled every seat in Gillette Stadium and was the main reason most fans flocked to the miniature city of shops and restaurants adjacent to the field called Patriot Place. The quarterback was the Krafts' cash cow, and letting him go now was unthinkable. The owner shot down Belichick's idea as quickly as a missile shooting down an enemy aircraft. The head coach didn't even have time to blink.

Belichick left the owner's office, seething. He got on the phone and told John Lynch that the deal was off.

As in any kingdom, the fortress walls of Foxboro had ears, and Brady quickly learned about Belichick's plot to send him into the pro football wilderness. But TB12 had his own card to play. The quarterback rushed to the owner and urged that a trade still be made with San Francisco, not for him, but for his young understudy.

Despite his genius, Belichick could be petulant and unforgiving at times. He had groomed Garoppolo from a second-round pick out of a small school to a highly touted superstar in waiting. By inserting Jimmy successfully into the lineup and making another Super Bowl run, the coach would prove once and for all that he was the one most deserving of credit for the Patriots dynasty. That dream was dashed now. The coach redialed John Lynch and told him that Garoppolo was available.

The San Francisco general manager was without a quality quarterback and ready to pay a hefty ransom for Jimmy G., but instead Belichick was willing to move him for next to nothing.

NFL insiders had previously speculated that there was no way that the Patriots would part with Garoppolo for anything less than a high first-round pick. Belichick stunned the sports world the next day when news leaked out of Foxboro that Garoppolo had been traded for no more than a second-round draft choice. Amazingly, Belichick managed to cannibalize his own needs and the needs of his team to exact some kind of retribution against the owner for backing Brady. But by this time, treachery had become commonplace inside Fortress Foxboro.

Prologue

SAN FRANCISCO, CALIFORNIA

May 19, 2015

New England Patriots owner Robert Kraft strode to the podium dressed smartly in a blue suit, blue dress shirt with contrasting white collar, and a red tie. It was a look fans had become accustomed to. In fact, Kraft had worn the attire for his nearly two decades sitting in the owner's box at Gillette Stadium and other modern-day coliseums while watching his team evolve into the greatest sports dynasty of the twenty-first century.

On May 19, 2015, Kraft had joined his fellow NFL owners at the San Francisco Ritz-Carlton for their spring meetings to discuss, among other things, the league's potential return to Los Angeles for the first time in twenty-one years. The owners—nineteen billionaires, including Kraft—sat through updates on competing stadium proposals, and while this topic was of interest to sports reporters in L.A., San Diego, and even St. Louis, the real focus of attention centered on the eroding relationship between Robert Kraft and Roger Goodell, commissioner of the National Football League. Ever since the league had accused New England of deliberately deflating footballs during the AFC championship game against the Indianapolis Colts, the two men had been locked in a bitter battle over the future of Patriots quarterback Tom Brady.

When Kraft arrived in the city two days earlier, the normally affable owner politely stiff-armed Boston reporters who were seeking any new nugget of information about the feud. The next day, he went on the record with *Sports Illustrated* columnist Pete King, calling the league's treatment of Brady unfounded and unfair. When asked whether he'd sue the league in an effort to save his quarterback's reputation, Kraft wouldn't confirm or deny taking such drastic action. The media prepared for a thermonuclear showdown between two of the most powerful men in the most popular sport in America.

But on the morning of May 19, ESPN reporter and respected league insider Adam Schefter turned the doomsday narrative on its head in a tweet that read, Roger Goodell and Patriots owner Robert Kraft already have met, spoke and even hugged, per an industry source who witnessed it. The headline was re-tweeted 738 times along with comments comparing their embrace to Michael Corleone's kiss of death planted on the lips of his traitor brother Fredo in *The Godfather Part II*. Was this Kraft's strategy? To keep his friends close but his enemies closer?

Moments later, Schefter added that the two perceived enemies had attended a sixtieth-birthday party for Sean McManus, chairman of CBS Sports, in New York City that past weekend and that Kraft and Goodell were "spotted on a couch, talking by themselves for quite a long time."

Schefter's tweets immediately transformed the lobby of the Ritz into a land of confusion as veteran reporters scratched their heads and texted their editors about this potential thaw in the NFL's most recent cold war.

A few hours later, their suspicions were confirmed when Kraft walked out to face a media ravenous for information. The owner shifted his feet and stared down at his prepared comments. He began the news conference by acknowledging the emotionally charged statements made in recent weeks by both Patriots fans and those who openly called for the proud franchise's painful demise. Kraft then complained about the "ongoing rhetoric that continues to galvanize both camps." It appeared as if the NFL had been split up into blue and red states, with partisans on both sides holding their ground and their grudges.

"I have two options," Kraft said about his war against the NFL. "I can either end it or extend it."

The Patriots owner paused before describing the goose bumps he felt being welcomed into "the room" by other owners after purchasing the team. Kraft expressed his allegiance to his fellow owners and their ultra-exclusive club he called the "full thirty-two."

"So in that spirit, I don't want to continue the rhetoric that's gone on for the last four months," he told reporters. "I'm going to accept, reluctantly, what he [Goodell] has given us, and not to continue this dialogue and rhetoric, and we won't appeal."

Kraft's star quarterback Tom Brady watched the news conference along with millions of others on television. He was devastated and angry. Brady grabbed his cell phone and punched in the contact number for DeMaurice Smith, executive director of the National Football League Players Association.

"What the fuck?" Brady shouted over the phone. "Why am I not getting the support I deserve on this thing?"

Smith tried to console his client and friend.

"No matter what Kraft says, it has no bearing on our appeal of the four-game suspension," he told Brady. "We'll be ready for that. Trust me."[1]

In a moment, the man hailed as arguably the greatest quarterback ever to play the game had to put his faith in another team, one of battle-tested attorneys in a war against, perhaps, the most formidable opponent of his life: the NFL.

PART I

Chapter One

A COLD RAIN

January 18, 2015

Indianapolis sports columnist Bob Kravitz squinted wearily through the frames of his prescription eyeglasses and ran his fingers through the gray whiskers that covered his chin. *Something's weird*, he thought to himself.[1] It had indeed been a strange game for fans of the Indianapolis Colts to watch thus far. On the drenched Gillette Stadium turf, the Colts, playing behind third-year quarterback Andrew Luck, were committing countless mistakes, and their opponent, the New England Patriots, had made them pay dearly. Early on, Colts punt returner Josh Cribbs mishandled a kick that hit him flush on his face mask before the football tumbled to the field, where it was scooped up and recovered by Patriots linebacker Darius Fleming.

New England's offense then took over. It was the second possession of the game for Patriots quarterback Tom Brady, and he fed the ball to running back LeGarrette Blount, who chewed up yard after yard before stampeding into the end zone for the first score of the AFC championship game. Seemingly unimpressed with his team's fast start, head coach Bill Belichick brooded on the sideline, his trade-mark navy blue hoodie surprisingly dry considering the weather.

That night, the temperature hovered just above freezing, bringing with it dense fog and a cold rain, instead of the light snow that had fallen in Foxborough, Massachusetts, during previous midwinter matchups between these storied rivals. But much had changed within the Colts organization since those epic and unforgettable snow bowls. Gone was legendary quarterback Peyton Manning, the proverbial face of the franchise and poster boy for the scorn of Patriots fans from Caribou, Maine, to Cumberland, Rhode Island. Manning had been vanquished and replaced by the first pick in the 2012 NFL draft, Andrew Luck, who had since broken Manning's franchise record for passing yards in a single season and had most recently beaten the Manning-led Denver Broncos in the divisional round of the playoffs. The outward identity of the Colts had also changed. They were no longer considered, as the Patriots were, perennial conference favorites destined to wreak havoc throughout the AFC. The Colts were now playing the role of the underdog behind a talented and modestly likable quarterback. Without Peyton Manning behind center, most Patriots fans no longer recoiled at the mere sight of the horseshoe-bedecked helmets. The intensity and excitement over the rivalry had waned in New England. But that sentiment was not shared by those toiling inside the Indiana Farm Bureau Football Center, the Indianapolis headquarters of the Colts.

The team had been taught to despise the Patriots. This was a deeper hatred than is normally found among business competitors. This was loathing on the level of rival nation-states with opposing ideologies. Colts owner Jim Irsay, the silver-haired, goateed man-child who had inherited the team from his father, Robert, viewed the Patriots the way Ronald Reagan once regarded the Soviet Union: they simply were not to be trusted. Irsay himself, however, had his own problems. In 2014, he had been arrested for

drunk driving and felony drug possession, which probably didn't
ease his decade-old grudge against the Patriots. The bad blood
went all the way back to a regular-season showdown in 2003,
when the Colts accused Patriots linebacker Willie McGinest of
faking an injury during a critical fourth-quarter play to stop the
clock, the Patriots eventually going on to pull out the victory in
typical Tom Brady fashion. Irsay's suspicions about the deceptive culture of the Patriots, however, were proven correct in 2007,
when Coach Belichick was caught videotaping play calls and signals of opposing coaches in a scandal that would come to be
known as Spygate.

Bob Kravitz looked at the scoreboard late in the second quarter
of the AFC championship game and saw that the Colts were down
ten points to the Patriots. The score was 17–7, but the game did
not appear that competitive. New England had complete control
over Indianapolis, the Colts weren't exactly playing perfect football, and no sports reporter, let alone Kravitz, had any reason to
believe that the Patriots were practicing any illegal sleight of hand.
But as the halftime whistle blew, Kravitz noticed Colts general
manager Ryan Grigson leave his seat in the press box, walk over
to the team's designated PR spot, and reach for the phone. Grigson began talking excitedly to someone on the other end of the
line. Kravitz, however, could not imagine what the conversation
was about. The columnist simply rubbed his chin and thought the
exchange was, in his words, "weird."

Kravitz watched the Patriots increase their dominance over the
Colts in the second half. Through a driving rain, Tom Brady drove
the offense down the field early in the third quarter and lobbed a
pass to hulking left tackle Nate Solder, who steamrolled into the
end zone, where he was flanked by the other beefy offensive linemen in raucous celebration. As sometimes seems to be the case for
Brady, the game was proving to be easy.

Less than seven minutes later, he struck again, this time it was a touchdown pass to his all-world tight end Rob Gronkowski. With the extra point, the score was now 31–7. Coach Belichick and Patriots offensive coordinator Josh McDaniels could have taken their foot off the gas pedal at this point, but it wasn't their style. As the New England defense and its mercenary leader, cornerback Darrelle Revis, continued to confuse Andrew Luck and keep the Colts out of the end zone, the Patriots offense kept hammering Indianapolis through the air and on the ground. LeGarrette Blount added two more touchdowns in the rout. The final score was 45–7, and with the win, the Patriots secured their sixth trip to the Super Bowl under Coach Belichick. Tom Brady completed twenty-three of thirty-five passes for a total of 226 yards, while Luck finished with just twelve completions and two interceptions. Soon the rain in Foxborough gave way to a shower of red, white, and blue confetti as players donned championship baseball caps and shirts, dancing in jubilation while the Lamar Hunt Trophy was handed to team owner Robert Kraft.

"You did your job," Kraft told the sold-out crowd. "Now we must go to Arizona and do our job."

CBS sports anchor Jim Nantz then pulled in a grinning Bill Belichick, who once again echoed that season's memorable mantra. "I only have one thing to say. We're on to Seattle!"

Finally, the microphone was presented to Brady, the one man every fan was waiting to hear from. Nantz reminded Brady and the frenzied crowd that he would be setting a new record, becoming the first quarterback to play in six Super Bowls. Number 12, wearing glare-deflective eye black, his wet hair matted, did his best to deflect attention from his personal accomplishment and praised his fellow players.

"My teammates...I couldn't be more proud of them," he said. "We put a lot of work in this year, worked our tails off to get to this point...we've got one more to go."

Hoisting the Hunt Trophy and flashing the smile that had

graced the cover of countless major sports and lifestyle magazines
in America, Brady then addressed the fans. "I know we've had
some ups and downs this year, but right now we're up, baby, and
we're gonna try to stay up for one more game."

The Patriots had approached each game that season with a similar mentality. After suffering a humiliating defeat to the Kansas
City Chiefs in week four, a loss that had both team beat writers
and chest-beating fans finally questioning whether the team and
its legendary quarterback were now approaching a steady decline,
Bill Belichick had refused to take the bait. When asked about
the performance of his thirty-seven-year-old quarterback during a
press conference after the game, the coach quickly cut off the reporter. "We're on to Cincinnati," Belichick barked. "It's not about
the past. It's not about the future. We're preparing for Cincinnati."
The team bounced back against the Bengals the following week
and soon regained control of the conference before marching
through the playoffs. In other words, there would be no more talk
about the Colts after this night. The team's sole focus would turn
to the Seattle Seahawks, the defending NFL champions. The players would be allowed to celebrate for a few more hours before
placing the victory in their rearview mirror.

Meanwhile, Patriots fans wanted to savor this victory longer,
as for them it was yet another coronation for the most dominant
sports team of the twenty-first century. For Colts fans, of course,
it was a car crash, and Bob Kravitz had witnessed the fiery wreck
close enough to smell the burning rubber. This was more than
a playoff loss. It was the worst defeat for the Colts against the
Patriots in a big-game situation. There were no silver linings to
write about for next season. Even with a star quarterback like
Andrew Luck, the Colts were simply not in the Patriots' class, and
as long as Tom Brady remained on the field, the outlook would
not change.

Kravitz made his way to the losing locker room and the Colts' postgame press conference, where he spotted the team's brain trust—owner Jim Irsay, head coach Chuck Pagano, and general manager Ryan Grigson—huddled in a corner in a heated pow-wow. The columnist figured that the owner was demanding heads roll after such an embarrassing defeat. It was understandable, Kravitz thought, and over the next couple of hours he stuck to his script and conducted player interviews that would make up his Monday-morning hit piece. It was late in the evening when he returned to the press box to fetch his laptop and cell phone. After packing away his computer, he reached for his phone and noticed that he'd received a message from someone in the NFL league office. The text read, Something you need to know. Give me a call.

Kravitz waited until he got to the parking lot at Gillette Stadium and then got out his phone.

"The Patriots are being investigated by the league for deflating footballs," the source told him.

"Get the fuck outta here," Kravitz responded incredulously. "I don't believe it."

"Believe it," the source told him.

"I can't run with the story unless I get confirmation."

"Then I suggest you do."

Kravitz hung up and began texting and tweeting other league sources and soon got ahold of another trusted NFL insider.

"Is it true the Patriots are being investigated for deflating footballs in the AFC championship?" he asked.

"If you write it, you won't be wrong," the insider replied.

Kravitz's mind was now racing. He still had to get back to his hotel room in nearby Smithfield, Rhode Island, to finish his column about the Colts' blowout loss. But the game itself seemed like an afterthought to him now. He had been given the opportunity to break a major story, and it couldn't wait for the morning news cycle. The columnist decided to report the allegations in a tweet. He began to type—Breaking: A league source tells me the NFL is investigating the possibility the Patriots deflated footballs Sunday night. More to come.

He showed his phone screen to his boss, WTHR Indianapolis sports director Dave Calabro.

"You know this is gonna raise holy hell," Calabro warned.

Kravitz nodded. He had begun to sweat in the cold New England night. Taking a deep breath, he pressed his thick index finger on the send button. The time was 1:55 a.m.

"Here goes nothing. Let's go break the Internet."

Chapter Two

STORM FRONTS

Bob Kravitz placed his head on a pillow and stared at the ceiling of his small hotel room. He closed his eyes but sleep would not come. He'd been a sports reporter and columnist for thirty-five years, and he describes his knowledge of the inner workings of the NFL as "a mile wide and an inch deep. Just enough to be dangerous."[1]

His social media post was potentially the most dangerous dispatch of his career. He lay awake wondering if he would even have a career in the morning.

There's a chance you could be wrong, Kravitz told himself. *Your balls are now on the line.*

Unlike Kravitz, Tom Brady slept soundly that Sunday night. After the game, he had returned home to his supermodel wife, Gisele Bündchen, and his mansion in Brookline, a tony Boston suburb, where team owner Robert Kraft also resided. Brady's body felt strong and healthy. He hadn't been punished by the Colts defense as he had been the previous week during an epic and physically draining come-from-behind win against the rugged Baltimore Ravens at Gillette Stadium. In that game, Ravens defenders repeatedly broke through the barrier reef formed by

Brady's offensive line to agitate the quarterback with angry shoves and violent pro wrestling–style hits.

While the aging legend struggled early, opposing Ravens quarterback Joe Flacco was going for the kill. Flacco had been a mystery to Patriots coaches, players, and fans throughout his career. He had never been intimidated by the aura of Bill Belichick and was immune to the three championship banners hanging from the rafters above the south end zone inside Gillette Stadium. Historically, Flacco performed well in New England, especially in the playoffs. He'd thrown five touchdowns and passed for more than five hundred yards over their past three showdowns and had two big wins over Brady and the Patriots to show for it. The six-foot-six signal caller had also thrown thirteen touchdowns with zero interceptions over his last five playoff appearances. The 2015 divisional playoff game appeared to be following Flacco's script. In the first quarter, he threw a nineteen-yard touchdown strike to wide receiver Kamar Aiken, himself a former Patriot, and then followed it up with a nine-yard score to respected veteran Steve Smith Sr., who caught cornerback Darrelle Revis on the inside for an easy touchdown.

The rambunctious hometown crowd grew quiet and waited to see how Brady and the Patriots would respond. It was now time to release the kraken. Patriots offensive coordinator Josh McDaniels summoned the pass-catching beast known as Rob Gronkowski and called his number 87 for two big pass plays, one for sixteen yards and another for a whopping forty yards down the left seam on the edge of the Ravens' coverage. Brady capped the drive with a scrambling run into the end zone. The Patriots were alive again and would soon tie the score, when Brady found slot receiver Danny Amendola, who pulled in a short pass and leaped for a touchdown. But Flacco and the Ravens soon countered with two more scores, and the pendulum continued to swing drastically back and forth as the two quarterbacks battled like prizefighters.

Down 28 to 14, Brady brought his team back with a touchdown to Gronkowski. Then slot receiver Julian Edelman, Brady's favorite target, found a target of his own. Josh McDaniels called a trick play, allowing Edelman, a former Kent State University quarterback, an opportunity for highlight-reel glory. The receiver took a pass from Brady behind the line of scrimmage and then paid it forward with a perfect spiral down the sideline to Amendola, a similarly built receiver twin, for a fifty-one-yard touchdown. There was jubilation in Foxborough.

A Baltimore field goal put the Ravens back in the lead, but once again, Brady charged back with his third touchdown pass of the game to veteran wide receiver Brandon LaFell. The strike was history in the making as it placed Brady in front of his boyhood idol, San Francisco 49ers legend Joe Montana, and Packers great Brett Favre, as the quarterback with the most postseason touchdowns—forty-six.

On this night, however, records meant little to Brady. The game was still tight, and the Patriots were holding on to a precarious four-point lead. The ball was now back in Joe Flacco's hands, and the Ravens quarterback showed why he'd earned the nickname "Joe Cool," which had been Montana's moniker a generation ago. He completed a critical fourth-down pass as the clock approached the two-minute warning. But a field goal would do Baltimore no good. The Ravens had to score a touchdown. Two plays later, Flacco heaved the ball to Steve Smith Sr., who was flanked by two Patriots defensive backs near the end zone. Safety Duron Harmon turned toward the play at the optimum moment and made a game-saving interception. Flacco would get one more shot, but a Hail Mary pass came up short and the Patriots were headed to the AFC championship game, where they would go on to trounce the Colts.

The Ravens, on the other hand, were headed home to Baltimore. They were beaten and angry. Before hopping on the team charter, head coach John Harbaugh addressed the media in a news conference at Gillette Stadium. Harbaugh was outraged that the Patriots had used an unorthodox blocking scheme during the game on a critical third-quarter drive where only four offensive linemen took position at the line of scrimmage. The team still needed a fifth player on the line, so running back Shane Vereen checked into the game as an ineligible receiver and rarely used tight end Michael Hoomanawanui moved over to the left tackle position. The chess move left Harbaugh and Ravens defensive coordinator Dean Pees no time to adjust and figure out who the eligible and ineligible receivers were. As the ball was snapped to Brady, Hoomanawanui raced upfield unchallenged and hauled in the pass. The tight end–turned–left tackle had open room and ran for several more yards before getting pulled down deep in Ravens territory. As the Patriots walked back to the huddle, a bewildered Harbaugh had no idea what he'd just witnessed and marched onto the field to cry foul. The coach drew a penalty for screaming at the officials and was forced to bite his lower lip until the postgame, when he took the podium and blasted the Patriots to reporters.

"We wanted the opportunity to ID who the eligible receivers were," Harbaugh said. "They [the Patriots] would announce the eligible player and then time was taken [off the game clock] and they would snap the ball before we had a chance to figure out who was lined up where, and that was the deception part of it. And that's where it was clearly deception....Nobody's ever seen that before."

When a reporter asked the coach whether he thought the play was cheap or dirty, Harbaugh responded with a terse no comment. The Ravens coach had just chummed the water with raw meat, and the sharks smelled blood. For the NFL beat writers, it was an easy and tantalizing story to write. The Patriots were being accused of deception once again. For the legion of football fans across the nation who despised Brady, Belichick, and company, it offered the opportunity to resurrect the Spygate scandal in bar-room and online conversations.

For Harbaugh's part, his tacit insistence that the Patriots were playing dirty or cheap could have been interpreted as a cheap shot against the organization. The Ravens coach claimed no one had ever seen a play like that before, when in reality the University of Alabama had run a similar play back in November 2014 in an over-time win against the Louisiana State University Tigers. Harbaugh noted that Bill Vinovich, the referee for the Patriots–Ravens game, had also made clear announcements in the stadium that certain Patriots receivers were ineligible, in essence telling the Ravens' de-fenders they didn't need to cover them.

When John Harbaugh's comments reached the ears of Tom Brady, the quarterback shot right back during his own postgame press conference.

"Maybe those guys [the Ravens] gotta study the rule book and figure it out. We obviously knew what we were doing and we made some pretty important plays. It was a real good weapon for us. Maybe we'll have something in store next week. I don't know what's deceiving about that. They [the Ravens] should figure it out."

The NFL backed up Brady's statement, ruling that nothing was illegal about the play in question, but the quarterback's counter-punch did not sit well with Harbaugh and other members of the Ravens organization, and the repercussions would be gigantic.

Number 12 later attempted to defuse the situation by saying he had a lot of respect for John Harbaugh as a coach, but the damage was already done and Baltimore plotted its revenge.

In the days leading up to the AFC championship, Ravens as-sistant head coach and special teams coordinator Jerry Rosburg placed a phone call to his friend Colts head coach Chuck Pagano. Pagano had close ties to the Baltimore organization, having served as the team's defensive coordinator in 2011. Rosburg informed his former colleague *of something rotten in the state of Denmark*. The special teams coach believed that within the palace walls of Gillette Stadium there lurked corruption and deceit on a scale that would have inspired William Shakespeare. Rosburg explained that the Ravens had experienced serious issues when they were in kicking or punt situations during their game with the Patriots. Each time, before they lined up a kick, the Ravens were handed new footballs instead of the balls Rosburg and his team had prepared themselves.

"Be careful," he warned Pagano.

That conversation was then relayed to Colts equipment manager Sean Sullivan, who pushed it up the chain of command to general manager Ryan Grigson. Sullivan surmised that the problems with the footballs went far beyond the kicking game.

"As far as the game balls are concerned, it is well known around the league that after the Patriots game balls are checked by officials and brought out for game usage by the ball boys, the Patriots will let out some air with a ball needle because their quarterback likes a smaller football so he can grip it better," Sullivan wrote in an e-mail. "It would be great if someone would check the air in the game ball as the game goes on so that they don't get an illegal advantage."

As the Colts' coaches prepared their game plan for New England, the Indianapolis front office hatched a plan of its own for the AFC championship.

Tom Brady, of course, was oblivious to the cloak-and-dagger operation. He had routed the Colts in one of the most decisive playoff wins of his storied career. After that game, Brady made sure he did not get lured into another controversy and was at his controlled best during the postgame press conference, praising both the Colts and the Patriots' opponent in the upcoming Super Bowl, the Seattle Seahawks.

On Monday morning, January 19, 2015, while the football universe was reacting to Bob Kravitz's tweet, Brady was still unaware of the allegations that broke in the predawn hours. The quarterback called into the Boston sports radio station WEEI for his weekly interview on the *Dennis & Callahan Show*. As with his previous on-air conversations on the program, Brady expected to discuss candidly the key plays from the previous night's game, endure some good-natured ribbing from the hosts, and possibly get lured into reliving his two most recent Super Bowl appearances, both ending in crushing losses to the New York Giants. Instead, he was confronted by cohost Kirk Minihane, the show's resident instigator, about the veracity of the Kravitz tweet. But at this point, even the sports radio jocks were skeptical.

"We didn't really give any weight to the story at the time," Minihane recalls. "Our producer, Chris Curtis, had the Kravitz nugget laid out for us when we arrived at the studio around 5:30 a.m., along with every other news item about the game. We knew that Kravitz was a shit-stirrer and Patriots hater so we just decided to ask Brady the question as a throwaway line, as a punch line."[2]

The interview had approached the nine-minute mark before Minihane asked Brady if he had heard about the Kravitz story. The quarterback said he hadn't heard about or read the story.

"Did you have a sense that you had a better grip on the ball than the Colts?" Minihane pressed.

Brady let out a nervous laugh. "I think I've heard everything at this point."

Following that interview the quarterback received a text from team equipment assistant John Jastremski. Call me when you get a second, the message read. It was his job to oversee Brady's footballs, and while the two men had a congenial relationship, it was the first time they had corresponded by text or a phone call in six months. Jastremski was a Massachusetts native and lifelong Patriots fan who grew up in the small town of Hopedale, located in the heart of the Blackstone Valley, midway between Worcester, the state's second largest city, and Foxborough. He'd played basketball in high school and had an affinity for computers, and, like many kids raised in New England, Jastremski bled Patriots red, white, and blue. He landed a job as a Patriots ball boy in 1994, the year coach Bill Parcells and the organization's top draft choice, quarterback Drew Bledsoe, joined the team during Robert Kraft's first year of ownership. Together, the three men resurrected the moribund franchise, and young Jastremski had been given a front-row seat to the dramatic turnaround. But what happened after the Parcells-Bledsoe era was more than any diehard Boston sports fan could wish for. Jastremski graduated Bryant University with a degree in computer information systems but kept his job with the Patriots, where he had celebrated three Super Bowl wins while forging a bond with a quarterback many were already calling "the greatest of all time."

Jastremski lived quietly in a condo a few miles away from Foxborough but spent most of his time within the confines of Gillette Stadium, working in the equipment room adjacent to the locker room, where players were always stopping by to pillage and plunder whatever they needed before practices and home games. Like other equipment assistants, Jastremski handed out player jerseys, adjusted helmets, and distributed the proper cleats to satisfy any change in field and game-day conditions. But over the past three seasons, his role had been elevated to "game ball maker." The designation allowed him to work directly with Brady in preparing game-day footballs. Each NFL team received nearly eight hundred footballs per season, and Jastremski treated each one like a coveted bejeweled Fabergé egg.

Less than a minute after Brady received the text from Jastremski, he placed the requested call to his "game ball maker," who answered immediately after seeing the contact TomBrady2 appear on his cell phone screen.[3] Their discussion lasted thirteen minutes and four seconds. Jastremski would later claim that the tone of the conversation was lighthearted and that he was "semi-busting Brady's chops." The ball handler hadn't heard the WEEI radio interview but had been alerted to its content by his girlfriend. Jastremski was obviously curious about the details of the allegations, since he was responsible for "making" Brady's footballs and it would be his neck on the chopping block if something went wrong.

The two men discussed what they had learned of the morning's media coverage. After Bob Kravitz's initial tweet, the NBC Pro Sports Talk website had posted a related story at 2:19 a.m. *Newsday* ran a story almost two hours later with National Football League spokesperson Michael Signora confirming that the league was "looking into the matter." Signora also stressed that there was no timetable on the investigation and that NFL rules prohibit teams from underinflating footballs during games. There was no indication from either Jastremski or Brady that this initial phone call included discussion of what seemed to be the elephant in the room at that time—the fact that Jastremski's coworker Jim McNally, the New England Patriots' official locker room attendant, had been questioned about the team's footballs by two members of NFL security immediately after the Colts game. Jastremski knew this because McNally had called him at 12:15 a.m. during his ninety-minute drive from the stadium to his home in New Hampshire.

Jastremski could only imagine what McNally would say under the scrutiny of NFL security. During the initial questioning following the AFC championship, McNally told league security representatives that he had walked the footballs (thirteen game balls stuffed into a sack) onto the field at Gillette Stadium without an escort before the game. Oftentimes, he would be joined on such a walk by game officials or Richard Farley, the NFL security representative for the Patriots.

"Nothing unusual happened during the walk from the locker room to the field," McNally insisted during the interview.

What McNally failed to mention was the fact that he had taken the game balls with him into a bathroom before continuing on to the field.

NFL director of investigations John Raucci, a twenty-five-year veteran of the FBI, had asked McNally to make himself available for a follow-up interview the next day. At first, the locker room attendant said that he would not be available for such a conversation because he had another full-time job and would not return to Gillette Stadium until August 2015 for the Patriots' first preseason game. Unbowed by this apparent evasion, Raucci stressed the importance of the follow-up interview, and McNally acquiesced. The two men scheduled to speak again on the evening of January 19.

Later, when asked to describe the purpose of their early-morning phone call, McNally and Jastremski both claimed that it was merely a congratulatory conversation about the team's big win but conceded that some of the talk did focus on the subject of the inflation level of the footballs.

The anxiety increased for Bob Kravitz as he made his way to the airport on the morning of January 19. Although he trusted his NFL sources, he also feared that he was being used as a pawn. As far as he was concerned, his was the only name attached to the story thus far, and those who had served up the narrative would remain hidden in the background, unidentified and protected by the rules of journalism. "What if I'm wrong?" he muttered to himself. Kravitz checked in on the Twitter universe and noticed the *Newsday* piece and began to breathe a little easier. Hours later, after he had returned to Indianapolis, the columnist let out a loud war whoop when ESPN reporter Chris Mortensen, one of the most respected media members covering the National Football League, fired off a tweet of his own—NFL has reported that 11 of the Patriots footballs used in Sunday's AFC title game were under-inflated by 2 lbs each, per league sources.

Chapter Three

PRESSURE

As the morning wore on, Brady continued his text conversation with Jastremski. The quarterback appeared to be gauging how well his "ball maker" was handling the pressure.

You good Jonny Boy? Brady asked.

Still nervous. So far so good though. I'll be alright, Jastremski typed in response.

You didn't do anything wrong bud, the quarterback insisted.

I know, I'll be all good, the ball maker replied.

Jastremski told Brady that Dave Schoenfeld, the team's head equipment manager, would be "picking his brain" about the situation later.

No worries bud. We are all good, Brady replied.

Jastremski handed over his cell phone to the Patriots security team later that day for forensic analysis.

Meanwhile, Tom Brady was attempting to smother the controversy in its cradle. To him, and most other quarterbacks, ball pressure came down to personal preference and was not something that could alter the course of a game, whether footballs were inflated or deflated on purpose or as the result of game-time weather conditions. Brady's friend and 2014 season MVP Aaron Rodgers, quarterback for the Green Bay Packers, would later admit that he liked his footballs to be overinflated. "I like to push the limit to how much air we can put into the football, even go over what they allow you to do to see if the officials take air out of it," Rodgers told Phil Simms, a former star NFL quarterback, Super Bowl winner for the New York Giants, and broadcaster for CBS Sports.[1] Brad Johnson, who also got a championship ring when he quarterbacked the Tampa Bay Buccaneers to a Super Bowl victory in 2003, said that he paid his equipment guys seventy-five hundred dollars to alter footballs before the AFC championship game against the Oakland Raiders. "I paid some guys to get the balls right," Johnson later told *Tampa Bay Times* reporter Rick Stroud. "I went and got all 100 [Super Bowl game balls] and they [equipment personnel] took care of all of them."[2]

Among the fraternity of NFL quarterbacks, ball manipulation was a commonplace, accepted bending of the rules.

But league officials did not see it that way, at least now, and the sharks were circling amid the hype machine over Super Bowl XLIX. On the afternoon of January 19, 2015, the head coaches of both the Patriots and the Seattle Seahawks were committed by the league to participate in a conference call with the media. Bill Belichick was historically notorious for his strategic refusal to offer reporters anything of substance during these exchanges. He could make the most exciting game seem as boring and painful as a visit to the dentist. Normally, only the most wonkish football fans paid close attention to the coach's comments.

But reporters were not interested in discussing X's and O's with the Patriots coach. By midmorning, news that the league was now investigating the Patriots over allegations of deflated footballs had grown from a small brushfire into a full conflagration. Now, news outlets such as CBS Sports, National Public Radio, and even the *Huffington Post* had latched onto the story.

"What's your response to the report on deflated footballs?" one reporter asked on the call.

"We'll cooperate fully in whatever the league wants us to," Belichick responded in his often imitated, grumbling monotone. "Whatever questions they ask us, whatever they want us to do."

The coach told reporters that he had no idea there were any concerns over the footballs during the game and that he had only heard about the potential issue that morning. However, given his reputation for control and for paying attention to each minute detail of the goings-on at Gillette Stadium, it seems unlikely that Jim McNally's interrogation by NFL security would have escaped Belichick's attention when it happened.

The media continued to pressure the coach. "What do you think of the topic and if that could potentially be an advantage for a team?"

"You're asking the questions, I'm just trying to answer them," he replied.

"Were the Patriots using deflated footballs?" one reporter asked pointedly.

"I just said the first I heard about it was this morning," Belichick fired back. "Whatever they need from the league, that's what we'll do."[3]

It was the last thing Bill Belichick wanted to be dealing with at the moment. He and his assistants had a Herculean task in front of them in developing a game plan against the reigning Super Bowl champions, and any talk about the inflation or deflation of footballs would divert attention away from this challenge. The coach repeated the season's rallying cry—*Do your job*— to the members of his staff and his players and attempted, at least initially, to block out the distraction and the tempest brewing outside Gillette Stadium. That day, David Gardi, senior vice president of football operations for the NFL, sent a letter via e-mail to Belichick, Patriots owner Robert Kraft, his son Jonathan Kraft, and league

Barnes & Noble Booksellers #3424
2401 US Highway 22 W STE 1F
Union Plaza
Union, NJ 07083
908-378-6472

STR:3424 REG:003 TRN:9284 CSHR:Gabriella C

MEMBER   EXP: 03/03/2024

Letters to Trump
  9781735503752   T1
  (1 @ 99.00) Member Card 10% (9.90)
  (1 @ 89.10)   89.10
12: Tom Brady and His Battle for Redempt
  9780316416429   T1
  (1 @ 18.99) Member Card 10% (1.90)
  (1 @ 17.09)   17.09

Subtotal   106.19
Sales Tax T1 (6.625%)   7.04
TOTAL   113.23
VISA   113.23
  Card#: XXXXXXXXXXXXX4162
  Expdate: XX/XX
  Auth: 001522
  Entry Method: Chip Read

  Application Label: US DEBIT
  AID: a0000000980840
  TVR: 8000088000
  TSI: 6800

Returns will be accepted with a receipt
within 30 days of purchase. Eligible refunds
will be made to your original form of
tender. For returns with a gift receipt, a
store credit will be issued in the form of
an electronic gift card for the purchase
price within 60 days of purchase.
Exceptions apply. Visit bn.com/returns
for full details.

MEMBER SAVINGS   11.80

059.02G   06/04/2023 12:54PM

CUSTOMER COPY

warranty.

Returns or exchanges will not be permitted (i) after 30 days or without receipt or (ii) for product not carried by Barnes & Noble.com, (iii) for purchases made with a check less than 7 days prior to the date of return.

Policy on receipt may appear in two sections.

Return Policy

<u>With a sales receipt or Barnes & Noble.com packing slip,</u> a full refund in the original form of payment will be issued from any Barnes & Noble Booksellers store for returns of new and unread books, and unopened and undamaged music CDs, DVDs, vinyl records, electronics, toys/games and audio books made within 30 days of purchase from a Barnes & Noble Booksellers store or Barnes & Noble.com with the below exceptions:

Undamaged NOOKs purchased from any Barnes & Noble Booksellers store or from Barnes & Noble.com may be returned within 14 days when accompanied with a sales receipt or with a Barnes & Noble.com packing slip or may be exchanged within 30 days with a gift receipt.

A store credit for the purchase price will be issued (i) when a gift receipt is presented within 60 days of purchase, (ii) for all textbooks returns and exchanges, or (iii) when the original tender is PayPal.

Items purchased as part of a Buy One Get One or Buy Two, Get Third Free offer are available for exchange only, unless all items purchased as part of the offer are returned, in which case such items are available for a refund (in 30 days). Exchanges of the items sold at no cost are available only for items of equal or lesser value than the original cost of such item.

Opened music CDs, DVDs, vinyl records, electronics, toys/games, and audio books may not be returned, and can be exchanged only for the same product and only if defective. NOOKs purchased from other retailers or sellers are returnable only to the retailer or seller from which they were purchased pursuant to such retailer's or seller's return policy. Magazines, newspapers, eBooks, digital downloads, and used books are not returnable or exchangeable. Defective NOOKs may be exchanged at the store in accordance with the applicable warranty.

Returns or exchanges will not be permitted (i) after 30 days or without receipt or (ii) for product not carried by Barnes & Noble.com, (iii) for purchases made with a check less than 7 days prior to the date of return.

Policy on receipt may appear in two sections.

Return Policy

<u>With a sales receipt or Barnes & Noble.com packing slip,</u> a full refund in the original form of payment will be issued from any Barnes & Noble Booksellers store for returns of new and unread books, and unopened and undamaged music CDs, DVDs, vinyl records, electronics, toys/games and audio books made within 30 days of purchase from a Barnes & Noble Booksellers store or Barnes & Noble.com with the below

commissioner Roger Goodell, stating in part that an initial investigation had found that none of the Patriots' game balls in the
AFC championship were inflated to the league-required 12.5 psi
(pounds per square inch). In the letter, Gardi stated that the footballs "may have been tampered with after the normal inspection
procedures were followed prior to kickoff."[4]

Fifty-five-year-old Roger Stokoe Goodell had been running the
most popular and lucrative league in all of professional sports for
more than a decade. The ginger-haired NFL commissioner was
the son of a United States senator appointed by New York governor Nelson Rockefeller following the 1968 assassination of New
York senator and presidential candidate Robert F. Kennedy. It was
the only time in his life that Charles Goodell had been handed
something he had not earned, something he had not fought for.
The elder Goodell came from modest beginnings in western New
York. He was a star athlete at Jamestown High School and played
both baseball and football at Williams College, in Massachusetts.
Known as "Charlie" to his friends, Goodell always kept a dictionary by his side, reading it incessantly to increase his vocabulary.
He joined the U.S. Navy in the mid-1940s, attended and graduated from Yale Law School and the university's graduate school of
government, and later enlisted in the U.S. Air Force as a first lieu-
tenant during the Korean War.

Charles Goodell got bitten by the political bug early. After a
brief stint as a law professor at Quinnipiac College, just down the
road from Yale, he went into practice briefly for himself before
heading to Washington, D.C., for a job with the United States Justice Department. A few years later, Goodell made his first run for
public office in a special election to fill a New York congressional
seat vacated by the death of Daniel Reed, a long-serving Republican and former head football coach at Penn State and Cornell.
Charles Goodell won the special election in 1959, when Roger, his

third son, was just three months old. The elder Goodell took in nearly double the votes of his opponent. He was reelected three times and emerged as one of the party's "young thinkers" at a time when House Democrats outnumbered Republicans two to one. He had voted against the "Great Society" bill, which outlined President Lyndon B. Johnson's so-called War on Poverty. Goodell submitted his own version but it went nowhere. As a Republican, he found himself in a perpetual minority, relegated to the sidelines of major policy issues along with his good friend and fellow Republican Donald Rumsfeld, a congressman from Illinois and future secretary of defense under President George W. Bush.

Charles Goodell's political future drew fresh breaths when Bobby Kennedy succumbed to bullet wounds fired by assassin Sirhan Sirhan in the kitchen of the Ambassador Hotel in Los Angeles. Governor Rockefeller needed to fill Kennedy's seat with a fellow Republican who would not be seen as repugnant to RFK's legion of supporters. As the nation mourned, the crafty New York congressman sent Rockefeller a secret letter that outlined the similarities he shared with the late Kennedy. Goodell was appointed to Kennedy's seat three months after his death.

But even with fair warning, Nelson Rockefeller could not imagine the sea change that would come through Goodell's political metamorphosis. Charles Goodell became a progressive. James Buckley, brother of noted conservative William F. Buckley and a staunch critic and rival of Goodell's, called him a "Republican whose level of liberalism approached the indecent" and said that he was making a career for himself by embarrassing the administration.[5] Goodell marched with Coretta Scott King, wife of slain civil rights leader the Reverend Martin Luther King Jr., was endorsed by the likes of liberal political activist Noam Chomsky, and even took on the leader of his own party—President Richard Nixon—voting against two of Nixon's nominations to the United States Supreme Court.

Then, in September 1969, Senator Goodell introduced a bill that would require all American troops out of Vietnam by December 1, 1970. He gave Henry Kissinger, Nixon's national security adviser, a heads-up about his plan during a phone call that was secretly recorded. Goodell then placed a similar call to Nixon's secretary of defense Melvin Laird. Despite being an early advocate for the war in Vietnam, Goodell now felt that the United States should not be engaged in a land war 10,000 miles away. Overall support for the war had dropped precipitously after the Tet Offensive in 1968, when news crews captured the intensity of battle between American soldiers and the Viet Cong. In reality, the fight resulted in an overwhelming victory by U.S. forces, but the tenacity shown by North Vietnamese troops caused influential Americans, most notably CBS news anchor Walter Cronkite, to question whether a successful resolution to the war was achievable. Those doubts soon echoed across college campuses, and Senator Goodell listened to the cries of outrage with both ears. The war had changed him, and he would soon be labeled a traitor for taking a conscious stand against his party and against his president. Therefore, he had to be brought to heel or destroyed. As Charles Goodell fought hard to become a hero to young Americans, he was being vilified by the Nixon White House. GOP operatives called him "Changeable Charlie" and "Instant Liberal." One fellow lawmaker compared Goodell's political conversion from conservative to progressive to Saint Paul's journey on the road to Damascus.[6] President Nixon quietly offered Goodell a job in his administration if he would tone down the rhetoric. But Senator Goodell only spoke louder. He entertained antiwar activists like Jane Fonda and met with defense analyst Daniel Ellsberg to discuss strategy for leaking the explosive Pentagon Papers.

Like an NFL coach whose goal is to isolate and take away the best player on the opposing team, Nixon and his aides focused their attention on Charles Goodell's demise. Vice President Spiro

Agnew became Nixon's hired gun and verbal assassin. He told fellow Republicans that "Senator Goodell has left the party." He compared Goodell to Christine Jorgensen, the first recipient of a sex-change operation. Those smears stuck. Charles Goodell lost his bid to win a full term, and his political career was over at the age of forty-four.

His eleven-year-old son, Roger, cried on election night.

The younger Goodell idolized his father. Yet Charles Goodell, despite his earnest connection with young people and those opposed to the war, remained aloof to the responsibilities of parenthood and distanced himself from Roger and his siblings. Charles Goodell moved his family to New York City, where he practiced law while his son Roger was given all the advantages and opportunities that his father had earned himself through hard work as a youth.

Nevertheless, there was resentment from the father toward the son. Roger fought for Charles's attention and love by excelling in the classroom and on the ball fields. He was a three-sport star athlete at Bronxville High School, where he captained the Broncos football team during his senior year in 1977. When his coach demanded that Goodell notify him if any teammates were drinking alcohol or experimenting with drugs, the 170-pound tight end did just that. Roger Goodell was willing to name names for the welfare of the team and also to endear himself to his coach. Injuries, including a concussion suffered during his senior year playing baseball, kept him from playing football in college, so after high school graduation, Roger attended Washington & Jefferson College, a small liberal arts institution spread across a leafy campus in Washington, Pennsylvania, some thirty miles south of Pittsburgh. The institution boasted its fair share of influential alumni, including a United States senator, treasury secretary, and attorney general. Washington & Jefferson provided students with the proper track toward a career in politics, but Goodell had no interest in following in his father's footsteps to Capitol Hill. In 1981, after graduating magna cum laude with a degree in economics, Roger composed a letter to his father offering thanks for putting him through college. "The only thing I want to do in life, other than to be the commissioner of the NFL, is to make you proud," he wrote.[7] The letter wasn't so much a pledge as a plea by a son for his father's blessings.

Goodell then wrote letters to all twenty-eight NFL teams, begging for an opportunity to prove his worth.

He also penned a letter to league commissioner Pete Rozelle on July 2, 1981, that read,

Dear Mr. Rozelle,

I am writing you in reference to any job openings you may have at your offices. Having just finished my undergraduate education at Washington and Jefferson College this past May, I am presently looking for a position in the management of professional sports. Being an avid football fan, I have always desired a career in the NFL. Consequently, as a great admirer of you, it would be both an honor and a pleasure to work for you in any position that may be available.

He signed the letter "Respectfully, Roger S. Goodell."[8]

Later he received a noncommittal reply from Rozelle's office: "Stop by if you're ever in the area," the note read. Young Roger wasted no time. He immediately phoned the league office and said that he was close by and could drop in the next day. This was a lie. Goodell was seven hours away in Pittsburgh at the time. Still, he got in his car and drove to NFL headquarters the following day for an informational interview. Roger made a positive impression and was awarded an internship as an administrative assistant a few months later.

Goodell, however, needed a mentor as much as he needed a job. Indeed, young Roger was searching for a father figure, and as luck would have it, the NFL was then being run by (Alvin) Pete Rozelle, a fifty-five-year-old former sports publicist and marketing genius who had grown the league from twelve teams to twenty-eight through a merger with the rival American Football League. Rozelle had also created the Super Bowl, professional sports' biggest spectacle, and birthed the long-running *Monday Night Football* television franchise with Roone Arledge, head of ABC.

Young Roger would learn a great deal from Rozelle, a true visionary. As commissioner, Rozelle introduced revenue sharing to the league, which allowed small-market teams like the vaunted Green Bay Packers to share equally in television revenues with big-market teams like the New York Jets and Giants, the Chicago Bears, and the Los Angeles Rams, thus creating a more level playing field than that of Major League Baseball, the NFL's chief rival. Rozelle had also honed his managerial and leadership skills through his work as general manager for the Rams and as a marketing executive for the 1956 summer Olympics. The man could also be tough.

Early in Rozelle's tenure, in 1963, league investigators discovered that two of the sport's biggest stars, Green Bay Packers running back Paul Hornung and Detroit Lions All-Pro tackle Alex Karras, had placed bets on NFL games. Investigators conducted fifty-two interviews with players on eight teams and determined the two football stars had either bet on their own teams to win or had placed bets on other NFL games. Neither Hornung nor Karras was guilty of taking bribes, point shaving, or game fixing, but the reputation of the emerging phenomenon called the National Football League took a major hit. Without seeking counsel from the team owners who had elected him and paid his handsome salary, Rozelle dropped the hammer on both players for gambling and associating with "known hoodlums." He banned them indefinitely, sending shock waves around the league.

Hornung was the NFL's biggest attraction at the time. The "Golden Boy" had set an NFL scoring record with 176 points in 1960 and was awarded the NFL's most valuable player trophy in 1961. Karras was the anchor of the Lions' defense and an all-league selection three years running. Five other Lions players were fined for betting on the 1962 NFL championship game between the Packers and New York Giants. The Lions organization was also fined four thousand dollars for failure to adequately supervise its players. At the time, Rozelle called the decision the hardest of his life. What outraged the commissioner was Hornung's and Karras's flagrant disregard for league rules. Each player had been informed time and again of the league rule on gambling, and yet according to Rozelle, they had continued to gamble with no signs of slowing down. The commissioner considered banning each man for life. This would be the most severe penalty paid by a professional athlete since "Shoeless" Joe Jackson and seven Chicago White Sox teammates were handed lifetime bans from Major League Baseball for fixing the World Series in 1919. The Black Sox Scandal was one of the reasons Rozelle had his job as NFL commissioner. Major League Baseball had never had a commissioner before 1919, but the position was created in the wake of the scandal to police and control the players. Pete Rozelle decided that he would exact from Hornung and Karras "the most severe penalty short of banishment for life."[9] Both players were reinstated a year later.

By 1981, Rozelle had weathered two players' strikes and was locked in a heated battle with Al Davis, the renegade owner of the Oakland Raiders, who was hell-bent on moving his storied franchise from the Bay Area to Los Angeles.

Goodell had called himself a great admirer of Rozelle. Unlike the commissioner, Roger was not a forward thinker, but he would grow to understand Rozelle's philosophy of leadership: *control equaled power.*

Roger absorbed what he could in his junior role with the league and was hungry to learn more. The following year, he landed an internship with the New York Jets' public relations staff for the 1983 season. The Jets went 7–9 that year and finished at the bottom of the AFC East. Goodell, who had only played football in high school, was offered an entry-level job on the team's coaching staff for the following season but decided to return to NFL headquarters instead.

He stayed and never left.

When Pete Rozelle retired in 1989, the league owners went outside league headquarters for the next commissioner and elected Washington, D.C., power lawyer Paul Tagliabue to take his place. Tagliabue was well known to the owners, having served as a lawyer for the NFL. He also was very aware of the giant shoes he had to fill. After all, his predecessor had been inducted into the NFL Hall of Fame in 1985 while he was still commissioner.

Tagliabue's leadership style was vastly different from that of Rozelle, whose dominant personality and innovative ideas made him larger than life. Still, though Tagliabue was seen as a kinder, gentler commissioner, he was also one who understood the value of growth. He expanded the league with new franchises in Jacksonville, Florida, and Charlotte, North Carolina, while also looking overseas for the opportunity to build new marketplaces for the NFL brand. Soon, a European developmental program, awkwardly called the World League of American Football, and later known as NFL Europe, whet the appetite of sports fans in Barcelona, Frankfurt, and London. The commissioner also understood the value of having a strong team around him. One of the league office's brightest young stars was Roger Goodell. Tagliabue grew to trust the young executive and valued his judgment enough to appoint him as the go-between with Gene Upshaw, executive director of the NFL Players Association, during labor talks. Goodell was also chosen to lead the league's negotiations with the city of Los Angeles in its quest to return to the NFL market after losing both the Rams franchise to St. Louis and the Raiders back to Oakland. Roger found himself front and center in just about every important league economic decision during the Tagliabue era. He had also found the mentor he had so desperately been searching for.

"My advice to most people is just to be yourself and continue to be thoughtful," the paternal Tagliabue once counseled.[10]

Soon another father figure would enter Goodell's life, a man who would groom Roger for power and prestige and one whom Goodell would ultimately attempt to destroy.

Chapter Four

THE ULTIMATE FAN

Eleven-year-old Robert Kraft heard the news and wept. Bobby, as he was known to friends and family then, cried uncontrollably when he learned that his favorite baseball team, the Boston Braves, had decided to move to Milwaukee, the first relocation of a major league franchise in fifty years. Like other kids growing up in and around Boston, Bobby was devoted to the team that played on the 800 block of Commonwealth Avenue, now home to Boston University's Nickerson Field. The Braves boasted rising star Sam Jethroe, a former rookie of the year who had hit eighteen home runs in 1950. More importantly, the African-American Jethroe had broken the color barrier in Boston sports. But the Red Sox, that *other* team in town, had Ted Williams, who was arguably the greatest hitter in the game and one of the league's biggest gate attractions. The rise of the mighty Williams meant that Boston could not support two major league teams, so the Braves took their show on the road to Wisconsin. The day of the announcement became known as "Black Friday" to Boston sports fans, and none took the news harder than young Kraft, who sold newspapers at Braves Field. His parents, Harry and

Sarah Kraft, consoled their son and told him to "seek unity in family and community."[1]

Kraft's father, Harry, who owned a small garment business, was a deeply religious man who sent his three children, Bobby, Avram, and Elizabeth, to Hebrew school each day and abided by the strict rules of the Sabbath on weekends. Young Bobby made friends easily in his Brookline neighborhood and had a comforting demeanor that impressed his father. During one trip to the beach when Kraft was a child, his father took his hand and gazed out at the ocean waves.

"You have a wonderful way of not holding grudges that can hurt you," Harry told him. "Stay that way and you'll live a happy life."[2]

Those words stuck and provided the building blocks with which Kraft would build his empire.

In high school, he became president of his senior class and was awarded a scholarship to Columbia University. While in college, he met his future wife, Myra, a student at Brandeis University, who asked him to marry her at the end of their first date. After graduation, Kraft returned to the Boston area to attend Harvard Business School and later went to work for Myra's father, Jacob Hiatt, a former circuit judge who fled Lithuania in 1935 after the rise of Nazi Germany under Adolf Hitler. Many of Hiatt's family members, however, had remained in Eastern Europe and were killed in the Holocaust. Jacob Hiatt had hoped to continue his law career in the United States but found his way to the packaging industry instead. Hiatt had built the Worcester, Massachusetts–based company Rand-Whitney Group after learning how to make boxes for his brother's shoe store, which later became Stride Rite.

Meanwhile, Robert Kraft—no longer answering to Bobby— had a difficult time working for his demanding father-in-law, but he found solace in his growing family and the game of football. After his beloved Braves moved west and Boston lost out on the Hall of Fame career of home-run king Hank Aaron, Kraft turned his attention to the city's new professional football team, the Boston Patriots. The team was owned by Billy Sullivan, a Boston-based entrepreneur who had aspired to be a sportswriter. In 1959, Sullivan paid $25,000 to the upstart American Football League for the rights to bring a professional football franchise to Boston. The Patriots stumbled out of the gate in their inaugural season played at Nickerson Field, formerly Braves Field. The team finished dead last in the standings, but Kraft fell for the lovable losers. He enjoyed the game of football more than he did basketball in a city where the Celtics were hoisting championship banner after championship banner; more than baseball, as he still blamed the Red Sox for the Braves' exodus; and more than hockey, the Bruins then still six years away from Bobby Orr's rookie season. Indeed, Bob Kraft stuck with the Patriots through thick and mostly thin. The team appeared in only one playoff game during the decade, a massacre at the hands of the San Diego Chargers, 51–10, in the 1963 AFL championship. Still, Kraft enjoyed being a member of the fellowship of the miserable. It was considered a badge of honor to stand by the Patriots in a city that was anything but a football town. When Billy Sullivan moved the team from Boston thirty miles south to the town of Foxborough in 1971 and renamed them the New England Patriots, Kraft bought season tickets along a stretch of cold metal benches in section 217, row 23, seats 1–6, in the end zone of what was then called Schaefer Stadium, which resembled a giant tin can that had been pried open. The decision to purchase season tickets sparked a battle in the Kraft household, as Myra considered football a sport played by barbarians. Her husband disagreed and looked to football as a way to bond with his sons. Kraft would routinely dismiss them early from Hebrew school for the long drive from Brookline to Route 1 in Foxborough to watch Patriots home games. Time spent with his boys was important to him. Kraft was blessed with natural paternal instincts.

"I don't recall my father ever missing a birthday," eldest son Jonathan Kraft later recalled. "If he wasn't traveling, he would come home every night for dinner with the family. Even when he was traveling I spoke with him every day."[3]

The proud father would even kiss his sons in public. These traits would later endear Kraft to many partners in his professional life as well, including Roger Goodell.

As a new season-ticket holder, Kraft and his sons witnessed the Patriots go 6–8 in the first year in their new stadium, under rookie quarterback Jim Plunkett, who was awarded rookie of the year honors. Plunkett, the former Heisman Trophy winner from Stanford, appeared to be the franchise quarterback the team had long been waiting for. But the young signal caller would never get his chance to shine, at least with the Patriots. The team had a porous offensive line that kept Plunkett on his back most times and out of the end zone. He'd eventually get replaced by Steve Grogan, a running quarterback from Kansas State whose tough play and ever-present neck roll turned him into a fan favorite.

As Kraft sat with his sons in section 217, he began dreaming of owning the team one day. His paper products company was now earning millions, and Myra Kraft no longer had to worry about whether her husband could afford season tickets or not. But Billy Sullivan, though he was one of the most cash-strapped owners in the lucrative NFL and was barely able to keep the Patriots afloat, showed no signs that he was interested in selling the team. So Kraft then turned his attention to the World Team Tennis league, which boasted sixteen franchises, including the New York Apples and the awkwardly named Hawaii Leis. The league struggled to grow a fan base, with most teams selling fewer than three thousand tickets per season; nonetheless, Kraft took over the defunct Philadelphia Freedoms franchise in 1975, moving it to Boston and renaming the team the Lobsters.

"The lob is one of the most effective shots in tennis so we thought it was a pretty cool name," Kraft said years later. "If I've done anything right in the NFL, I think part of it was having the learning curve and experience of owning a team in the seventies."[4]

Kraft was not alone. Future Los Angeles Lakers and Los Angeles Kings owner Jerry Buss also received an early education in professional sports management as owner of the Los Angeles Strings, a team that included two of the sport's biggest stars, Chris Evert and Ilie Nastase. Kraft understood the need to have a star player and landed one of his own in Czech defector Martina Navratilova, whom he signed to the Lobsters in 1977. Navratilova was the world's number one–ranked women's tennis player at the time, but the sports fandom of Boston did not seem to care. If the Patriots were the fourth most popular professional sports team in New England, support for the Lobsters was so low that its matches didn't even garner a mention in the *Boston Globe* or *Boston Herald American.* The Lobsters struggled financially in part because Kraft had no control over parking or concessions at the team's small arena at Boston University. All revenue went to the venue, not the franchise.

Both the team and the league folded at the end of the 1978 season. But the experience was invaluable for the young businessman. If the opportunity came again to own a professional sports team, he would make sure that he also owned the team's facilities.

Although he flirted with the idea of bidding for the Red Sox and Celtics, Kraft always had his eyes on one day owning the Patriots. He did his research and learned that team owner Billy Sullivan had made a huge mistake when building his stadium. Sullivan owned the venue but had failed to buy up or control the property surrounding it. In 1985, Kraft began slowly putting his stranglehold on the Patriots by purchasing Foxborough Raceway, the 330-acre horse track next to the stadium. He would have to thank Michael Jackson for his next opportunity. Billy Sullivan and his sons sponsored the pop star's ill-fated 1984 Victory Tour and had put up the home of the Patriots, now called Sullivan Stadium, as collateral to guarantee a $36.6 million advance for the King of Pop and the Jackson brothers. But the Sullivans, all new to the world of concert promotion, were a disorganized bunch who had overestimated merchandising opportunities while underestimating the size of the show. The tour was a massive production that reduced seating at venues by up to 33 percent. The Victory Tour was a disaster for the Sullivan family, and they nearly lost everything. Sullivan was forced to sell controlling interest in the team to Remington shaving CEO Victor Kiam for $84 million, and the stadium fell into bankruptcy.

Bob Kraft seized the opportunity and outbid Kiam and others to buy the property for $22 million. He had learned from his earlier mistake with the Lobsters. *He who controls the land controls everything.* Kiam was about to learn that, too. The new team owner tried to move the Patriots to Jacksonville, Florida, but Kraft wouldn't let him break the team's lease with the stadium, which ran through 2001. Victor Kiam, now in a virtual choke hold, was forced in 1992 to sell the team to Anheuser-Busch heir James Orthwein, who had plans to move the Patriots to his hometown of St. Louis, which had not had a professional football franchise since the Cardinals moved to Phoenix in 1988. It was the business model of the NFL. Struggling teams either had to move or die.

But now the Patriots were showing value. Orthwein hired head coach Bill Parcells, the larger-than-life football genius and mastermind behind two Super Bowl–winning seasons with the New York Giants. Parcells came out of a brief two-year retirement to coach the Patriots and brought with him several former Giants assistants, with the exception of his trusted defensive coordinator Bill Belichick, who was still coaching the Cleveland Browns at the time.

Parcells used his first draft pick for the Patriots to select record-setting quarterback Drew Bledsoe out of Washington State. The six-foot-five, 238-pound passer proved as good as advertised in his rookie campaign. The team struggled as a whole, only earning five wins that season, but the quarterback threw fifteen touchdowns and showed a sense of poise and promise at the position that had been absent in New England for years. More importantly there was a buzz around the Patriots that hadn't been felt since their one trip to the Super Bowl in 1985, when they got stomped by the Chicago Bears. Bill Parcells brought instant credibility to a franchise that had long been considered the doormat of the NFL, and every press conference held by the commanding, quick-witted coach was must-see TV for Boston sports fans. But the new excitement surrounding the team was progressing toward a punch line to the ultimate cruel joke. Absentee owner James Orthwein was about to make good on his plan to uproot the team and move it to Missouri.

Before the last game of the 1993 season, angry fans burned empty cases of Budweiser in the stadium parking lot. If it was to be the final game ever played in New England, the rookie Bledsoe would give the Patriots faithful something to remember as he led the team to an overtime win against the Miami Dolphins with a touchdown pass to receiver Michael Timpson. Many of the nearly 54,000 fans in attendance began the rally cry "Don't take our team, don't take our team!" as Bledsoe and company jogged off the field. Bob Kraft heard the chant as he stepped into an elevator with his son Jonathan. This was the moment he had been waiting for since he watched helplessly as a boy as the Boston Braves left town. This time, however, he had the power and determination to make a difference. James Orthwein was courting potential buyers, and Kraft was among the bidders.

"There's no way we're not winning this," he told his son Jonathan as the elevator door closed.[5]

Kraft traveled to St. Louis for an audience with Orthwein three weeks after the season ended. He offered a bid of $125 million for the team, but the beer baron did not blink. Kraft would have to do better. The stiffest competition came from St. Louis businessman Stan Kroenke, who was willing to plunk down $200 million for the team but demanded that Orthwein pay league fees of about $20 million, for moving the franchise. A deal with Kroenke would also require Orthwein to pay Kraft to get out of the team's lease on Foxborough Stadium, which would not expire for eight more years. The owner turned his attention back to Kraft and said he'd be willing to part with the Patriots for $172 million. It was the steepest price ever paid in the history of the NFL, roughly $30 million more than Jerry Jones had paid for the Dallas Cowboys, "America's Team." Without consulting his wife, Myra, who later told him he was crazy, Bob Kraft accepted Orthwein's deal.

"I'm not going to be the most popular man in St. Louis," Orthwein said at the time. "As far as owning a team, I'm done with that."[6]

James Orthwein was right and couldn't show his face in his hometown, while Kraft was considered a savior back in Boston. He celebrated the purchase by taking Myra and their four sons to a Celtics game, where he was greeted with a standing ovation from the crowd.

The new owner pledged to work with his head coach to take advantage of the small window of opportunity under the NFL's new salary cap, which would force teams to bring player salaries in line. Bill Parcells had other plans. The coach understood that Kraft was a step up from previous owner Orthwein, who had invested nothing in the franchise. During Parcells's first year with the team, players had to drive their own vehicles in full pads to a nearby field to practice because there was no practice facility adjacent to the stadium. Under Kraft, there was now stability and a willingness to invest in a winner. But the head coach demanded total control of the team and wanted Kraft to sign the checks and stay the hell out of the way. This wasn't what Kraft had in mind when he bought the team. Parcells learned this fact the hard way during the 1996 NFL draft when the owner trumped his coach's plans to select a defensive lineman in the first round and, instead, ordered his personnel director Bobby Grier to pick talented but troubled wide receiver Terry Glenn. Parcells was outraged over the slight and made sure that the owner got the message. Kraft considered firing his bombastic coach right on the spot.

"Someone else was calling the shots," Parcells later told *Boston Globe* columnist Dan Shaughnessy. "That was something that bothered me because I wasn't 100 percent confident in the people that were doing it."[7]

But from the outside looking in, it was a match made in heaven. New England fans now had arguably the best coach in the league and an owner who was like them, one who bled Patriots red, white, and blue. The relationship between Kraft and Parcells appeared to work at least for the first couple of seasons, as the Patriots played before sellout crowds and had even managed to sniff the playoffs.

In 1996, Parcells reunited with defensive genius Bill Belichick, who had been recently fired in Cleveland. The two men had a long and successful history together since joining the Giants in 1981, Parcells as defensive coordinator and Belichick as special teams coach. During those early days in the Meadowlands, the pair had shared an office and stayed together at the Hasbrouk Heights Sheraton, where they forged a solid working friendship. Soon, Belichick began to assist Parcells with the defense, and when Parcells was handed the reins of the franchise in 1983, he promoted Belichick to defensive coordinator, despite the initial misgivings of the Giants' resident superstar Lawrence Taylor, who believed Belichick couldn't lead the defense because he'd never played the game.[8] Taylor, a future first-ballot Hall of Famer, became a quick believer in Belichick as the Giants racked up victory after victory and earned two Lombardi Trophies behind one of the league's greatest defenses.

Now Parcells introduced his protégé to Robert Kraft, who liked him and agreed to go over budget and hire Belichick as assistant head coach. Together, Parcells and Belichick mounted a solid season, winning eleven games behind Drew Bledsoe's twenty-seven touchdown passes and more than a thousand yards gained on the ground by running back Curtis Martin. That year also saw the emergence of defensive stalwarts Willie McGinest, Ty Law, and Tedy Bruschi. The Patriots knocked off the Pittsburgh Steelers and the Jacksonville Jaguars to secure a trip to Super Bowl XXXI against the mighty Green Bay Packers and all-world quarterback Brett Favre.

This marked just the second time the Patriots would be stepping onto the sport's biggest stage. But Parcells could not get over Kraft's constant meddling, despite the fact that Terry Glenn, the owner's draft-day favorite, had set a rookie record with ninety receptions. It eventually got so bad that Parcells and Kraft were no longer speaking to each other, so Bill Belichick often served as a go-between with the two. The head coach voiced his frustration to his close friend, *Boston Globe* columnist Will McDonough, who then splashed details of the soured relationship between owner and head coach across the front page of the newspaper in the days leading up to the big game. The rift, according to the longtime newspaper man, was more like a chasm. McDonough intimated that Parcells was done with the Patriots after the Super Bowl, win or lose. Kraft was especially hurt by the timing of the column, which ran just days before the game, in which the Patriots were already big underdogs. New England lost the game 35–21 to the Packers in a matchup that was never truly competitive. Bill Parcells did not fly back to Boston on the team plane, and the marriage was over. All that was left for the divorce lawyers to do was to divide the assets and agree on compensation. The league's worst-kept secret was that Parcells would head down Interstate 95 to coach the New York Jets, the Patriots' biggest AFC rival.

"It blew my mind, to be honest," Robert Kraft admitted years later in an interview with ESPN. "How does he go and accept another job somewhere?"[9]

Kraft said that he investigated the issue and believed that the NFL was working diligently behind the scenes to support the move. "The undercurrent was that having Bill Parcells back in New York running the Jets was good for the NFL," Kraft surmised. "It also told me that the league office was not as pure as I might have thought."[10]

Parcells would eventually be free to coach the Jets, and in return Kraft would receive a number of draft picks and a check for $300,000 to the Patriots' charitable foundation.

The Patriots' owner took Belichick and his wife, Debby, out to dinner to discuss the coaching vacancy and told him that although he thought he was a good coach, the timing was not right to hire him. The owner needed to make a clean break from Bill Parcells and his coaching minions.

Bob Kraft had rid himself of an insubordinate head coach, but he still had a young star quarterback named Drew Bledsoe to continue to build his team around as the Patriots looked toward the new millennium.

Chapter Five

THE UNDERDOG

As the 1997 NFL season began in Foxboro under new and untested head coach Pete Carroll, the young man who would determine the future of the New England Patriots was 805 miles away in Ann Arbor, Michigan, and wrestling with the biggest decision of his life to that point. Tom Brady had just turned twenty years old and he wanted to go home—back to San Mateo, California.

He had been playing or not playing for the University of Michigan for the past two years. Redshirted as a freshman, Brady was now officially entering his sophomore season with the Wolverines and had just received word that he was getting passed over for the starting job at quarterback in favor of fifth-year senior Brian Griese, son of Miami Dolphins great Bob Griese.

Michigan had been a long shot for Brady from the start, when his father, Tom Sr., a University of San Francisco graduate and owner of a small insurance agency in San Mateo, shelled out two thousand dollars to produce fifty-four highlight videos of his son's high school career. The reels included an introduction from Tom's high school coach Tom McKenzie, who described him as "a big, strong, durable athlete with an excellent work ethic."[1]

Stanford University, the University of California Davis, and even tiny St. Mary's College in nearby Moraga, were on the target list. The younger Brady tossed out the University of Michigan as another option. His dad didn't think it would hurt, so they sent a VHS tape out to Ann Arbor.

Brady was the only boy in a household with three older sisters, all great athletes in their own right. Sister Maureen, nearly five years older than Tom, was a star softball player in high school. As a seventeen-year-old pitcher, she played her way onto the U.S. junior Olympic team and won a scholarship to Fresno State University. Sister Nancy was also a softball standout, while middle sister Julie played soccer in high school and later at St. Mary's College. Young Tom's weekend schedule revolved around whatever sport his sisters were involved in at the time. Their mother, Galynn, would squire the brood from field to field. The Brady girls were routinely written up in the sports pages of their small local newspaper, and Tom lived deep in their shadows. Around town, he was known as Maureen Brady's little brother. As a youngster, Tom played basketball and baseball, and most observers figured his future glory as an athlete would be made with a catcher's mitt. But the idea that a kid from San Mateo could one day become a major sports star was not a novel one. It had happened three times before in two different sports. Future NFL Hall of Famer Lynn Swann caught his first passes as a member of the Junipero Serra High School Padres, while both Barry Bonds and Gregg Jefferies had competed on the same field of dreams as Brady before launching their storied careers in Major League Baseball.

Tom was consumed by baseball and didn't play organized football until his freshman year at that same private Catholic high school, when he was fourteen years old. At that stage, he was a doughy kid with a strange mopped mane of the kind popular with some skateboarders his age. Although he had turned heads on the baseball field, he was considered "just another kid" on the gridiron. Brady served as backup quarterback on a freshman team that played nine games without scoring a single touchdown en route to a winless 0–8–1 season. But his coaches soon discovered that he had a strong arm and natural command of the huddle, strengths he had developed as a baseball catcher. When Brady began playing junior varsity as a sophomore, he developed a sign language with his receivers that he continued to use throughout his career.

"When he saw a DB [defensive back] playing too tight, Tom would pull on his face mask and it would change a short route into a streak," said John Kirby, Brady's high school teammate. "I knew the ball would be coming to me and he'd put it right on the money. And he did it time after time. Just like he does now."[2]

Leading the varsity squad beginning his junior year, the young quarterback threw for 3,514 yards and thirty-three touchdowns over the next two seasons. Teammate John Kirby caught forty-two passes from Brady in their senior year. His feats on the baseball field were equally impressive. Over two years playing varsity baseball, Brady batted .311 and smashed eight home runs and eleven doubles. Pro scouts saw great potential in the six-foot-four, two-hundred-pound lefty. The Montreal Expos worked him out at Candlestick Park and were impressed by his arm strength, hitting power, and his presence. The stage wasn't too big for the young man from San Mateo.

Still, Brady seemed to have his heart set on a career in football. He earned MVP honors at the prestigious Cal State football camp heading into his senior year and was ranked among the top high school quarterbacks in California. Brady got his first taste of television as a senior when he was profiled by Bay Area football legend and NFL Hall of Famer Dan Fouts for KPIX in 1994. When the young quarterback came out of the Serra High School locker room and introduced himself to the San Diego Chargers great on the football field before the interview, Fouts sized him up and then whispered to his producer, "This is the guy. This is the guy to watch."[3]

The two quarterbacks sat on the Serra High bleachers, and Fouts asked Brady to describe his strengths as a quarterback.

"Everybody tells me I've got a pretty strong arm, which is good. I'm pretty accurate with it," he replied nervously with hands folded in front of him. "I think I need to work on my speed a little bit but hopefully that'll come in time. Pretty good work ethic so I think I can get the job done."[4]

Brady exuded a quiet confidence in the interview and not the cockiness projected by the other top prep players profiled in the story. Fouts's producer agreed with his assessment. Tom Brady was indeed the guy to watch.

But the big-time college football programs didn't see it.

Only a single college scout attended one of Brady's games during his senior year. The scout flew up from USC and liked what he saw but ultimately couldn't sell Brady to his boss, head coach John Robinson.

When Brady's highlight reel landed on the desk of Bill Harris, an assistant coach at the University of Michigan, Harris was impressed by the player's ability to make short, intermediate, and deep throws. He then shared the tape with the Wolverines' quarterback coach, who also thought Brady was worth taking a closer look at. Harris flew to San Mateo to meet with Brady, his parents, and head football coach Tom McKenzie.

"I found out that he played baseball and that he was a catcher. I'm thinking in my mind, you know, catchers have to be tough. So this kid is going to have that toughness you want if he's back there getting beat behind the plate," Harris recalled.[5]

Brady was invited to visit the Michigan campus and voiced his desire to play for the storied program, which had won ten national titles by 1994. Head coach Gary Moeller called Brady at home to say "We want you." It could have been the beginning of a beautiful friendship, but Moeller was fired in early May after punching a police officer during a drunken incident at a Detroit-area restaurant. Defensive coordinator Lloyd Carr took over the reins of the program as Brady entered Michigan.

When he arrived, there were seven quarterbacks ahead of him on the depth chart.

"I remember being out there on the first day of practice, thinking, 'Man, I'm better than these guys,'" Brady recalled. "But of course I wasn't. But that was always my attitude."[6]

During his sophomore season, with junior quarterback Scott Dreisbach on the sideline recovering from an injury, the starting job came down to a slugfest between Brady and the older Griese. Most observers called it a draw, but under Coach Carr's regime, the tie went to the upperclassman. Brady was hurt by the decision, and for the first time in his life, he actually thought about quitting. He contemplated relinquishing his dream to play for Michigan and transfer to another school, mostly likely Cal State. Brady then marched into Coach Carr's office to voice his frustration. The coach didn't coddle the quarterback.

"You know, Tommy, you gotta worry about yourself," Carr told him. "You gotta go out and worry about the way you play. Not the way the guys ahead of you are playing, not the way your running back is playing and not the way your receiver just ran the route."[7]

Brady chewed on Carr's words and wrestled with the decision overnight. He returned to the coach's office the following day with a renewed focus and determination. Brady pulled a chair in front of Carr's desk and looked him straight in the eye.

"Coach, I'm not gonna leave, and I'm gonna prove to you that I'm the best quarterback."[8]

Carr saw the fire in Brady's eyes, and that burning desire spilled over to the practice field and "The Big House," Michigan Stadium, where he led the team to ten wins. He threw for fourteen touchdowns and 2,427 yards. Brady was named team captain in his senior year, and his previous on-field performance should have been enough to secure him the starting job, but Coach Carr had other plans. He was coveting thy neighbor's house and looking toward the future. Carr had recruited local high school legend and All-America quarterback Drew Henson with the intention of starting him over the solid, reliable Brady.

Michigan teammates compared the rivalry to a race between a draft horse (Brady) and a quarter horse (Henson). From afar, Henson had everything. He had unbelievable quickness and a rocket-like throwing arm. He was the most talented quarterback Lloyd Carr had ever seen.

Tom Brady, on the other hand, was a slow, skinny fourth-year junior with average arm strength and the speed of a tortoise. But those closest to the two quarterbacks saw something else. "As a quarterback in practice every day watching this, it was never really a decision; it was always Tom's job," said senior backup Jason Kapsner. "Tom earned the job in practice every day. Drew was never a leader. He hadn't earned it in practice, but there was a lot of pressure to play Drew."[9]

The threat imposed by Henson's father was that if Drew didn't get the opportunity to play, he'd leave the program and focus solely on his promising career as a baseball player in the New York Yankees system. Once again, nothing came easy for Brady. He sat alone late at night inside the team's practice facility studying game film. He took extra snaps at practice and threw passes until his arm felt like it was hanging by a thread off his shoulder. Five days before Michigan's season opener, Coach Carr still hadn't announced his starting quarterback. When pressed by reporters, the coach replied, "What time's the game? 3:30? You'll see then."[10]

Unwilling to make a decision, Carr instead chose to play both quarterbacks in shifts. Brady would start the game, Henson would play the second quarter, and the hotter hand would emerge from the locker room after halftime to finish the contest. Brady finished four out of five of the team's first games. During a showdown with in-state rival Michigan State, Carr chose Henson over Brady in the second half, but the young phenomenon couldn't find the end zone and the Wolverines fell behind. Panicked, Carr sent Brady back into the game and watched him nearly pull off a comeback win. Michigan managed to hold on to its number nine ranking but lost again the next week to unranked Illinois and Carr threw up his hands, telling reporters, "I have no idea how this team will rebound."[11]

The answer was Tom Brady. Coach Carr gave up the idea of platooning his quarterbacks and decided to ride his draft horse the rest of the way. Michigan would not lose another game. Brady led the team in wins over Penn State and Big Ten archrival Ohio State and capped off the season with a stellar performance before a national audience in the Orange Bowl, defeating the Alabama Crimson Tide 35–34 in overtime. He threw four touchdowns in the win and set a school record for pass completions in a single game with thirty-four.

"He [Brady] won this game," Michigan's star receiver David Terrell said moments after the victory. "Tom Brady showed poise. He showed the heart of a leader, the heart of a lion."[12]

Yet, despite an epic performance on college football's big stage and the praise heaped upon him by his Michigan teammates, Brady found his pathway to the pros littered with land mines.

Chapter Six

GAME CHANGERS

The moment Bill Belichick returned to New England to take over the Patriots in February 2000, he realized that he had inherited a weak and dysfunctional team, one that was a far cry from the squad that played in the 1996 Super Bowl.

He also knew that the stadium on Route 1 in Foxborough would mark the end of the line for his head-coaching career if things didn't go right. As a defensive coordinator, Belichick had won two Super Bowls with the New York Giants under Bill Parcells and had appeared in a third as Parcells's assistant with the Patriots. But as a head coach, he'd tanked in his five-year stint with the Cleveland Browns, turning off media and fans alike with his prickly personality while sporting only one winning season. But as others, like former Giants general manager George Young, saw limited potential in Belichick as a head-coaching candidate for any team, Robert Kraft thought differently. He saw a coach whom he could trust and work with. The head-coaching job in New England was now open after the firing of Pete Carroll, who struggled to replace the larger-than-life Parcells and most recently had failed to make the playoffs. The timing was finally right to bring in Belichick, a man who could relate to Carroll in that he, too, was having difficulty trying to emerge from Parcells's big shadow. Kraft hoped to lure Belichick away from the Jets, where he had served once again as assistant head coach and defensive coordinator under Parcells. Kraft sent a fax to the Jets' front office requesting permission to interview Belichick. Parcells got his hands on the fax and immediately resigned from his position as head coach, which triggered a clause in Belichick's contract that elevated him to head coach following Parcells's departure. It was an attempt by Parcells to checkmate his former boss.

Belichick was furious that he had not been given the opportunity to interview for the Patriots job and was unwilling to play a pawn in his mentor's game of brinksmanship against Kraft. Belichick spent only one day as Jets head coach before writing on a napkin, *I resign as the HC of the NYJ*.

If Parcells's breakup with the Patriots was a messy affair, Belichick's divorce from the Jets was a true War of the Roses. The team refused to let him out of his contract, so Belichick filed an antitrust lawsuit against the franchise and the NFL. After weeks of demands and counterdemands, the coach finally dropped the suit when the Jets and Patriots came to a compromise on compensation. Kraft had just about given up on his dream to hire Belichick and was close to striking a deal with Jacksonville Jaguars defensive guru Dom Capers when Parcells called Kraft's secretary one evening and told her to tell the owner that "Darth Vader" was on the phone.

"I told him [Kraft] there was a way we could do this, but it wasn't getting done for free," Parcells later recalled.[1]

Robert Kraft agreed to give up a first-round draft pick in exchange for what he hoped was a first-rate coach. During his first appearance before the Boston media, Belichick admitted that the shopping list was long and that every phase of the organization had to be improved upon in order to build a winner. Most important, the culture had to change. When Pete Carroll ran the team, players who were disgruntled with the coach and his system could simply march up to the front office and seek asylum. This would not happen under Bill Belichick.

He needed to instill discipline, but he also needed the right players. The Patriots still had a core of stars and potential stars in Drew Bledsoe, linebacker Willie McGinest, and cornerback Ty Law. But the new coach was also looking for a different style of player, one who also had true grit and was easily coachable. He was looking for diamonds in the rough and would need to go mining for these unpolished gems in both free agency and the draft.

It was a tall order, however, and Coach Belichick would need help.

One of his first personnel hires was Dick Rehbein, a journeyman assistant coach who had worked with the Green Bay Packers and the New York Giants. Belichick put him in charge of his quarterbacks. Rehbein was excited to work with a talent like Drew Bledsoe, but first he had to write up the team's insurance policy for the quarterback position. He took two scouting trips, one to Louisiana Tech to work out Tim Rattay, who was a top-ten vote getter for the Heisman Trophy in 1998, and another to Ann Arbor to watch Brady. Neither player was projected to be drafted in the first round, which worked for the Patriots, since they did not have an early pick. Belichick and Rehbein both liked Rattay because he ran a spread offense and had put up gaudy numbers for the Bulldogs. He performed as advertised during the workout, and the Patriots put him on the board as a projected seventh-round pick. The visit to Michigan was almost perfunctory at this point.

Rehbein went to Ann Arbor looking for a player he could mold into a durable third-string quarterback, but what he found was a young man who would alter the course of history for the New England Patriots franchise and the city of Boston. And he knew it right away. When the special teams coach returned home from the scouting trip he told his wife, Pam, "Twenty years from now, people will know the name Tom Brady."[2]

Rehbein wasn't deterred by Brady's woeful performance at the pre-draft NFL Combine in Indianapolis, where he looked soft and ran a mule-like 5.3 forty-yard dash and scored a 33 on a scale of 0 to 50 on the Wonderlic, a test to gauge a player's overall intelligence. His vertical jump was the worst for a quarterback in thirty-two years. The scouting report on Brady was filled with negatives: "Poor build...Skinny...Lacks great physical stature and strength...Lacks mobility and ability to avoid the rush...Lacks a really strong arm...Can't drive the ball downfield...Does not throw a really tight spiral...System-type player who can get exposed if forced to ad-lib, gets knocked down easily."[3]

The positives were few, but to Dick Rehbein they were a better indicator of Brady's potential. "Very poised and composed...Produces in big spots and in big games...Team leader."

Still, the quarterback coach needed to convince his boss Belichick and Bobby Grier, the team's vice president of player personnel. While Grier would be fired two weeks after the draft as Belichick wanted to reshape the front office in his own image, before getting shown the door, the Patriots executive listened to Rehbein's glowing assessment of Brady and made a call to Michigan head coach Lloyd Carr. Grier was the only NFL front office guy to reach out to Carr about his quarterback. The two men had worked together on the staff at Eastern Michigan and Grier valued Carr's advice. Despite his early misgivings, Carr had become a true believer in Tom Brady and expressed some of the traits that could not be measured in a forty-yard dash.

"I told Bobby [Grier] that they'd never regret drafting him and that Tom had every intangible you could ask for," Carr recalls. "I remember his first scrimmage as a true freshman, when I was interim coach and Tom wasn't physically developed yet. The defense just knocked the hell out of him, and he kept getting up. He took a beating and kept standing in there throwing the ball, and that was the day the whole coaching staff realized just how tough Tom was."[4]

Still, if Carr valued Brady's toughness, why did he insist on platooning him with Drew Henson during his senior season? Bill Belichick had a hard time wrapping his head around that question.

"You say, okay, they don't really want this guy as their starting quarterback," Belichick said later. "They want another guy. What's the problem here? It was a bit of a red flag there."[5]

Another issue was the team's relative stability at the quarterback position. When Belichick took over the team a few months prior, the Patriots had forty-two players on the roster and were $10.5 million over the salary cap. New England's front office had to trim the roster to thirty-nine players to fit under the cap, and they already had three quarterbacks under contract, the twenty-eight-year-old Bledsoe, backup veteran John Friesz, and third stringer Michael Bishop. Could the Patriots even afford to draft a player like Tom Brady? What attracted Belichick and his coaches to the Michigan standout was his mental toughness, a characteristic that Lloyd Carr had put an exclamation point on during his phone call with Bobby Grier. Belichick particularly liked the way Brady would get thrown into games and lead the Wolverines back to victory.

The Patriots' brain trust decided it would take him in the third round of the draft, should he still be available. Brady figured that he'd be drafted in the fourth round or so and had even relocated to Metairie, Louisiana, to train with Tennessee quarterback Tee Martin and other NFL prospects in hopes of refining his skills and adding value to his stock before the draft.

Like every other player entering the draft, Brady had no idea where he'd be going and didn't know much about the Patriots other than the fact that the team was all set at quarterback. He hoped that on draft day he'd get a call from his hometown team, the 49ers, a team that failed to make the playoffs in 1999 after superstar quarterback Steve Young suffered a career-ending concussion. Brady participated in a local combine for San Francisco head coach Steve Mariucci and the team's special adviser, the legendary Bill Walsh, and failed to impress the man who'd drafted Joe Montana, Tom's idol. Brady and his father were sitting in the stands of Candlestick Park when Montana cemented his own legend by heaving the ball to tight end Dwight Clark in the end zone to win the NFC championship against the Dallas Cowboys, which propelled the San Francisco 49ers to their first Super Bowl appearance in 1981.

When it came to selecting a quarterback in the third round, the 49ers chose Giovanni Carmazzi, a six-two, 224-pound senior from Hofstra. Less than twenty miles south of San Francisco, Brady and his parents sat together in their living room watching the draft unfold on television and were stunned by the announcement.

"We had season tickets for the 49ers for twenty-five years and we were just hurt," recalled Brady's father. "We kind of took it personally."[6]

Carmazzi was just one of six quarterbacks called by then–NFL commissioner Paul Tagliabue to elevate lowly franchises around the league as Brady continued to wait. He could watch no more.

The fourth and fifth rounds came and went. As draft picks were being announced in the sixth round, Brady told his parents that he had to clear his head so he grabbed his baseball bat and left the house. He returned later to learn that another twenty-two players had been chosen and still his name wasn't called.

"I gotta get outta here," he told his dad.

This time, Tom Sr. and wife Galynn tagged along as Tom began walking back up the street. The young quarterback was confronted with the potential reality that he'd have to give up his dream of playing professional football and join his father's insurance practice.

What he didn't know was that his name was still up there on the Patriots' draft board. The idea of selecting him in the third round was quashed to address the team's more immediate needs. Belichick wanted to boost the offense, so he picked a couple of linemen to protect Drew Bledsoe and a running back to strengthen the ground game. In the fifth round, the Patriots selected a tight end out of Boise State named Dave Stachelski, who would play only nine games in the NFL and none with New England. As they entered the sixth round, it no longer made sense to pass on Tom Brady. The Patriots selected the kid from San Mateo with the 199th pick, a pick that has since gone down as the greatest steal in NFL history. But at that moment no one knew it, no one except maybe Dick Rehbein, who called his wife immediately from the team's draft-day war room.

"We got him," he told her. "We got him!"[7]

PART II

Chapter Seven

LEARNING CURVE

Tom Brady arrived in Foxborough without fanfare. He was invisible. There was no excitement surrounding the sixth-round choice and the only question tossed about by Patriots beat reporters was why the team had wasted a pick on another quarterback when they already had Bledsoe, a franchise player, plus two serviceable backups. Bill Belichick could ill afford a draft-day flop heading into his first season as head coach. But he didn't see it that way. Belichick was methodical. He had set out to build a skyscraper one steel beam at a time. Like the coach, the afterthought draft pick from Michigan also had an eye toward the future. When owner Robert Kraft first met Brady, the quarterback was carrying a pizza box and looked like a kid strolling across campus on his way to class, not a legitimate NFL quarterback. Kraft couldn't get over how skinny Brady was—a "beanpole of a kid" is how the owner remembers him. The rookie walked right up to Kraft and introduced himself.

"Hi, I'm Tom Brady."

"I know who you are," Kraft replied. "You're our sixth-round draft choice from Michigan."

Brady looked him right in the eye. "Yeah, I'm the best decision this organization has ever made."[1]

The owner looked at him curiously. Kraft smiled, nodded, and walked away. He was amused at first, but there was something in Brady's voice that stuck with the owner. He immediately called his son Jonathan and told him about the encounter he'd just had with the fourth-string quarterback.

"God, really? Was he cocky?" Jonathan asked.

Bob Kraft thought about the question. He didn't believe Brady had a cocksure attitude. Most players have that. It was something else.

"I'm telling you. There's something about the way he said it that I believe him."[2]

The owner didn't mention the conversation to the coach.

Brady was issued the number 12, a jersey number that held no significance for the franchise. It was a number that had been given to past quarterbacks like backup Matt Cavanaugh and even to a punter. No player had worn the number with distinction, but the rookie was determined to change that.

Jack Mula, a longtime agent and Patriots executive, recalled his first encounter with Brady at Foxboro Stadium shortly after the draft. Because the quarterback was a sixth-round pick, his contract was a standard late-round rookie deal, but Brady made it a point to go up to the business office on the fifth floor to meet Mula, who was then the team's director of legal and business affairs.

"I just want to meet the man who is going to sign my contract," Brady told him. Mula, a former agent who represented players for twenty years, said he'd never heard of a player going out of their way to meet folks in the business department. Brady also met with the team's salary-cap analyst, and introduced himself to everyone on the floor. And he asked Mula to send him a copy of his contract.

"That stuff is always left to the agents," Mula said. "He didn't have to do that. He was just a kid, but he came up as a mature businessman. He knew it wasn't the last contract he was going to be signing with us and he just wanted to meet the people up there."[3]

In the late summer of 2000, Brady purchased a spacious condominium in Franklin, Massachusetts, from fellow Michigan Wolverine and star Patriots cornerback Ty Law, conveniently located just ten minutes from the stadium. This same condo was once owned by former Patriots quarterback Scott Zolak, and was later passed on from Brady to another Patriots signal caller, Rohan Davey. From the outside, a professional athlete buying a condo near his team's facility may not appear to be anything out of the ordinary. But the NFL's non-guaranteed contracts and well-earned "Not For Long" moniker keep most players living as renters until they are in a long-term second veteran contract—unless they're a high draft pick with significant guaranteed money. That usually means first, second, and (maybe) third rounders. Brady's decision to buy a home as a sixth-round pick on a roster with four quarterbacks was tangible evidence that his famous declaration to owner Robert Kraft wasn't just bluster. Brady believed it, and made an unusual initial financial investment in himself.

Wisely, Brady took on rent-paying rookie roommates in the three-bedroom spread, adding fellow class of 2000 Patriots defensive end David Nugent from Purdue University, taken two picks after Brady at number 201, and tight end Chris Eitzmann, an undrafted free agent from Harvard University. First-year Patriots linebacker Matt Chatham, from the University of South Dakota, had been released by the St. Louis Rams prior to the start of the 2000 season but claimed by the Patriots for opening day. Chatham rented a cramped apartment in North Attleboro but became fast friends with the Franklin crew, crashing in the basement of the Franklin condo with regularity. He wasn't a paying customer, but to this day Brady affectionately calls him "roomie."

Coach Belichick had low expectations for the 2000 season. His players simply weren't tough enough. "We've got too many people who are overweight, too many guys who are out of shape, and too many guys who haven't paid the price they need to pay at this time of the season. You can't win with 40 good players while the other team has 53," he groused during training camp.[4]

The team stumbled out of the gate, losing its first four games. The offense led by Drew Bledsoe would score thirty points only once that season, during a December victory against the Kansas City Chiefs. The Patriots managed only five wins and finished dead last in their division, the AFC East.

The 2000 Patriots season is often overlooked in the meteoric rise of this franchise, but the shared experiences of that painful 5–11 campaign is the thorny bush that roster survivors had to crawl through to get to the luxurious promised land of Patriots Place as we know it today. Belichick was intent on finding his kind of players, and weeding out those that wouldn't commit to his brand of smart, tough, and emotionally challenging professional football. "This ain't Club Med" was a constant reminder that the coaching staff used to chide the players. The 2000 Patriots were known to practice longer, with far more physical practices, than was the NFL norm of the time—meeting at all hours of the day when players in other organizations were happily at home. This was Belichick's litmus test. It was not like this elsewhere in the NFL. You had to want to be a part of this unique culture, or you would soon be gone. Adopt his vision of the football work grind, or quickly lose the opportunity to play football for work.

And for Tom Brady, who survived as the rare fourth quarterback on that 2000 roster, the exhausting schedule that Belichick put before the players was never enough.

"Brady and I would stay out after practice a minimum of thirty minutes, where it's just me running routes and him throwing to me…over and over and over again," recalls former tight end

Chris Eitzmann. "A lot of days we'd basically be out there right up until the next meeting, so sometimes it would be as much as an hour. It was fucking horrible. Brady just wanted to keep going and going and going. I wanted some extra work, too, because I was always on the bubble, but this was different. He'd move me around, split me out some, but basically he'd have me run the entire tight-end route package. We would just run them until I was dead."[5]

Matt Chatham spent each practice working against Brady, testing him, disrupting his pre-snap reads and passes. Coach Belichick would also pour water from his personal Gatorade bottle onto the football just before the snap to make it difficult for the center and Brady to handle. The defense would be told the coming route combinations to jump. Everything during the practice week was set up to make life hard on this ascending young quarterback and the offensive group he was charged with leading.

After one rough late-season practice, Coach Belichick laid into his young quarterback with a vicious tongue lashing. It wasn't that Brady was playing poorly or having an off day, the offense had merely stalled out because the defense was given the game plan ahead of time and could predict Brady's every move.

"I went up to Tom in the lunchroom after practice to try and explain that we were being encouraged to be assholes, to jump certain routes, grab and hold, and make life unusually difficult for them," Chatham recalls.

He told Brady that he would be happy to back off so that the quarterback could find his rhythm again.

"No. Fuck that, Chatham," the rookie replied angrily. "Keep it coming. We need it."

Meanwhile, the Franklin condo became a post-practice safe haven for this crew of exhausted and battered young Patriots clinging to their coveted roster spots. Their bruised bodies covered in ice bags, the players would drink beer, play video games, and then fall asleep with their playbook. Each day was a carbon copy of the next. *Wash, rinse, repeat.*

But despite all the extra work, Brady remained the last quarterback on the totem pole for most of his rookie season, behind Bledsoe, John Friesz, and second-year pro Michael Bishop. This meant twenty-two-year-old Brady rarely traveled for away games. Fellow rookie Dave Nugent played as a backup defensive tackle, so he traveled and saw limited playing time. When he returned from one particular away game, he was struck by how Brady was dealing with the frustration and disappointment of not yet having the role he so craved. "I get back to our condo. It's a crazy-late hour. But Tom was still up, sitting in the living room with his offensive playbook out studying," Nugent said. "I set my bags down and walked into the den. He puts his playbook down on the coffee table and starts eagerly asking me all about the game and how I did."[6]

Nugent was initially thrown off by Brady's genuine excitement. He had a real interest in the tight end's performance, but he was also eager to know all the details of the game. The quarterback wanted to know *everything.*

"As I went through it all and answered all his questions, I felt for him because I knew the interest was from how much he wanted to be a part of it all. But at the same time, he showed so much excitement and happiness for me. I'd never seen anything like this before."

Nugent asked Brady how he kept such a positive attitude when it really didn't seem like the coaches knew he existed. He wasn't given many chances in practice and was lucky to get scout team snaps.

"All I can do is focus on what I can control," Brady told him.

He could not control what the coaches thought, what other players thought, how the quarterbacks in front of him performed, how the receivers he threw to performed, or whether or not he was getting enough reps.

"All I can do is focus on how hard I practice, how much I study, and how prepared I am when I get my snaps. When my time comes, I'll be ready."

This wasn't something Brady had been programmed to say. Nugent remembers the conviction in his voice during their conversation as well as the determination in his eyes.

"Even now, when I think about how he looked at me, how oddly sincere he was, and knowing how it all turned out, I still get goose bumps."

Brady carried that authenticity and quiet confidence with him onto the practice field.

Being in the huddle with any of the other Patriots quarterbacks was different. "You get in the huddle, and you feel like you're part of a business—just do your job and don't fuck up," Eitzmann recalls. "It was just an entirely different experience with Tommy. This is what made him so great. Guys get in his huddle and they want to win for him. It's such a weird, rare thing. His magic is that guys will get cut, but still feel like they let Tommy down as much as themselves."

During home games, Brady stood on the sideline while Drew Bledsoe ran the huddle, but with each play he would imagine himself right in the middle of the action.

"I take a lot of mental reps," the rookie told a reporter midseason. "I see what Drew does out there and I know the play and I'm looking at the defense and when the ball snaps, I'll think 'what would I have done on that play? Why did Drew throw it there?...What would I have done differently? If you apply that throughout the game, let's say you're the backup and you're put in during the fourth quarter, that first snap in the fourth quarter can't be the first snap you've taken all day mentally, or you're gonna be so far behind you'll never catch up."[7]

Without an offense of his own to lead on game day that first year, Brady had to have a place to focus all that competitiveness. The rookie dorm-like culture of the condo provided the perfect outlet, with downtime almost always including some tinge of competition. Nights off were frequently spent in Boston at The Rack, a sprawling sports bar filled with pool tables where Brady and his teammates would frequently wager on games of "3-ball." Another favorite spot was F1 Boston, in Braintree, for indoor go-cart racing, where these giant men would squeeze into tiny motorized cars not made for football frames. In nearly every endeavor, there was a thread of competition. None of the guys were that big into video gaming, but one day Brady went out to a local pawnshop and bought an old Nintendo system, including some classic games like Tecmo Bowl and Mario Cart. The teammates competed in all-day Tecmo Bowl tournaments. They didn't have a lot of disposable cash in those days, so sometimes the wagering would take on a more creative form with public shame as the currency: *a naked lap around the roundabout in front of the condo for the loser.* It was largely a community with a lot of older couples, and naturally, this wasn't the most family-friendly display. Without fail, the loser would take his lap. And with similar certainty, the winners would lock the front door and close the garage, just long enough to make it sufficiently uncomfortable.

A well-earned hatred of losing was strong in the condo. In the off-season following Brady's rookie year, the four teammates took to playing frequently in celebrity charity softball and basketball games. In one basketball game in East Boston against their local fire department, Brady began screaming at the group of current and alumni Patriots players about their lack of effort. Veteran quarterback Damon Huard had been signed that spring to compete for a backup quarterback position and was part of the group that received Brady's scorn as the team fell behind in the charity contest.

"Brady just started going off on us. *We're fucking losing to a bunch of firefighters!* Everyone just looked at each other like 'Is this guy serious?' Next thing you know we're in the most competitive charity basketball game you'll ever see and Brady's banking in three-point shot after three-point shot. And this steamy little high school gym just starts going crazy," Huard said.[8]

Those who packed the small East Boston gym had no idea who Brady was. He'd only played in one NFL game so far against the Detroit Lions, where he completed only one pass for six yards in a lopsided loss. The fans had flocked to the charity basketball game to watch more established Patriots players, but suddenly all eyes were on the team's fourth-string quarterback and his thorough command over his more seasoned teammates. The players also recognized the unique character of this former unsung draft pick.

Brady's leadership skills were first heralded by coach Dick Rehbein before the 2000 draft, and his early prognostication was proved correct during the quarterback's rookie year. Rehbein would hurry home from practice each day and tell his daughters Betsy and Sarabeth all the progress Brady was making on the field and behind the scenes. The coach talked about Brady as if he were his own son and charted his development in a journal. Rehbein saw the player's potential, but was also quick to point out his deficiencies. One day when the coach stepped away from his office, Brady sneaked in and took a peek at Rehbein's journal. He flipped through the first couple of pages and found his name along with a notation that "everything he does is slow."

Rehbein had to teach him how to react to the tempo of the professional game and how to overcome the fog of war and improvise when a play broke down.

"Tommy, you're trying to see everything," Rehbein warned him. "But instead you're seeing nothing."[9]

Brady continued to study and take reps long after practice was called for the day. He was learning the game at an accelerated level but physically he had yet to grow into his tall, lanky frame. Rehbein urged him to spend more time in the weight room during the off-season, and Brady did just that, returning for his second training camp in Smithfield, Rhode Island, with twenty pounds of added muscle. He was no longer the skinny kid that Robert Kraft had encountered the year before, but he carried the same confidence. While others saw Tom fighting for a backup job against Damon Huard and Michael Bishop, Brady was preparing to wage a competitive battle with the face of the franchise.

"I'm gonna beat out Bledsoe," Brady told Chris Eitzmann. "You watch."

The quarterback's words lacked all sense and logic. The Patriots had just signed Drew Bledsoe to a record ten-year $103 million contract, and owner Robert Kraft was building a shiny new palace to replace the old tin can, Foxboro Stadium, considered by many to be the worst pro football stadium in America.

Chapter Eight

TAKING HITS

The abysmal performance by the Patriots during Belichick's first season as head coach was not to be repeated, and he was intent on weeding out the players that did not fit his mold. The draft had been a good one, with prime picks such as defensive tackle Richard Seymour and offensive left tackle Matt Light joining the roster. New England also brought in veterans with true grit and character, including linebackers Brian Cox, Mike Vrabel, and Roman Phifer. The pieces of Belichick's puzzle were beginning to fit into place. The team looked stout on the defensive side of the ball, but what would the 2001 Patriots offense bring?

Dick Rehbein's job was to get more production out of Drew Bledsoe, who had thrown seventeen touchdowns with thirteen interceptions the past season. He was now entering his ninth NFL season, and despite his physical gifts, the six-foot-five, 238-pound quarterback was still prone to head-scratching mental mistakes and one of the worst "tells" in the league. Indeed, Bledsoe had a nasty habit of patting the football before each throw, which alerted defensive backs as to where the ball was headed. Tom

Brady, however, didn't make those mistakes. Unlike Bledsoe, who relied more on his physical prowess, Tom was a true student of the game. Rehbein recommended that he read books about other NFL quarterbacks like Ken Anderson and Phil Simms and even suggested that his young quarterback pick up a biography of General George S. Patton. Brady's assignment wasn't only to read the books, but write a report on them as if he were in high school. The coach wanted his protégé to understand every facet of leadership and commanding an army of his peers. The homework assignments weren't something Rehbein could give to a veteran like Bledsoe, who lived in a $10 million home. Instead, he became a sounding board for Bledsoe if something wasn't going right on the field or with the other coaches.

While at training camp that summer of 2001, Rehbein had been given a rare couple of days off along with other Patriots coaches, so he took his twelve-year-old daughter Sarabeth to their local gym for a quick workout. The coach practiced what he preached and believed in the value of conditioning. He ran four times a week despite the fact that he'd been diagnosed with cardiomyopathy, or an enlarged heart. Rehbein had been treating the condition with daily medication for years. As he ran on the treadmill, no doubt thinking about practices and coaches' meetings to come, he suddenly felt light-headed and then everything went black. As he collapsed, someone yelled, "Man down, man down." His daughter was at the other end of the gym when she heard the shouts. Rehbein quickly regained consciousness and managed to walk himself into the ambulance for the ride to Massachusetts General Hospital for tests. Doctors kept the coach hospitalized overnight and ran him through several exams. A stress test was scheduled the following morning, and Rehbein called Patriots offensive coordinator Charlie Weis and told him not to worry and that he'd see him later that day at a coaches' meeting scheduled for 7 p.m. Rehbein completed his stress test and was in the cool-down period when he lost consciousness again. This time, his heart stopped beating and he couldn't be revived and died.

Dick Rehbein was only forty-five years old.

The team was devastated, and nobody more so than Brady. The coach had believed in him when so many others had not. Rehbein had tutored the second-year quarterback with just the right combination of nurturing and tough love. Now he was gone. Bill Belichick did not replace his late coach, but instead, the team dedicated its entire season to his memory. At first, it looked like a most dubious honor as the Patriots lost the season opener to the Cincinnati Bengals 23–17.

By this time, Brady had earned the role as Bledsoe's primary backup. After Rehbein's death, Belichick tasked himself with the mission of mentoring his quarterbacks. He'd never spent much time with Tom Brady until then. The head coach recognized quickly that the Michigan product had both the skills and an understanding of the game that would allow him to compete and succeed in the league. If Brady's trajectory continued upward, the coach would eventually be forced to make the difficult decision on which quarterback gave the team the best chance of winning for the future. Number 12's teammates were also impressed.

Patriots tight end Jermaine Wiggins was one of those players with nothing guaranteed to him in that 2001 training camp, fighting for a roster spot alongside Tom Brady. "The biggest thing I noticed about Brady right off was his intensity during camp. You could see his competitive nature real easy as he was fighting to get snaps and make the team. I'd be in the huddle with Tom during camp practices with the second or third team, and you'd see that same fight that you see today—he wanted to win every rep no matter who he was playing with or going against. It speaks highly of what's inside him—how badly he wanted to show everybody he deserved to be there."[1]

According to 2000 draft classmate running back Patrick Pass,

"Tom spent his downtime in that 2001 camp trying to get extra reps with the receivers—and that's not unusual for a quarterback trying to work his way up a roster. But he also wanted them from the running backs—guys like myself, J. R. Redmond, and Kevin Faulk. *That's different.* He'd try to polish his game with everybody. These are the things most other QBs overlook. But look how important those relationships with his backs have been over the years!"[2]

The topic of football and just about everything else was placed on hold, however, two days later when the United States came under attack on 9/11. For a team still numbed by the sudden death of their beloved quarterback coach, the shock and horror of September 11 brought their grieving to a new and unimaginable level. Drew Bledsoe was filming a television commercial for Papa Gino's pizza when he heard the news, while his understudy Brady was driving his yellow Jeep to the stadium when the alerts came over the radio. He immediately turned around and drove back to the condo in Franklin and turned on the television and watched the nightmare of the morning continue to unfold. Patriots offensive lineman Joe Andruzzi was sitting in a dentist's chair when he first heard that a small plane had struck the World Trade Center. He immediately thought about his three brothers, all New York City firemen, who had responded to the disaster. All three managed to narrowly escape with their lives that day while 343 fellow firefighters perished underneath the rubble of the twin towers. The league suspended play for September 16 and resumed the season the following week.

The entire world, however, would change over the next twelve days. The United States was now at war against the Taliban in Afghanistan, while at home the wounds were still raw and emotions remained high. The nation was in need of healing and the game of football, a symbol of American toughness and pride, allowed fans to begin that process.

When the Patriots took the field against the New York Jets at Foxboro Stadium, the team was led by Joe Andruzzi, who charged across the turf waving two small American flags before joining his brothers in their NYFD uniforms at midfield. The game itself could have been an afterthought given the magnitude of the moment. But instead, it was one that altered the course of the franchise forever. The game was a low-scoring affair, one plagued by four Patriots turnovers, including an interception thrown by Bledsoe in the red zone. From the looks of it, the team was headed for another loss and fans were ready to buckle themselves in for yet another disappointing season. Brady watched the action on the sideline, still mentally taking every snap alongside the starting quarterback.

And then it happened.

Brady didn't just see it. He could feel it. It was the loudest hit he'd ever heard. The Jets were ahead 10–3 with just five minutes left in the fourth quarter. Bledsoe was facing yet another long third down, and as the ball was snapped, he searched for an open receiver but was chased out of the pocket by a defensive swarm. He decided to run toward the first-down marker but was met by a 260-pound freight train, Jets linebacker Mo Lewis, who threw his shoulder and body into the chest of Bledsoe, knocking him down on the sideline. The quarterback suffered a concussion and worse. His mind was scrambled. Bledsoe didn't know where he was and couldn't remember his two-minute plays, which he had run and practiced for years. It was a vicious hit that should have kept any player out of the game. Instead Bledsoe returned to action after a series and even managed to complete a two-yard pass to fullback Marc Edwards. But he was merely relying on muscle memory now, and Belichick finally decided to take him out of the game in the final two minutes and replace him with Tom Brady.

As Joe Andruzzi revealed, "When Drew went down, it wasn't really known to the guys in the huddle that Tom would be coming out. We had [Damon] Huard as the vet…but then came Tom jogging in. We all knew his work ethic, all the work he'd done in the off-season. But it's not like we'd worked with him a bunch."

Up to this moment, number 12 had only thrown six passes in the NFL. Everything was happening so fast, and the second-year quarterback was reacting to the moment, yet there was a sense of calm that came over him.

"I felt prepared," he recalled. "And it really felt like football, like something I had done many times before."[3]

Tom entered the game and completed six out of eleven passes and also made a nice nine-yard run. Barely anyone in the stadium that day paid much attention to Brady during those final minutes as concern was focused on the face of the franchise.

Meanwhile, Bledsoe was rushed by ambulance to the hospital, but not for a head injury. He'd complained to Patriots team physician Dr. Thomas Gill of intense pain in his shoulder. Gill considered the possibility that Bledsoe's C3 nerve, which aerates the diaphragm and allows breathing, could be in distress. The nerve goes to the top of the shoulder, but the real problem was in the abdomen.

Bledsoe's stomach and chest were filling with blood. He lost consciousness on the way to the hospital. When he arrived, doctors found that he had torn a blood vessel behind his rib, which was now filling his chest with three liters of blood. They managed to drain the blood quickly and stabilize Bledsoe. Had Dr. Thomas Gill not made the initial diagnosis, Drew Bledsoe could have died. The starting quarterback would need more than a month to recover, which meant the team's playoff hopes would be determined by Tom Brady—even though the team was considering chasing after retired quarterbacks Jim Harbaugh and former Patriot Scott Zolak to fill the void.

Brady's first NFL start came the following week against the quarterback he would be measured against for the rest of his career—Peyton Manning. To this point, their journeys could not have been more different. While Brady had been largely unheralded, Manning was a former number one overall draft choice coming out of the University of Tennessee. Not only had Manning been anointed by his new team, the Indianapolis Colts, but the league looked at him as the heir to the quarterback throne previously held by legends like Dan Marino and John Elway. The NFL's future rested largely on the shoulders of number 18 for the Colts, while no one gave more than a passing glance at number 12 for the Patriots.

The only person to discuss Brady and Elway in the same breath at that time was Bill Belichick, and the comparison wasn't a good one.

"I don't think we're talking about John Elway here, but I don't know how many of those there are," the frustrated coach told reporters, who wondered why the team hadn't turned to a more seasoned backup like Damon Huard. "He's [Brady] got a good NFL arm. I really don't think I'm going to be standing here week after week talking about the problems that Tom Brady had. I have confidence in him."[4]

The game was played in Foxboro in front of a crowd mostly wearing Bledsoe jerseys. Manning's backup, Mark Rypien, who won a Super Bowl with the Washington Redskins, didn't see anything to fear in the young, opposing quarterback.

"You looked at Tom and it's not like anything just stood out about him," Rypien remembered. "There are kids you see in warm-ups and you go, 'Wow!' Nothing Tom ever did was just an awe factor."[5]

Patriots star Willie McGinest rallied his troops on the defensive side of the ball. If the team had a chance of winning, it would be the job of the defense to carry the day. Belichick, already considered by most as a defensive genius, devised a plan to pressure Manning from the middle and left side, confuse him, and force him out of the pocket. But it was the Colts defense that drew first blood, sacking Brady on the very first offensive play. After throwing some incomplete passes, he finally settled down and managed the game with handoffs to running backs Antowain Smith and Kevin Faulk. He also completed thirteen out of twenty-three passes that day with no interceptions but no touchdowns either. Manning, on the other hand, had one of his worst outings as a pro, getting picked off three times, including a return for a touchdown. Brady won his first game as a starter 44–13 over Indy and his first head-to-head matchup against Manning in what would become the greatest rivalry in NFL history.

Fans got a glimpse of the future when the team traveled to San Diego for game five and Tom led the team back from a ten-point deficit with just four minutes left and won it in overtime. Brady threw for 364 yards that day and shared star billing with receiver David Patten, who was another player that Dick Rehbein had fought hard for.

Belichick offered a posthumous thank-you to his late coach after the game for insisting they sign Brady and Patten. "Even though he's gone," he said of Rehbein. "He's not forgotten by any of us."

The Patriots had three wins against one loss over their next four games as fans waited for Drew Bledsoe to heal and return to the lineup. Coach Bill Belichick was having different thoughts. He liked the way Brady managed the game and played within himself instead of relying on talent and instinct the way Bledsoe often had.

Tom Brady played smart, and it seemed to have an effect on the defense, which had come together with an aggressiveness that kept them in games. The team was trending up, so why change things now?

"Brady was out of sorts when he was first learning to be a starting quarterback," Andruzzi recalled. "He held his press conferences in his locker, so we just hosed him down with silly string in front of all the reporters—anything to bust his chops. Our offensive line was a bunch of jokers back then, but we helped keep Brady grounded, keep things light in a new and tense situation."

Bledsoe was cleared to play after a fifty-one-day recovery during week eleven of the 2001 season. The news came in a press conference with his doctors at Massachusetts General Hospital.

"I'm itching to get back there," Bledsoe told reporters. "I feel strong and I've been working out for the last couple of weeks and I feel great."[6]

But to Bledsoe's dismay, Belichick kept the franchise quarterback on the sidelines in favor of Brady. The replacement responded that week with a four-touchdown performance in a big win over the New Orleans Saints.

It was the beginning of a magical run.

Chapter Nine

IT'S GOOD!

The Brady-led Patriots would win the rest of their remaining regular-season games in 2001 to finish first in the AFC East with an 11–5 record. The team was headed back to the playoffs behind its second-year head coach and second-year quarterback.

Despite the team's late-season run, however, there was at least one Patriots player that didn't believe Brady had what it took to lead the team into the postseason. Drew Bledsoe met privately with Coach Belichick near the end of the season and warned him that the team could not win with Brady, who was virtually a rookie quarterback. It was the franchise QB's attempt to regain control of his team and his career. Belichick didn't agree, but it would not be the last time that he would be confronted with the question.

The Patriots were scheduled to play host to the Oakland Raiders in their first playoff game, the last one played in that old tin can, Foxboro Stadium. Owner Robert Kraft planned to open a new state-of-the-art stadium the following year and the renewed fan frenzy surrounding the team could not have come at a better time.

The playoff showdown with the Raiders would later be known

by two distinct nicknames, one for Patriots fans and one for all those others living outside New England. Locals nostalgically refer to it as "the Snow Bowl," while members of Raider Nation bitterly call it "the Tuck Rule game."

There was a real animosity between the two franchises that had been festering for decades. The teams first met in the divisional round of the AFC playoffs in 1976, when the Patriots fell victim to a hotly disputed roughing-the-passer call against defensive tackle Ray "Sugar Bear" Hamilton on Raider quarterback Ken Stabler that led to an Oakland win. Nearly a decade later, in January 1986, New England would exorcise those demons by defeating the Raiders in the playoffs 27–20. Patriots general manager Patrick Sullivan taunted Raiders defensive end Howie Long after the game and was punched in the head by Long's teammate Matt Millen.

Those players and executives were all long gone, but the bad blood remained between the two teams. New Englanders were bracing for the first significant snowfall of the season as Patriots fans piled into their cars and headed to Foxboro to renew their tailgating rituals on Saturday, January 19, 2002. As the snow began to fall that day, traffic halted to a crawl along Route 1 in both directions leading to the stadium. Tom Brady, the young player with the hopes of the Patriots faithful on his shoulders, was one of those stuck in the game-day traffic tie-up. Two and a half hours before kickoff, Brady had to call the team's head of security to coordinate a police escort to get him to the game. Meanwhile, a biting wind enveloped the stadium and the snow fell harder as the teams took to the field. Old man winter had arrived just in time to serve as the Patriots' twelfth man, but the Raiders weren't intimidated.

"They [Patriots] wished for snow, they wished for it to be cold," shouted Raider linebacker Travian Smith during warm-ups. "But there's one thing they didn't wish for, they didn't wish for the Raiders."[1]

The prophecy proved true, at least in the first half. Brady and the offense were stuck and there was no police escort in sight. The Patriots entered the locker room at halftime down seven points, but the game did not appear competitive. The Raiders had dominated both sides of the ball on a sloppy, snow-covered field. This wasn't the kind of effort that fans expected, and Brady and his teammates were roundly booed as they marched into the locker room. The natives might have been getting restless, but both the quarterback and Coach Belichick knew that it was no time to panic.

On a day of brutal weather, which made consistently completing downfield throws a mere fantasy, feeding a sure-handed tight end Jermaine Wiggins with shorter, sticks-moving completions was an absolute must for the Patriots to win. "I've always prided myself on being able to catch everything, on having really good hands. We ran a little tight-end screen against Oakland where I went in motion and I dropped the ball. I was on the sidelines really upset because it was such an easy catch—I just took my eyes off it trying to run. Tom comes up to me and says, 'Hey, listen, don't worry about that. We gonna keep feeding you.' Here comes the quarterback giving me confidence to know he's not going to give up on me, he still trusts me. Then he says 'Just keep getting open' and walks away. I ended up getting opportunities throughout the rest of the game to do my part to contribute."

As the second half unfolded, Brady sent a jolt of electricity through the stadium as he scrambled through five inches of snow and found the end zone, where he spiked the ball and then himself as he toppled onto the powder. In a moment, the Patriots were back in it. The score was now 13–10 in favor of Oakland, but fans could feel the momentum shifting. New England had the ball with just a minute and fifty seconds left to play. Brady ran over to the sideline to consult with offensive coordinator Charlie Weis and told him that he wanted to throw a slant pass on the next play.

Oakland cornerback Eric Allen overheard the exchange and reported it back to his teammates. The Raiders were ready.

As Tom took the direct snap, he dropped back, looking for an open receiver running the slant pattern, but an opposing linebacker had closed that window. He pumped the ball and was suddenly struck by a small missile, former Michigan teammate Charles Woodson, blitzing from Brady's right. Woodson swatted Brady's right arm during the hit and the ball came loose. Another Oakland player pounced on it and the play was immediately ruled a fumble. With the Raiders now in possession of the football with less than two minutes left, they could run out the clock and begin making arrangements for the AFC championship game. Oakland's players started celebrating on the sideline while Brady and the Patriots were now faced with the realization that their season was coming to an end.

At that moment, the replay buzzer held by Walt Coleman, the game's head referee, went off. He had issued the ruling on the field although he hadn't seen for himself what had happened to the ball or when it came out of Brady's hand. Coleman ran over to the replay screen, where he reviewed video taken from the front of the play. This angle clearly showed that Brady's throwing arm was coming forward at the exact moment of the Woodson hit before the ball fell out of his hand. Coleman recognized immediately that the play was not a fumble but an incomplete forward pass under NFL Rule 3, Section 22, Article 2, Note 2.

The play was overturned to the relief of Brady and the Patriots and to the dismay, if not outright anger, of the Raiders. Brady knew that he'd been given a fortunate call from the NFL gods, as the play sure felt like a fumble to him. He wouldn't be branded the goat after all. But he wouldn't be the game's hero either. That distinction would be saved for the team's kicker, Adam Vinatieri, who belted an impossible forty-five-yard field goal through a wall of wind and snow to tie the game and send it into overtime, where he gave a repeat performance, this kick from twenty-three yards out to seal the win.

The AFC championship game was held the following week in Pittsburgh, where the Steelers were heavy favorites. Some players wearing the black and gold thought very little of the Patriots and believed that a trip to the Super Bowl was a foregone conclusion, so they confidently began making travel plans for their families. This line of thinking could not be found anywhere in Foxborough, as Belichick routinely drilled into his players the mantra of "one game at a time." Dick Rehbein's wife and two daughters were named the Patriots' honorary captains for the game.

Under a sea of waving "terrible towels," the Patriots drew an early lead in the game, thanks to elusive receiver Troy Brown, the team's MVP of the season, who fielded a punt and scampered fifty-five yards for a touchdown. Late in the second quarter, Brady looked to add to that score by completing a critical third-down pass to Brown, who ran for a large gain. But it would be the last play of the game for number 12. As he released the throw, Brady was hit low and his body twisted like a pretzel. The second-year quarterback limped off the field with an ankle injury and was replaced by the man he'd replaced. Was Brady's improbable season coming full circle? Drew Bledsoe entered the game and, despite some early boneheaded plays, led the Patriots the rest of the way to a 24–17 victory. Later, Belichick admitted that Brady could have gone back in the game but that the team was better off with Bledsoe. Now the quarterback controversy that the coach had worked so hard to contain was filling up the phone lines across Boston sports radio programs leading up to the final game of the season—Super Bowl XXXVI in New Orleans against the high-flying St. Louis Rams, the "Greatest Show on Turf."

Tom Brady had taken over the leadership of the team and had proved his worth. A twist of fate gave him the opportunity and he made the best of it, but now it seemed another twist of fate could take it all away. Reporters peppered Belichick with questions about which player would be starting, and the coach promised that he'd have an answer by midweek. Bledsoe fans hung on to the hope that the nightmare season for their favorite quarterback would culminate in a major plot twist that would bring number 11 back where he belonged in time for the biggest game of the year. But the Patriots coach didn't believe in fairy tales. Belichick still felt that, if healthy, Brady gave his team the best chance to win.

He met with both players and told them that Brady would play in the Super Bowl, but only if he was physically able to practice with the team. Bledsoe was outraged, which was a natural response from such a tough competitor. Still, he remained relatively quiet for the good of the team. Brady was happy to see that the coach believed in him. It was a different feeling than he had experienced in college, and the support given to him added confidence leading up to the biggest game of his young life.

During practice that week, offensive coordinator Charlie Weis stressed one thing above all else from his quarterback—*Take care of the ball. No turnovers.* Brady wasn't called upon to engage in a shooting match with Rams quarterback Kurt Warner, the league's MVP. Instead, he had to play within himself and within the game. Coach Belichick and defensive coordinator Romeo Crennel had devised a plan to release the dogs of war on Warner and the Rams offense, showing them a level of physical play they hadn't seen all season.

Brady felt calm as he entered the Superdome on Super Bowl Sunday. In fact, he took his shoulder pads off before the game, laid them down, and fell asleep for about thirty minutes as the pregame pageantry continued on the field. He'd played in big moments before, surely nothing this big, but that's why the Patriots had drafted him. He was ready to show owner Robert Kraft why he was the best decision the franchise had ever made. When Brady woke up, he changed his shirt, put his shoulder pads on, and waited just twelve minutes for the team to take the field.

Instead of getting introduced individually, the Patriots rumbled out of the tunnel as one. The act crystallized the yearlong message that no player was above the team. The spirit carried into the game as the players carried one another. The St. Louis offense had scored five hundred points that season and entered the game as fourteen-point favorites. Most sports reporters figured the Rams receivers would race up and down the field as if at a track meet. But the offense led by Kurt Warner and Marshall Falk only managed to score three measly points in the first quarter. Not stopping there, the Patriots defense would put New England on the scoreboard in the second quarter, thanks to a Ty Law interception return for a touchdown. It was obvious. The Patriots weren't intimidated. In fact, they were in charge. Brady then doubled the score with an eight-yard touchdown pass to David Patten.

The Patriots were now leading the Rams 14–3.

"At that point, we were feeling pretty darn good about the score," Brady recalled later. "We went into halftime thinking it's gonna be tough for them to beat us."[2]

In the third quarter, the Patriots defense continued to swarm Kurt Warner and his receiving corps, shutting them down once again while stretching the lead with an Adam Vinatieri field goal. But by the fourth quarter, the Rams had finally made adjustments and were prepared to mount a counterattack. Warner cut the lead with a two-yard touchdown run and later hit receiver Ricky Proehl with a twenty-six-yard completion and touchdown. An extra point would tie the game 17–17. The Rams now had the momentum and their swagger back. Just before kickoff, Proehl had predicted a St. Louis dynasty in the making, and now in the final minutes of the game, Rams cornerback Dexter McCleon sat comfortably on the bench and shrugged, saying, "Tom Brady? Overrated."

On the opposite sideline, meanwhile, kicker Vinatieri was smiling. He placed his arm around the equipment manager. "They screwed up," he told him. "They gave us too much time."

As Brady took the field deep in his own territory with no time-outs left, coordinator Charlie Weis was once again in the quarterback's ear with an all-too-familiar order. "Hey, take care of that ball!"

At that moment, Brady's mentor-turned-rival Drew Bledsoe piped in.

"Fuck that!" Bledsoe told his replacement. "Go out there and sling it!"

His enthusiasm wasn't shared by TV commentator and legendary coach John Madden.

"Now with no time-outs, I think the Patriots with this field position, ya have to just run the clock out," Madden told a worldwide television audience. "You have to play for overtime now."

"We were huddled on the field after a play stoppage," Jermaine Wiggins remembered. "Charlie, Drew, and Tom are over on the sideline going through their communication. We're out on the field wondering what's gonna happen, and Tom finally joins the huddle and says, 'Listen, we're gonna drive the ball down the field and win this football game.' Everyone got kind of hyped. We were like 'Let's go!' We talked about ball security, making sure we got out of bounds, not making any critical mistakes, but Tom got it set in our minds that we were going to go down and kick that field goal."

Number 12 almost got strip-sacked on the first play as he barely completed a short shuffle pass to running back J. R. Redmond.

"I don't agree with what the Patriots are doing right here," Madden continued. "I would play for overtime."

Tom Brady wasn't listening. He threw another completion to Redmond to secure a first down. The Patriots needed to march another forty yards to get into field goal range. On the next play,

Brady found Redmond once more for yet another first down. The running back fought his way out of bounds at the 40-yard line to stop the clock with thirty-three seconds to go.

"Now I kinda like what the Patriots are doing," Madden exclaimed.

Brady was pressured on the next play and was forced to throw it away. But he got right back to work and hit Troy Brown for a big gain with just twenty-one seconds remaining. On the following play, Brady avoided a Rams blitz and dumped the ball to Wiggins, who fought his way to the 30-yard line.

"Tom says to me, 'Hey, I'm coming to you on this one.' This was because I was the closest one to him in the trips set we were running. Tom knew this would be the easiest throw," Wiggins recalled. "We could safely get seven or so yards to set up Vinatieri in a more comfortable distance. I would just have to catch the ball, secure it, get down, and get the ball to the referee so we could spike it. They dropped defensive end Leonard Little into coverage to my side, so when I started running a return route against this guy, he's not used to being in coverage. He thinks I'm running across the field, so he starts to turn and run and I just put the brakes on. It was pitch and catch, easy money."

They were now in field goal range with twelve seconds left on the clock. Number 12 took the ball from center Damien Woody and spiked it with seven seconds remaining.

Brady and the Patriots weren't playing for overtime. They were playing to win. The young quarterback embraced the historic moment. *This is for the world championship*, he thought to himself.

John Madden was now a believer. "I'm telling you, what Tom Brady just did gives me goose bumps."

Those Patriots fans who were listening to the game on the radio could not see Brady's mastery, but they could hear it through the enthusiastic play-by-play calling of longtime announcer Gil Santos, who like them had suffered through decades of humiliating losses. He watched as Adam Vinatieri was called out to attempt a forty-eight-yard field goal.

"Set to go. Snap. Ball down. Kick up. Kick is on the way," Santos shouted into the microphone.

Patriots fans in the stadium, watching on television, and listening on the radio held their collective breath as the ball sailed toward the goal post.

"It's good!" Santos screamed. "It's good...and the game is over and the Patriots are Super Bowl champions. The Patriots are Super Bowl champions, the best team in the National Football League!"

The confetti rained down in the Superdome as Patriots players ran onto the field. From Cranston, Rhode Island, to Camden, Maine, New England's long-suffering fans leaped for joy, hugged, and even wept. Tom Brady, the accidental quarterback, was named the game's most valuable player.

As he reached the podium to hoist the Lombardi Trophy, the first in franchise history, Brady caught the eyes of his three sisters in the stands. He placed his hands to his head and mouthed the words *Can you believe this?*

Months later, when the team handed out diamond-studded championship rings to the players and members of the coaching staff, Pam Rehbein received one in honor of her husband's contributions to the season, primarily, championing the young quarterback out of the University of Michigan who would bring the first Lombardi Trophy to Foxboro.

Rehbein's widow spoke of the honor. "It's his legacy to his children."[3]

PART III

Chapter Ten

LEGENDARY STATUS

In early 2015, Tom Brady and the Patriots found themselves headed back to the Super Bowl, and they were underdogs no more. They were no longer the Cinderella team that had delivered one of the greatest upsets in Super Bowl history against the mighty Rams. New England was now the gold standard by which all other teams were measured. Few could have predicted the team's decade-long run of success that would earn them two more Vince Lombardi trophies in 2003 against the Carolina Panthers and 2004 versus the Philadelphia Eagles and a total of four more trips back to the Super Bowl. Fans could not imagine that their team would celebrate a perfect regular season in 2007. But it all had happened. It wasn't a dream. The Patriots had built the greatest sports dynasty of the twenty-first century under the architectural guidance of Brady and Bill Belichick.

For Tom, the comparisons to Drew Bledsoe were long gone now. Bledsoe, as good a professional quarterback as he was, would go down in history as a footnote to the Brady legend. The Patriots star wasn't just Tom Brady anymore. He was TB12, a one-man corporation with multimillion-dollar contracts to endorse Uggs boots, Under Armour, and other high-end products. He was also building a new health and wellness business with his nutritionist, fitness trainer, and best friend, Alex Guerrero, who was placed in charge of Brady's training after he suffered a torn ACL during the first game of the 2008 season and was kept out for a year.

The yellow Jeep and the cramped Franklin condo were also distant memories. Brady now drove around in a Rolls-Royce Ghost and lived in two huge mansions on both coasts with his supermodel wife, Gisele, and their two young children, Benjamin and Vivian. He also shared custody of his firstborn son, John Edward ("Jack"), with actress Bridget Moynahan.

Most important, the 2000 NFL draft-day afterthought was rightly considered to be among the greatest quarterbacks ever to play the game. For a decade, he competed against career rival Peyton Manning for recognition as the NFL's top gun. Now entering his sixth Super Bowl against the Seattle Seahawks, he had pulled ahead of Manning in the eyes of most NFL observers, with just one quarterback blocking his way toward the rarefied title of greatest quarterback of all time—Joe Montana.

Brady's boyhood idol was teetering on the top of the sport's Mount Olympus, poised to get knocked off by the Patriots quarterback if he could lead his team to victory over the Seahawks. A fourth Super Bowl win would tie Brady with Montana. Championship rings were the most important measuring stick with which to judge any NFL quarterback. Number 12 was on the cusp of matching number 16 in Super Bowl wins, but he dominated his idol in every other quarterback category.

By 2015, Brady had thrown for more than four thousand yards in seven different seasons, while Montana had never eclipsed four thousand yards passing in a single season throughout his entire lofty career. Brady had thrown twenty-five touchdowns or more in ten different seasons, including a record-setting fifty in 2007, while Montana had done it just six times. Brady had even thrown fewer interceptions than his idol. He had won more regular-season and playoff games than Montana but had also lost the two Super Bowls to the New York Giants in heartbreaking fashion. The 49ers legend, on the other hand, was a perfect 4–0 in world championship games. With four rings, Joe Cool was alone on the mountaintop looking down at TB12. Another win would give Brady sports immortality and his fans plenty of ammunition in their barroom and golf course GOAT (greatest of all time) debates.

"Brady's made a mockery of the man many believed was the greatest quarterback in football," said Kerry Byrne of Cold Hard Football Facts. "Statistically speaking, there is no comparison between the two. Montana peaked at age 33 when he was the most efficient quarterback in the game but he was not considered among the best at his position in the later years of his career. Tom Brady is still the best at what he does."[1]

The Brady–Montana story line heading into the Super Bowl against Seattle was drowned out quickly, however, by the controversy that was swirling around number 12 and allegations that he had performed with deflated footballs in the AFC title game against the Colts. The story was still fluid, changing by the minute. *Newsday* circulated a report that the issue had been first brought to the attention of the Colts staff by linebacker D'Qwell Jackson, who had intercepted a Brady pass in the second quarter of the game. Jackson reportedly gave the ball to a member of the Colts equipment staff who then alerted head coach Chuck Pagano that the ball appeared to be deflated. This story belies the fact that Pagano had already been notified about the Patriots' ball situation by Ravens special teams coordinator Jerry Rosburg in a phone call the week before the game. Jackson would later claim that he had no suspicion that the football he intercepted had been tampered with.[2]

Now both sides in this drama were working hard to get their stories straight.

The night after the story first broke, DeMaurice Smith, executive director of the NFLPA, was enjoying dinner out with his wife, Karen, near their home in a suburban Maryland town. He glanced at the large television above the bar and his eyes were drawn to the ticker at the bottom of the screen, where the words *deflated footballs* and *Tom Brady* flashed before him.

"Fuck," he muttered.

His mind began to race. *In what number of directions can this possibly go?*

Karen gazed at her husband. She knew that look. It was the look of a fighter. She had seen it when the two were classmates at the University of Virginia Law School. She had seen it during the nine long years he had worked for United States Attorney General Eric Holder in the Justice Department. Karen understood the look because she was a fighter, too. She was a breast cancer survivor and the strongest person her husband had ever known.

Dinner ended quickly. It was time for Smith to assemble his team and go to work.

The story was spiraling out of control. It led news coverage on every network and now had its own name—Deflategate.

The drumbeats were getting louder. As Tom Brady and the Patriots coaching staff tried to block out the media distractions and focus on preparations to face the Seahawks, DeMaurice Smith and his NFLPA legal team analyzed each step taken by Roger Goodell and the NFL up to this point in the case.

Smith had already developed a close relationship with Brady over time.

"Tom was one of the lead plaintiffs back in 2011 with Peyton [Manning] and Drew [Brees] to sue the league for locking the players out," he explained.[3]

That battle was over a new collective bargaining agreement (labor agreement between the owners and players). Team owners wanted a cutback in player salaries and health benefits, but the

NFLPA fought hard against this plan. When the players could not come to a consensus with the owners, all thirty-two owners imposed a work stoppage and locked the players out of team facilities and halted league operations. The stalemate lasted from early March to late July that year.

"He [Brady] was a union rep at the time and the statement by him and those other quarterbacks was not only a bold statement by them as union members, but it was nearly unprecedented to have what everyone would consider to be future Hall of Famers as lead plaintiffs fighting for the union," Smith said.[4]

Brady had agreed to designate himself as lead plaintiff, knowing full well that Patriots owner Robert Kraft was the principal owner in the process of locking out the players.

"He went against his own boss," Smith continued. "The decision by that quarterback in particular was a direct choice to express clearly which side they were on."

Brady stood tall for the union at a time when they needed him most, and now it was Smith's turn to pay back the favor.

Number 12 was now getting pinned down by the media. What he thought was a small issue over deflated footballs had grown into a national scandal. He figured the best way to control the media-fed wildfire was simply to address the allegations during an NFL required pre–Super Bowl news conference at Gillette Stadium in Foxborough. DeMaurice Smith adamantly opposed the strategy.

"Stay cool, man. Don't discuss it," Smith warned Brady. "You can't address it. We need to get a handle on this, man."

Tom did not listen. Instead he went rogue. He stepped up to the podium wearing a Patriots winter cap complete with pom-pom and told the crush of reporters, flatly, "I didn't alter the ball in any way. I have a process that I go through before every game where I go in and I pick the footballs that I want to use for the game. Our equipment guys do a great job of breaking the balls in. They have a process that they go through. When I pick those balls out, at that point to me they're perfect. I don't want anyone touching the balls after that. I don't want anyone rubbing them, putting any air in them, taking any air out. To me those balls are perfect and that's what I expect when I show up on the field. That happened obviously on Sunday night. It was the same process that I always go through. I didn't think anything of it."

From there, Pandora's box was opened.

"Are you comfortable that nobody on the Patriots side did anything wrong?" one reporter asked.

"I have no knowledge of anything. I have no knowledge of any wrongdoing," Brady replied, sounding like a politician on the wrong side of a story.

"Are you comfortable that nobody did anything?" another writer pressed.

"Yeah, I'm very comfortable saying that. I'm very comfortable saying that nobody did it, as far as I know. I don't know everything. I also understand that I was in the locker room preparing for a game. I don't know what happened over the course of the process with the footballs. I was preparing for my own job, doing what I needed to do."

For fifteen minutes, he was peppered with question after question. One particular query hit him square in the solar plexus.

"This has raised a lot of questions around the country from people that view you, a three-time Super Bowl champion, as their idol," the reporter stated. "The question they're asking themselves is, 'What's up with our hero?' So can you answer right now...is Tom Brady a cheater?"

Brady smiled and let out a nervous laugh as he tried to maintain his composure. For the first time in his life, reporters were questioning his heart and his character. A stain on his credibility and work ethic would not only impact his legacy but also his relationships with all those he knew and loved.

"I don't believe so," Brady responded. "I feel like I've always played within the rules and would never do anything to break the rules."

I don't believe so. These are the four words that would haunt him. Instead of emphatically denying any wrongdoing, Brady offered a safe response—a "lawyered up" reply. The superstar quarterback was rattled, and many in the media pool questioned whether he was advised by legal counsel beforehand about what to say and how to say it. The odd response struck cynical reporters the same way that President Bill Clinton's phrase "it depends upon what the meaning of the word *is* is" did during the Monica Lewinsky probe.

Watching the news conference from his office at NFLPA headquarters, DeMaurice Smith grimaced. He certainly hadn't advised Brady to use such language. Smith didn't want Tom to talk at all. As a professional football player, Brady was used to answering questions about his performance on the field, but he was now out of his comfort zone.

Earlier in the day, Bill Belichick had defended his own actions and perceived lack of knowledge of any wrongdoing.

"I'm not a scientist, I'm not an expert in footballs, I'm not an expert in football measurements. I'm just telling you what I know," Belichick said during a news conference. "I'm not saying I'm the Mona Lisa Vito of the football world as she was in the car expertise area."

The coach was making a reference to Marisa Tomei's character in the Joe Pesci comedy *My Cousin Vinny,* a film he'd seen numerous times.

New England fans were captivated by the news conference and the coach's attempt at dark humor. One fan, Michael Curley from Cape Cod, found something artificial in Belichick's words. He remembered bumping into the coach on Nantucket one summer day. Curley was biking around the island with his wife when the pair stopped at Sconset Market for a bite to eat. They saw Belichick pull up in a mud-covered Jeep.

"Hiya, Coach," Curley said.

Belichick looked at his dirty vehicle and remarked, "This is what happens when you lend your Jeep out on Nantucket."

Curley noticed that the Jeep's tires were very low and offered to pump them up with air while Belichick went grocery shopping. (Drivers on the island are encouraged to lower the tire pressure on their vehicles when they drive on sand.) His wife looked at him curiously, but Curley was a diehard fan and it was the least he could do for his favorite coach. Belichick obliged and Curley went to work. When the coach finally emerged from the market, the job was done. Curley thought he'd get a big thank-you and maybe even an autograph. Instead, Belichick pulled a small pressure gauge from the pocket of his shorts and proceeded to inspect each tire for proper air pressure. Curley's wife thought it was an odd gesture, but her husband stood and marveled at the way Belichick examined each tire.

"It's that level of scrutiny in everything he does that makes him the greatest coach in history," Curley remarked to his wife later.

Now, watching the coach's news conference, Curley asked himself why, if Belichick applied such focus and knowledge about tire pressure to his beat-up island Jeep, he did not understand or care about the air pressure of a football.[5]

Reporters had their own questions about the veracity of Belichick's words. After all, this was the coach that had built "Fortress Foxboro," an impenetrable football stronghold where he oversaw every detail. When pressed further by the media, Belichick uncharacteristically said they should "ask Tom" about the balls, seemingly throwing his star player under the bus. Now the bus was on top of Brady.

This was a much different Belichick than anyone, including DeMaurice Smith, had seen before. The coach had mastered the art of saying basically nothing to the press, but here he was animated, angry, and pointing the finger at his own quarterback.

"When you have a coach putting all that pressure on a player, it makes me very nervous," Smith told his legal team. "We need to reach out to Tom and advise him not to speak about this."

Brady didn't take Smith's advice. Instead, he dug himself into a deeper hole with the public and the league. "Tom gave the news conference because he didn't think the situation was a big deal and that he hadn't done anything wrong. He thought he would address it once and move on," Smith recalled. "But I know the way the NFL works. They try to find a murder behind every bush. Once they target you, they do not stop."

Chapter Eleven

"IT'S ABOUT HONOR. IT'S ABOUT RESPECT."

Despite the circus atmosphere that had enveloped Fortress Foxboro, there was still a game to be played—the biggest game of the season and the biggest game of most players' careers. For Brady, Super Bowl XLIX offered him the opportunity to pull the monkey off his back after the two championship losses against the New York Giants. In each of those games, number 12 had put the Patriots in a position to win despite early struggles, only to see the team's fate sealed by miraculous catches made by Giants receivers. A third consecutive loss in the Super Bowl would quell any comparisons to Montana. Instead, Brady would find himself discussed alongside Denver Broncos quarterback John Elway, who won two Super Bowls but lost three. Elway was an all-time great, but those big losses kept him out of the conversation with Montana. Tom Brady was a student of history, and despite his public comments that team success was the only success that mattered to him, he was maniacally driven to be the best. Like the fictional Roy Hobbs, he wanted people to walk down the street and say, "There goes Tom Brady, the best there ever was in this game."

Initially, the Las Vegas odds makers had given the defending champion Seahawks a slight edge over the Patriots, but the game was now a pick 'em. More than 70,000 fans packed the University of Phoenix Stadium in Glendale, Arizona, while a record 114.4 million viewers watched the NBC telecast at home. Brady was ready. He'd spent sixteen hours per day on football, waking up in the predawn hours to study film and hold meetings with his offensive coordinator, Josh McDaniels. Brady tried to eliminate all distractions, which was a Herculean effort, since the Deflategate controversy was now the hot topic not only for sports commentators but for news pundits on CNN, Fox News, and all the major television networks. Jimmy Garoppolo, Brady's young backup at the time, marveled at number 12's dedication to preparation.

"He'd come in [to quarterback meetings] and already be a day ahead of everybody," Garoppolo recalled. "If we were on third down, he'd studied third down yesterday... being that far ahead of the game, it gives you an edge."[1]

Brady was mentally prepared, but physically he was fighting a nasty cold that he'd caught from his kids, which had him eating raw garlic to boost his immune system. He was dogged by illness and questions about his integrity that were not going away. Fox Sports reporter Jay Glazer had just broken a story that the NFL had surveillance footage of one of the Patriots' locker room attendants taking footballs from the officials' locker room into the bathroom at Gillette Stadium before taking them onto the field for the AFC championship game.

By now the league had appointed Ted Wells to investigate the matter. The sixty-three-year-old New York–based attorney and senior partner with the powerhouse firm Paul, Weiss, Rifkind, Wharton & Garrison had counseled several high-profile clients, including former New York governor Eliot Spitzer in a scandal involving a prostitute and Scooter Libby, the onetime adviser to Vice President Dick Cheney, who was indicted and later convicted for his role in leaking the name of CIA covert agent Valerie Plame to the press. Wells had conducted the investigation into Syracuse University's response to sexual assault accusations involving assistant basketball coach Bernie Fine, and most recently he had spent eighteen months on behalf of the NFL investigating a scandal involving Miami Dolphins lineman Richie Incognito, who was accused of bullying offensive linemate Jonathan Martin. Ted Wells issued a statement about the Deflategate probe, saying that the investigation was proceeding expeditiously but that it was unlikely to come to a conclusion for several weeks.

It was now time for the Patriots to dig their trenches and prepare themselves for a long and bloody war.

In an attempt to show support for his star quarterback, Robert Kraft hijacked a news conference held for Brady and Belichick the Monday before the Super Bowl and read a statement to reporters.

"I want to make it clear that I believe unconditionally that the New England Patriots have done nothing inappropriate in this process or in violation of NFL rules," Kraft said. "Tom, Bill, and I have been together for fifteen years. They are my guys. They are part of my family. Bill, Tom, and I have had many difficult discussions over the years. I have never known them to lie to me. That's why I am confident in saying what I just said. It bothers me greatly that our reputations and integrity, and by association that of our team, has been called into question this week."[2]

He spoke for three minutes and did not take questions.

"If the Wells investigation is not able to definitively determine that our organization tampered with the air pressure of the footballs," Kraft concluded, "I would expect and hope the league would apologize to our entire team, and in particular Coach Belichick and Tom Brady, for what they have had to endure this past week."

Kraft was markedly absent when Roger Goodell gave his annual state of the NFL speech a few days later. During his hour-long address to reporters, the commissioner was pressed repeatedly about the investigation. When asked about Kraft's demand for an apology, Goodell snapped back, "That's my job. This is my responsibility to protect the integrity of the game. I represent thirty-two teams. All of us want to make sure the rules are being followed, and if we had any information where the potential is that those rules were violated, I have to pursue that, and I have to pursue it aggressively."

Later when asked whether the NFL had ever previously tested the air pressure of footballs during halftime, the commissioner said simply, "I don't know the answer to that question."

Patriots fans, who had mostly held a benign attitude toward Goodell during his tenure, were now sharpening their long knives for the commissioner now deemed public enemy number one in New England. But Goodell did have his supporters. Former Jacksonville Jaguars quarterback Mark Brunelle broke ranks from the NFL QB fraternity and said during an emotional rant on ESPN, "I don't believe what Tom had to say [during his previous news conference]. Those balls were deflated. Someone had to do it and I don't believe there's an equipment manager in the NFL that would on his own initiative deflate a ball without the starting quarterback's approval."[3]

Retired Dallas Cowboy great Troy Aikman, another quarterback with three Super Bowl rings, agreed with Brunelle, telling listeners on his radio show that he believed Brady had something to do with the deflated balls. Fellow Hall of Famer Fran Tarkenton echoed Aikman's sentiments. "Tom Brady knows exactly what was done to the ball and what wasn't done with the ball as every other quarterback in the National Football League is," he said.

From his laptop in Indianapolis, columnist Bob Kravitz continued to sling arrows toward the Patriots but saved most of his vitriol, not for Brady but for Belichick.

"If Patriots owner Robert Kraft has an ounce of integrity, he will fire Bill Belichick immediately," Kravitz wrote. "There's only one way that this [deflated footballs] could happen and that's with Belichick's full knowledge and approval."

The coach gathered his players and assistants and told them point-blank not to concern themselves with the outside distraction as they had a world championship to prepare for.

"Take all of that garbage that's on the exterior, get that outta the way," Belichick told the team in Glendale. "Get focused on our jobs to go out there and have a helluva night, Sunday night."[4]

But the national media had no interest in letting the story die, so Brady sat down for an interview with Bob Costas, which ran during NBC's marathon pregame coverage on Super Bowl Sunday. Brady had agreed to the sit-down while Roger Goodell had declined, but Tom remained elusive in answering questions about whether he had direct knowledge or involvement in deflating footballs. Once again, he had the opportunity to say emphatically that he was innocent of the allegations, yet still decided to stay guarded. He told Costas that he wasn't concerned the night of the AFC championship with how the balls were inflated, just how they felt, and they felt good.

"Is it a fair assumption that a Patriots employee would deflate the footballs only after your input?" Costas asked.

"Absolutely, I think absolutely. I can understand why people feel that way," Brady replied. "There is an investigation going on. I'm sure all the things will come out. It's been a lot of speculation and I think that has led to my hurt feelings."

This was the first time that the Patriots superstar admitted publicly that the accusations swirling around him had left their mark. Brady had never faced this kind of heat before. He had kept out of trouble despite being in the public eye. While other players attracted public scorn for beating up their wives and girlfriends or for using performance-enhancing drugs, Brady's image and reputation had remained clean—until now.

Toward the end of the interview, Costas asked Brady whether, in the end, fans would be able to say they have no doubt about him and that he's "on the up and up."

"Not a lot of people know who I am and what I am about," he replied. "The people who know me, they know what I'm about and what I stand for."

Fifty-two of those who could vouch for his character, Brady's teammates, were now in the locker room with him as he prepared to take the field for a record-breaking sixth Super Bowl appearance.

The storm had abated, at least for now. For the next few hours, there would be no talk about deflated footballs. Brady felt in control again. The only thing that mattered to him was putting points on the board and getting his team in a position to win.

Number 12 jogged onto the field echoing his familiar rally cry. "Let's go. Let's go!" he urged his teammates. On the opposite sideline, Seahawks quarterback Russell Wilson let out a few motivational woot-woots of his own.

The stadium had not been kind to Brady and the Patriots. They had been denied a perfect season here in February 2008 with a shocking loss to the Giants that left an indelible scar on every New England fan. It was now time to exorcize those demons. But neither history nor the top-rated Seahawks defense appeared to be on their side.

"I feel good," Brady told Josh McDaniels before kickoff. "I feel great, ready to roll."

After the Seahawks took the field waving a flag symbolizing the Seattle fans as their twelfth man, the Patriots' number 12 pulled his team together.

"It's our time," he told them. "It started seven, eight months ago, right? All for this moment, all for this moment. It's about honor. It's about respect."

Brady's strong voice was demonstrative of the fire that was fueling him.

"You win this game, you're honored," he shouted. "Your kids are honored. Your families are honored!"

The first quarter of Super Bowl XLIX was a scoreless affair for both teams, and fans on each coast prepared themselves for a tough defensive battle. Brady was intercepted by Seattle cornerback Jeremy Lane in the end zone, washing away hopes for an early lead.

But early in the second quarter, Brady put the offense in gear, marching the Patriots downfield before hitting receiver Brandon LaFell for an eleven-yard pass in the end zone. The extra point made by kicker Stephen Gostkowski put New England out in front 7–0. The Seahawks countered with a three-yard run for the goal line by their one-man Sherman tank, Marshawn Lynch. Unfazed, the Patriots battled back with Brady finding his favorite target, tight end Rob Gronkowski, for another touchdown. But with six seconds left on the clock before halftime, Seattle, benefiting from a face mask penalty against New England, took one last shot at the end zone. Quarterback Russell Wilson convinced his coach, Pete Carroll, who had been jettisoned from New England years before, to call the field goal kicker back to the sideline and go for it from the 11-yard line. The gamble paid off as Wilson hit receiver Chris Matthews for an easy score that would tie the game. Like two prizefighters, the teams stood toe-to-toe in the first half, each taking big swings packed with heavyweight power and landing crushing blows against the other. Bloodied but unbowed, the Patriots and Seahawks retreated to their neutral corners for halftime.

It was still anyone's game.

The third quarter of Super Bowl XLIX belonged to the Seahawks, and it was beginning to appear that the city of Seattle would need to finalize plans for a second straight championship parade. A field goal put them up by three. On the Patriots' next possession, Brady threw another costly interception, this time to

Seattle linebacker Bobby Wagner. Russell Wilson made New England pay, driving his team fifty yards before connecting with receiver Doug Baldwin for another touchdown. The score was now 24–14 heading into the final quarter.

"You win this game, you're honored," Brady had told his teammates before the coin toss. Now he had just fourteen minutes to determine their fate. The Patriots' running game stalled in the second half, gaining only four yards on the ground. New England's chances for victory rested solely on the shoulders of number 12 against a defensive unit that had allowed the fewest passing yards of any team during the regular season. Bill Belichick consulted with his quarterback.

"Try no negative plays," the coach stressed as he squatted in front of Brady on the bench. "Ya know, if you gotta get rid of it, you gotta get rid of it. The chances of them playing three good defensive plays in a row don't look very good. The pass rush…everyone's running by you. They're getting displaced in their zone. Just no negative plays and we'll keep it close."

Brady nodded. The NFL championship was on the line but so was his legacy. The quarterback strapped his helmet back on and went to work.

"Hey, we've been in worse situations than this, huh?" he reminded his teammates. "C'mon now!"

In a performance for the ages, he completed thirteen of fifteen passes in the fourth quarter, spreading the ball around, hitting all his receivers, including Danny Amendola for a touchdown and another touchdown toss to his close friend Julian Edelman on a play that had just been put into the game plan the night before the Super Bowl. Following that score, Brady raised his fist high in the air, pumped it, and pointed to the crowd. The Patriots had retaken the lead 28–24 with just over two minutes left. Brady's passer rating for the quarter was an astounding 140.7.

"When things seem dire, what do you do in life?" asked Patriots color commentator and former quarterback Scott Zolak in a speech reminiscent of Russell Crowe in the film *Gladiator*, whipping the radio audience into a frenzy. "You go right to people that you can depend on—Julian Edelman!"

Brady butted helmets with Edelman and congratulated him for the catch.

"Way to go. Nice job," he told the receiver. "That's a championship drive, Jules."

It was time for the Patriots defense to protect the lead.

"Remember, we're staying aggressive," defensive coordinator Matt Patricia ordered his troops.

The Seahawks, however, were unfazed, as Wilson had led the team to come-from-behind victories throughout the season. Seattle players and coaches did not think much of a defensive adjustment by the Patriots to replace defensive back Kyle Arrington, who had struggled all day, with Malcolm Butler, an undrafted free agent from Division II Western Alabama. The unheralded twenty-four-year-old Butler, who had worked at a Popeyes Chicken in college, had a vision that he'd make a big play in the game. But on the final drive, all the plays were going Seattle's way. First, Wilson connected for a big pass with Marshawn Lynch. Then he threw it up for receiver Jerome Kearse, who juggled the ball as he fell and yet somehow managed to pull it in for a thirty-three-yard catch at the 5-yard line. The ghosts of Glendale, Arizona, had come back to haunt the Patriots. On the same field in Super Bowl XLII in 2008, Giants receiver David Tyree had made a similar improbable grab, that one on his helmet, to help defeat the Patriots 17–14.

"Aw, we have no fucking luck." Robert Kraft sighed from the owner's box.

It was happening again, and this time, the quarterback who had just completed one of the greatest performances in Super Bowl history could only watch helplessly from the Patriots bench.

"Man, the D's gotta make a play," Brady told Josh McDaniels.

Malcolm Butler had given up the play to Kearse and nearly tore his chin strap off in frustration as he returned to the sideline. On the next play, Wilson fed workhorse Marshawn Lynch, who powered his way to the 1-yard line. Lynch, who had earned the nickname "Beastmode" for his tough, physical play, had run the ball successfully against the Patriots defense throughout the game.

It was now second and goal, and Seattle sent a third receiver onto the field. The Patriots countered by sending the rookie Butler back into action. The Seahawks were going to throw. Butler recognized the call; it was the exact play he'd been burned on in practice earlier in the week. He had begged off the receiver and it had cost him. But practice is practice. Lessons learned there needed to be executed when it counted. There was no moment that counted more than right now. As Butler got into position, he saw Wilson's eyes dart his way. He lined up four yards off the line, facing Seattle receiver Ricardo Lockette. The ball was snapped and Butler exploded, freed up by fellow defensive back Brandon Browner's jamming of Jerome Kearse. Butler stepped in front of the throw and hauled it in for the game-saving interception.

Tom Brady leaped to his feet screaming. He jumped in the air and spun around in disbelief before hugging his coordinator.

"Oh my God. We did it, Josh. We did it!"

Brady and the offense returned to the field to run out the final seconds of Super Bowl XLIX. Number 12 took the snap and then a knee. Victory was theirs.

Once again the confetti at the Super Bowl rained red, white, and blue. Edelman hugged Brady and told him what nearly all football fans had finally come to recognize without dispute.

"You're the greatest quarterback in the world, man!"

Brady was named Super Bowl MVP for the third time. The quarterback fought his way through a sea of players until he found Malcolm Butler, the game's most unlikely hero.

"Malcolm, are you kidding me?" Brady said joyously. "You're unbelievable, man!"

Number 12 was given a 2015 Chevy Colorado in conjunction with his Most Valuable Player Award. He gave the vehicle to number 21, Malcolm Butler.

Brady then received a hug and kiss from wife Gisele, who had a complicated relationship with some Patriots fans who had blamed her for the team's losses in their past two Super Bowl appearances. The so-called Gisele Curse had now been lifted. The animosity had always been unwarranted, as she had expressed nothing but support for her husband's career. Bündchen posted a photo of her husband on Instagram that summed up her feelings in both English and her native Portuguese.

We are so proud of you daddy!!!, she wrote. Congratulations!!!! Estamos muito orgulhosos de você papai! Parabéns!!!!

Chapter Twelve

BRADY'S NEW TEAM

New England Patriots fans were almost denied the chance to celebrate their world championship. Boston was in the midst of a record-breaking winter, and a total of nine feet of snow had fallen on the city by early February. There was simply no place to put it all as snowbanks towered on street corners and walking paths were treacherous and few. Robert Kraft strongly considered cancelling the event over safety concerns. He was also worried about the prospect of terrorism. Bostonians were still recovering physically and emotionally from the 2013 marathon bombings, and Kraft had consulted his own intelligence network about potential threats beforehand to ensure that his team and their fans would be safe. After also speaking with Boston mayor Marty Walsh and police commissioner William Evans, one of the heroes of the marathon bombings, Kraft decided to go ahead with the parade, which was pushed back a day to Wednesday, February 3, 2015.

It was the team's first championship parade since 2005, but the city itself had become accustomed to the spectacle. The Patriots had opened the floodgates after their surprise win in Super Bowl XXXVI. Since that time, New England sports fans had celebrated

eight more world championships, three for the Patriots, three for
the Red Sox, and one apiece for the Celtics and Bruins. Boston
had gone from sports world laughingstock to Titletown, U.S.A., in
less than a decade, and many fans credited Tom Brady and the
Patriots for inspiring the turnaround in the region's professional
sports cultures.

Wearing the same ski cap he had sported during the awkward
Deflategate news conference two weeks before, Brady, now a four-
time Super Bowl champion, stepped onto the duck boat with his
five-year-old son, Benjamin, and wife, Gisele, for the ride down
Boylston Street in the heart of Boston. Number 12 was given the
honor of carrying the Lombardi Trophy and was met at each turn
of the ninety-minute parade by cheering fans whose screams hit
a decibel level not reached in Boston since the Beatles played the
Suffolk Downs racetrack in 1966. Despite the frigid temperatures,
little Benny Brady danced for the crowd, kissed the trophy, and
then fell asleep on his dad's shoulder as the line of duck boats arrived at city hall.

Number 12 had been right. His family was indeed honored
with his victory. Brady had gone ten years between Super Bowl
victories, the longest stretch of any quarterback in history. The
fact that he was still playing at the highest level astounded both
adoring fans and hard-bitten reporters alike. On the night of the
Super Bowl, the team had hired country rocker Darius Rucker
to entertain the crowd at the postgame victory party. He played
one of his most popular songs, "Time," from his days with
Hootie & the Blowfish, which included the lyric *Time, why you
punish me? Time, time, you ain't no friend of mine.* At thirty-seven,
Brady had not just defeated the Seahawks, he'd also beaten time.
Joe Montana was in the last year of his playing career at the
same age, but Brady had proven that he was still at the top of
his game with no end in sight. All was right in the world again
for Patriots fans. The team was primed for more championships,

and Deflategate looked as if it would end not with a bang but with a whimper.

While Brady, his teammates, and their fans basked in the glow of their championship season, DeMaurice Smith sat in the fifth floor conference room at NFLPA headquarters on 20th Street in Washington, D.C., with two of his toughest attorneys, forty-five-year-old Heather McPhee and general counsel Tom Depaso, a fifty-nine-year-old former Penn State linebacker who had served on the union's legal team for over three decades. They were trying to predict the league's endgame for number 12. Heather McPhee had been Smith's professional right hand for more than a dozen years; the pair had represented mega-corporations and executives together, first at renowned international law firm Latham & Watkins and then at the most powerful lobbying law firm in the United States, Patton Boggs. Since moving to the NFLPA, Smith and McPhee had successfully battled Roger Goodell and the NFL billionaire owners in several high-profile cases, including most recently the suspension of Baltimore Ravens running back Ray Rice, who was caught on videotape punching his then fiancée unconscious in a hotel elevator.

Defending a domestic abuser like Rice was difficult for McPhee, who was forced to put her moral judgment aside to do her job. Ray Rice had been urged by Ravens team president Dick Cass to soften his language when describing the incident.

"It would be truthful to say that you laid your hands on her," Cass told him.

McPhee, like Cass, was a Princeton graduate and sophisticated lawyer who understood the "word management" that Cass was suggesting. But she knew this wasn't the time to deploy semantics. She smiled at Cass, whom she knew, respected, and liked, tossed her wild blond hair and smiled. "Come on, Dick, that phrasing evokes visions of televangelists on late-night cable TV," she said.

Despite the nerves and intensity in the room, Rice slightly smiled at the remark. And soon thereafter, when asked by Goodell what happened in the elevator, Rice looked the commissioner in the eye and said, simply, "And then I hit her." He had wisely followed McPhee's advice.

The disgraced player told the commissioner that he hit his girlfriend.

Goodell handed down a mere two-game suspension for Ray Rice and hoped the incident would quickly go away.

Three months later, the case returned like a clap of thunder after *TMZ* published a security video showing Rice punching his fiancée. The video immediately went viral, and critics and reporters voiced their outrage at the running back, the Baltimore Ravens, and Roger Goodell for his decision to suspend the player for only two games. The NFL league offices went into spin control, with Goodell stating publicly that he was appalled by the video and that he had increased the punishment from a pair of games to an indefinite suspension. The commissioner also claimed that Rice had not been honest with him during their disciplinary meeting.

Heather McPhee knew this was a lie, and the intense, detail-oriented lawyer had the proof. During that meeting, as she always did, McPhee had taken copious notes, including a record of Rice's simple, raw words, "And then I hit her." She underlined the words on the legal pad; Rice had followed her guidance. When Goodell tried to justify the new punishment of Rice, McPhee and the NFLPA resoundingly won the case on appeal. For her, it was not a victory for Ray Rice but a victory for the truth.

The saga was a near fatal blow for Roger Goodell. His handling of the affair was roundly criticized, and many were now calling for his job. The once mighty commissioner was wounded, vulnerable, and under threat of losing what he craved most—total power.

Now, two months later, McPhee stared across a conference table at her boss, DeMaurice Smith, as they attempted to determine the motive behind Goodell's new investigation against Tom Brady— the proverbial face of the NFL.

Smith was a high-powered white-collar lawyer with the experience and instincts that came from his background as a criminal prosecutor. He and his team had quickly gathered information that triggered more questions than answers. They had learned that the Baltimore Ravens had tipped off the Colts to allegations that the Patriots mishandled game balls during their win over the Ravens in the divisional round of the NFL playoffs. Colts general manager Ryan Grigson had brought the matter to the attention of league officials.

Normally, the league would notify a team that was accused of a rules violation, especially if the infraction was minor. The proper inflation of a football had never been an issue in the long history of the NFL, as teams and quarterbacks often deflated or overinflated balls for personal preference. This custom was almost universally viewed as having no effect on a player's performance or the outcome of a game.

"The league should have simply called the Patriots and put them on notice, but instead they stayed quiet," Smith observed out loud. "Why?"

"Maybe they wanted to catch them in the act," replied McPhee. "Like a sting operation."

"Sting operations don't happen in the spur of the moment," Smith added. "This one took careful planning."

The NFLPA attorneys continued to pore over their notes. Smith and McPhee noticed that Goodell had sent his director of football operations, Mike Kensil, to the Patriots–Colts game to keep a close eye on New England's equipment guys. At halftime, he had approached equipment manager Dave Schoenfeld, who supervised both John Jastremski and Jim McNally.

"We weighed the balls," Kensil told him. "You are in big fucking trouble."[1]

Smith could hardly believe what he was reading. The league was aggressively crafting its own narrative that the Patriots were cheaters from the get-go.

Roger Goodell had orchestrated an elaborate setup to expose a rule violation that few players, including Brady, knew even existed.

The NFL had never tested footballs at halftime before.

Once again, the NFLPA's top lawyer asked himself the question—why?

He called the meeting, grabbed his jacket, and took a walk around the block. Smith needed to think. He believed that he understood Goodell, his primary adversary, better than most, but still—this was bizarre. As Smith strolled down K Street, another narrative began to form in his mind. The other NFL owners had been breathing down the commissioner's neck to punish the Patriots in some way to make up for his egregious behavior during the Spygate scandal in 2007. No one had forgiven Goodell for destroying the videotaped evidence to protect his mentor Robert Kraft. The commissioner needed to do something to protect his salary, an estimated $42 million per year, and to reassert himself and salvage the power that he had recently lost.

"In order to regain control of the league, he must kill his father," Smith surmised metaphorically. "He must tear down Robert Kraft."

The saga had a Shakespearean ring to it.

But why go after somebody like Tom Brady, who has had an unblemished Hall of Fame career?

Smith came back to the one word he often used when describing Goodell—*power.*

If he can assert his power over Brady, the league's number one attraction, he can make all other players bend to his will, Smith thought.

For decades, Roger Goodell had quietly built a base of power through relationships with team owners, most importantly Patriots owner Robert Kraft. In Kraft, Goodell had not only found a professional mentor but a true father figure. The benevolent owner took Goodell under his wing and tutored him on the finer points of running a business as large and as powerful as the National Football League. Goodell proved to be an apt and loyal pupil. When his predecessor Paul Tagliabue announced his retirement in 2006, Goodell was just one of several candidates being discussed to replace him. Others considered for the job included Fidelity Investments honcho Robert Reynolds, Washington lawyer Gregg Levy, and Cleveland attorney Frederick Nance. Robert Kraft campaigned vigorously on Goodell's behalf, and through a savvy combination of hand holding and arm twisting, convinced his fellow owners to appoint his young protégé as the new commissioner of the most lucrative and important professional sports league in America.

The choice was made in a hotel in a Chicago suburb. The selection process was supposed to have been decided over three days by the league's thirty-two owners, but on day two the choice was whittled down to two candidates, Goodell and Gregg Levy, the NFL's chief outside counsel. The owners could have gone with another lawyer like the outgoing Tagliabue, but instead they chose Goodell, the company man who had overseen the league's lucrative television contracts. The owners voted with their wallets. They chose Goodell on their fifth ballot. The vote was twenty-three to eight in his favor (with Oakland owner and league agitator Al Davis abstaining). Goodell had one more vote than the required two-thirds majority, and the owners made it unanimous. Robert Kraft got his man.

But shortly after Goodell's ascension, the corporate culture inside the NFL offices began to shift. The new commissioner took control of all disciplinary procedures across the league and was heaped with praise by national sports reporters for tightening the reins on players for their illegal actions off the field and their use of performance-enhancing drugs to give them a competitive edge on the field. It was a feeling of power that Goodell had never experienced before, and it began to manifest in peculiar ways.

NFL staffers were told to avert their eyes when the commissioner strolled down the halls at the league offices. Lunchtime strategy sessions were transformed into royal courts where executives were not allowed to speak or reach for a slice of pizza until Goodell had done so first. The commissioner kept a mental list of his enemies and was morphing into a Nixonian type of leader— the kind of leader that his father Charles Goodell would have despised.

Roger went after players and teams with a heavy hand. He was quick to punish teams with sanctions for salary-cap violations, and as league owners grumbled, Goodell could always count on the support of his friend and mentor Kraft. The two men had a personal relationship that went beyond the business they were in.

But their close bond was put to the test in the fall of 2007 when the New England Patriots were accused of videotaping New York Jets defensive coaches' signals during a Patriots win in early September. The accusations ignited a firestorm across the sports world, and Goodell felt compelled to act. He took a coveted first-round draft pick away from the team and fined Patriots head coach Bill Belichick $500,000. The penalties were deemed stiff by some, but not the league owners who whispered among themselves that Robert Kraft's team had been given a break, thanks to his cozy relationship with Goodell. After all, the case resulted in no suspension for Belichick or any member of his staff, and the Patriots went on to win all of their regular-season games before losing to the Giants in the Super Bowl. Goodell even took it upon himself to destroy the videotaped evidence and notes at the heart of the scandal now known as Spygate.

"I think it was the right thing to do," Goodell said at the time. "I have nothing to hide."

The NFL owners, however, believed that Goodell had betrayed their trust because of his loyalty for one man—his father figure Kraft. The Patriots owner later returned that loyalty in the Ray Rice case. He privately counseled the commissioner and publicly supported him by appearing on *CBS This Morning*, where he stressed that Goodell had no knowledge of the video and that anyone who second-guessed the commissioner did not know the type of man he was. Kraft also called his fellow owners, urging them to release statements of support for Goodell.[2]

The other owners resented the close friendship between the commissioner and Kraft, who was called "the assistant commissioner" behind his back. But the money was rolling in, so Goodell's position was protected. Each team was worth more than ever before and total league revenues had skyrocketed 65 percent. Only those nostalgic for the way things once were would still refer to the game of baseball as "America's pastime." Football, and most notably the NFL, had supplanted Major League Baseball as the nation's dominant sports league. This unmatched level of success emboldened the commissioner over time. Later, when negotiating a contract extension, Goodell asked the owners for a yearly salary of approximately $49.5 million, lifetime health insurance for himself and his wife and their kids, and lifetime use of a private jet.[3] He had earned a mind-boggling $212.5 million through 2015. This was unheard-of for a commissioner. It was more money than any of the NFL's marquee stars, including Brady, Peyton Manning, and Aaron Rodgers, had made. Only two athletes, baseball star Alex Rodriguez and NBA legend Kobe Bryant, earned more money over the same stretch of time.

But a debt needed to be paid. If Goodell was to maintain his lofty position and continue to justify an obscene salary, he had to build alliances with not just Robert Kraft but also the other thirty-one league owners, who had their own franchises to run, and each owner looking for a way to knock the Patriots from their throne as the league's winningest modern-day dynasty. They bided their time and waited for New England to slip up again. And this time, there would be no cover, or cover-up, by Goodell.

Chapter Thirteen

POWER PLAY

Allegiance to the other NFL owners was incentive enough for Roger Goodell to go after the New England Patriots, but why put the bull's-eye on Tom Brady's back? He'd had an unblemished career to this point and appeared to be the poster boy for everything the league was selling. He was clean, rarely said anything wrong or incendiary, and he proselytized team success over individual accolades.

Even Peyton Manning, the NFL's other cornerstone quarterback, had not escaped controversy. While in college at the University of Tennessee, he was accused by former athletic trainer Jamie Naughright of exposing himself and placing his genitals against her face. Manning claimed that he "mooned" another Tennessee player in the female trainer's presence but had long denied allegations of sexual harassment. Naughright later settled her case with the university for $300,000. Manning was also accused in an article published by Al Jazeera America of receiving supplies of HGH (human growth hormone) in his wife's name from an anti-aging clinic in Indianapolis. Manning had never failed a drug test, and a subsequent seven-month investigation by the NFL cleared him of all charges.

DeMaurice Smith sat behind the desk in his office and wrestled with the question about why number 12 was now being targeted. He came back to the word he often used when describing Goodell—*power.*

"Those low-level draft picks fighting for a spot in the league can see what Tom's going through and will come to the conclusion that they have no rights," he would later say.[1] It was up to Smith and his team of union litigators to protect them. Early on in the Brady case, the key was to establish the rules of engagement with NFL investigator Ted Wells. NFLPA attorney Heather McPhee had worked closely with Wells on the Incognito bullying case and had gained respect for the opposing lawyer.

"In that case, Ted only asked for what he was entitled to, which included Incognito's phone records," McPhee recalled. "It was all very civil under the circumstances."[2]

Civility was a trait shared by McPhee, but she was also tough and battle tested. The attorney grew up in Natick, Massachusetts. Her mother, Sharon, was a schoolteacher, and her father, Neil, a retired shortstop for the Minnesota Twins. The couple met while Sharon attended her first Major League Baseball game with a friend who was dating another Twins player. After his career in the pros, Neil McPhee returned to his native Massachusetts and coached baseball at Northeastern University, his alma mater, for twenty-nine years.

As a child, Heather delivered newspapers for extra money and earned a scholarship to a local private school where she rode horses. Later, she followed her older brother Dan to Princeton University. From an early age, Heather had developed goals for herself and then worked furiously to achieve them. She carried that tenacity with her into adulthood, where she developed into a skilled lawyer and expert negotiator. McPhee worked tirelessly and earned both the loyalty and the trust of her boss DeMaurice Smith.

She was also greatly admired by Tom Brady, who shared a similar work ethic and keen attention for detail. The two spent time on the phone together in the weeks after the Super Bowl while Ted Wells was conducting his investigation.

"He always maintained such a positive attitude during that time," McPhee recalled. "He believed the case was overblown because of the hype surrounding the Super Bowl and thought that it would die down."

But McPhee knew that Ted Wells was a formidable opponent and would not rest until every detail of the case was scrutinized. The NFL had become a very important client for him. The league had paid Wells's firm more than $45 million for both the Bullygate and Deflategate investigations. Wells was known to lock himself in hotel rooms for weeks at a time while poring over mountains of evidence in the various cases. As with the Incognito case, Wells asked McPhee for Brady's phone records. The attorney then reached out to Brady's agent, Don Yee, in Los Angeles to get the ball rolling on the request. She was stunned by the reply.

"Yee's office told me flat out that they weren't going to comply and that they would handle things moving forward," McPhee said. "He [Yee] didn't feel like Tom owed anything to Wells and his team."

The NFLPA lawyer explained to the agent that the league was entitled to any information in Brady's phone, but Yee refused to budge. The agent then informed McPhee that his team would deal directly with the NFL.

"I knew this was a huge mistake and that it would only piss Wells off," McPhee claimed. "Don Yee is an agent, not a litigator. Tom Brady was about to get some bad advice, but he was loyal to Don so he didn't question it."

McPhee believes that Yee's refusal to cooperate turned what was a professional investigation into a personal vendetta for Ted Wells.

Brady thought he was in good hands. He escaped the snow

and cold of New England for a family trip to Costa Rica, where he dove off a cliff, much to the dismay of his coaches and fans, rode horses with Gisele, and chased their kids across the beach. The weather was beautiful and there were no storm clouds in sight. Number 12 appeared to be blocking everything out to spend quality time with his family.

Meanwhile, Ted Wells kept working.

On May 6, 2015, Wells released a 243-page report outlining the NFL's case against Tom Brady. Investigators had interviewed nearly seventy witnesses, including the Patriots quarterback and head coach. The report stated that all eleven footballs used by the Patriots in the 2015 AFC title game against the Colts had tested below the minimum air pressure level of 12.5 psi, while the four Colts balls tested measured within the 12.5 to 13.5 psi allowed by the league.[3]

But was it a deliberate act? Ted Wells and his team, which included NFL executive vice president Jeff Pash, concluded that it was "more probable than not" that Patriots employees Jim McNally, the team's official locker room attendant, and equipment assistant John Jastremski colluded in a deliberate effort to break the rules. Most important, the report stated that it was more probable than not that Tom Brady himself was at least generally aware of the plot. Referee Walt Anderson went on the record to say that McNally had violated pregame protocol by taking the balls out of the officials' locker room without permission. It was the first time in Anderson's nineteen years in the league that he could not locate the game balls at the start of the game. The video-taped surveillance showed that McNally carried two large bags of footballs down the center tunnel toward the playing field and made a curious pit stop into a bathroom, where he locked the door and remained inside for approximately one minute and forty seconds. The video showed him then leaving the bathroom with the ball bags and heading to the field.

According to Wells, the real smoking gun against number 12 could be found in the dozens of text and phone records retrieved from the key players in the case, specifically those of McNally and Jastremski. NFL investigators found a disturbing thread of texts between the two equipment guys dating back to the 2014 off-season. In May of that year, the pair exchanged texts about what would become a running theme between the two: McNally's demand for free stuff from Brady.

McNally: you working?

Jastremski: yup.

McNally: nice dude...jimmy needs some new kicks...lets make a deal...come on help the deflator.

McNally: Chill buddy im just fuckin with you...im not going to espn...yet...

The word *deflator* jumped out to investigators. Wells and his team also found it damning that McNally had offered a veiled threat to go to ESPN.

Two questions needed answers. Why did McNally refer to himself as the "deflator," and what information did he threaten to give the television sports network?

The text conversations continued into the season after a Thursday night game between the Patriots and Jets in October 2014, when Brady complained angrily about the inflation levels of the footballs. The quarterback's criticism was met with scorn by McNally.

McNally: Tom sucks. I'm going to make that next ball a fucking balloon.

Jastremski: Talked to him last night. He actually brought you up and said you must have a lot of stress trying to get them done...

Jastremski: I told him it was. He was right though...

Jastremski: I checked some of the balls this morning. The refs fucked us...a few of then [them] were at almost 16.

Jastremski: They didn't recheck then [them] after they put air in them.

McNally: Fuck tom ... 16 was nothing ... wait til next Sunday.

Jastremski: Omg. Spaz!

McNally blasted Brady over the next several days in texts to Jastremski. He threatened to blow up the footballs to the size of rugby balls and even watermelons. When Jastremski pointed out that the texts sounded so angry, McNally replied, The only thing deflating sun [son] ... is his [Brady's] passer rating. According to the texts, he later asked the quarterback for cash and new "kicks" (sneakers). If Brady didn't come through with the items, McNally warned his friend Jastremski that it would be a "rugby Sunday."

In January 2015, McNally continued to press Jastremski to ensure that Brady delivered the new sneakers plus some autographed footballs.

McNally: Remember to put a couple of sweet pigskins ready for tom to sign

Jastremski: You got it kid ... big autograph day for you.

McNally: nice ... throw some kicks in and make it real special.

Jastremski: it [if] yur lucky. 11?

McNally: 11 or 11 and half kid.

McNally eventually received an autographed jersey and two signed footballs from Brady.

The conversations between Jastremski and McNally were alarming and did not bode well for Brady's case. But the evidence was circumstantial at best. Ted Wells needed science to back up his claim that the footballs used by the Patriots in the AFC title game did not lose air pressure naturally over the course of the game. He hired a Menlo Park, California–based company called Exponent to dig in further. Researchers at a company site in Phoenix, Arizona, used a forty-foot-long thermal chamber to re-create the environment inside Gillette Stadium on that fateful night. The chamber floor was covered in green artificial turf and the temperature inside was set at forty-eight degrees Fahrenheit. In another windowless space, they attempted to re-create the exact setting of the officials' locker room at Gillette, where the balls would have been at room temperature.[4]

Four primary Exponent scientists spent three months on their part of the investigation. After several experiments, they concluded that "the reduction of pressure of the Patriots game balls cannot be explained completely by basic scientific principles."[5] Those scientific principles included what is known as the Ideal Gas Law, which suggested that a given mass and constant volume of a gas, plus pressure exerted on both sides of an object, was directly proportionate to its absolute temperature. It was a wonky way of stating that the pressure drop of the Patriots balls was greater than the pressure drop of the Colts footballs in the exact same climate. Scientists also simulated how quickly someone could deflate thirteen balls and found that the task could indeed have been completed in the minute and forty seconds Jim McNally was alone in the bathroom with the Patriots' footballs.

The finger of suspicion was clearly pointed at McNally and Jastremski, but did they act alone?

The Wells Report could not offer a definitive answer but concluded that Brady was most likely involved. Investigators pointed to the volume of telephone and text conversations between number 12 and Jastremski right after the Deflategate story broke. Neither had communicated by phone or text in the six months prior to January 2015. Ted Wells also found it suspicious that Brady had then invited Jastremski to a private meeting in the quarterback room. It was the first such invitation in Jastremski's twenty-year career with the team. Wells believed that the two equipment guys were merely lackeys who would not consider deflating footballs without Brady's knowledge.

When number 12 sat down with investigators, he denied having any involvement in deliberate efforts to deflate footballs and claimed that he did not know McNally's name or what his role was regarding game-day footballs. His testimony contradicted the fact that he was present when McNally received the autographed jersey and balls and Jastremski's claim that he had spoken to Brady about McNally. Was the quarterback misremembering or was he lying? Ted Wells believed that Brady wasn't telling the truth. The report also noted that Brady had refused to turn over his phone to Ted Wells. Heather McPhee's plea that Brady cooperate with investigators had fallen on deaf ears.

The report was a bombshell, and reaction came swiftly from Brady's fellow NFL players. Colts linebacker Erik Walden said it was "gross" that Brady resorted to cheating but also acknowledged that Brady and the Patriots put a "whupping" on his team during their march toward the Super Bowl. Former Broncos star Shannon Sharpe fired off a tweet demanding a severe punishment against the Patriots because spygate taught them absolutely nothing about adhering to the rules.[6]

Number 12 did have his defenders, and they were close to home. Chased by reporters for his reaction, Rob Gronkowski simply flexed his enormous biceps. Agent Don Yee released a lengthy statement that said, in part, "The Wells report, with all due respect, is a significant and terrible disappointment. It's [*sic*] omission of key facts and lines of inquiry suggest the investigators reached a conclusion first, and then determined so-called facts later." Yee pointed out correctly that the report strangely omitted nearly all of his client's testimony and only summarized Brady's response to investigators' questions. Brady's father, Tom Sr., expressed his outrage to a reporter from *USA Today*. "The thing is so convoluted; they say that possibly, possibly he [Brady] was aware of this. The reality is if you can't prove he did it, then he's innocent, and lay off him. That's the bottom line.... This was Framegate from the beginning."[7]

Number 12 kept a low profile on the day the report was released but emerged the following afternoon for a prescheduled speaking event at Salem State College, just north of Boston, with veteran sports reporter and friend Jim Gray. Like an embattled head of state, the Patriots quarterback rode a helicopter to campus, where scalpers were getting big money for tickets to hear him offer his first public words since the release of the Wells Report. Brady took the stage to thunderous applause from the sellout crowd chanting, "MVP, MVP, MVP." He was tan, smiling, and appeared relaxed.

"Tom, it looks like you've picked a pretty friendly place to reappear," Gray said, staring out at the adoring crowd.

As the applause died down, Gray opened with the question on the mind of everyone in the sports world. "What is your reaction, Tom, to the Ted Wells report?"

Before Brady could respond, someone in the audience yelled out, "Who cares?"

"I don't have really any reaction," Brady said. "It's only been thirty hours so I haven't had much time to digest it fully, but when I do I'll be sure to let you know how I feel about it."

Tom Brady the quarterback had become Tom Brady the politician. He had learned a hard lesson since fumbling while addressing the allegations in that initial news conference. This time, he did not misspeak.

"I've had a lot of adversity over the course of my career, my life," Brady told the crowd. "And I'm very fortunate to have people that love me, support me. Life so much is about ups and downs, and certainly I accept my role and responsibility as a public figure, and I think a lot of it, you take the good with the bad...so we'll get through it."[8]

Gray asked if the controversy took away the enjoyment of winning the Super Bowl.

Number 12 smiled. "Absolutely not."

But inside, Tom Brady was seething.

Five days after the release of the Wells Report, the NFL announced that Brady would be suspended without pay for the first four games of the regular season. In a letter to Brady, Troy

Vincent, a former player and one of Goodell's top lieutenants, told the quarterback that "there is substantial and credible evidence to conclude you were at least generally aware of the actions of the Patriots' employees involved in the deflation of the footballs and that it was unlikely that their actions were done without your knowledge."[9]

Don Yee vowed that he would appeal the decision to the commissioner.

The Patriots were also slammed with a $1 million fine, the biggest in league history. The seven-figure punishment was matched only by the fine levied against former San Francisco 49ers owner Ed DeBartolo Jr., who pleaded guilty to a felony gambling charge in 1999.

The bleeding didn't stop there.

The Patriots had to give up two draft picks, a first-round pick in 2016 and a fourth-round pick in 2017. And almost as an afterthought, two team employees were now out of jobs. The league suspended Jim McNally and John Jastremski "indefinitely."

In a show of solidarity, the Patriots swapped their Twitter avatar showing the team logo for an image of Brady's jersey. The wife of New York Jets owner Woody Johnson also shared her feelings on social media. Suzanne Johnson tweeted out the news of Brady's suspension along with a happy-face emoji.

Chapter Fourteen

KRAFT'S COUNTERATTACK

Robert Kraft was outraged by the assault on his quarterback and his team at the hands of Roger Goodell, the man he had mentored, protected, defended, and even welcomed into his home. It may have been called the Wells Report, but Kraft believed the scathing indictment against the Patriots and subsequent suspension and penalties were orchestrated by the commissioner alone. Kraft had owned up to the Spygate scandal, calling his coach's flagrant rule violations stupid. But with Deflategate, he was ready to mount a counterattack. He felt that the latest controversy was being fueled by the jealousy of his fellow owners and people working in the league office who had ties to the Jets, the Patriots' hated AFC East rival. Mike Kensil, who had participated in the sting operation during the championship game, had previously worked in the Jets front office for twenty years and was there when Bill Belichick abruptly resigned as head coach to go to New England in 2000. Omitted in the Wells Report was any mention of Kensil's heated rant directed toward Patriots equipment manager Dave Schoenfeld at halftime of the Colts game, when he allegedly warned him that he was in "big fucking trouble." The report only alluded to a conversation between the two men about the testing of footballs.

Wells had made no effort to interview D'Qwell Jackson, the Colts linebacker who intercepted Brady in the AFC championship game and was said to have given the ball to a member of the Colts' equipment staff, despite the fact that Jackson's name is mentioned several times in the Wells Report. "Throughout the NFL investigation, no one reached out to me. No one asked me about the football," Jackson said in a 2018 radio interview. "Not a peep. Silence. I would have loved to catch them [the Patriots] in the act because we got our tails kicked... but no, I had no idea [about the ball being deflated]."[1]

There was also the disturbing case of Jeff Pash, the NFL executive and labor lawyer who had helped negotiate the collective bargaining agreement with the NFLPA in 2011. He worked side by side with Ted Wells on the so-called independent investigation. Kraft didn't trust him. Pash had drawn the owner's ire for refusing to correct misinformation that had been sprinkled across the media from league sources—most notably, ESPN NFL reporter Chris Mortensen's claim from January, later proved not to be true, that the league had found that eleven of the New England Patriots' twelve game balls were inflated "significantly below" the NFL's requirements at two pounds under the psi minimum. The truth, according to the Wells Report, was that only one Patriots football had tested two psi below the league threshold.

Allegations of the Patriots' wrongdoing continued to pile up. Less than a month later, ESPN aired another false report claiming that Jim McNally had attempted to slip an unapproved ball to the referee in charge of overseeing footballs for special teams in the same game. The story carried a cloak-and-dagger, underhanded tone. It was just another example of the Patriots getting caught cheating. But the reality was quite different. The ball in question, referred to later as K-Ball #1 in the Wells Report, had been taken out of play by league employee Scott Miller after kickoff to auction off later. It was replaced with a new ball that was described by Patriots staff as "crappy" and insufficiently broken in. Patriots placekicker Stephen Gostkowski was outraged over the switch and demanded that the ball be returned for the remainder of the game. Schoenfeld, Jastremski, and McNally then went hunting for the ball. An NFL official said he saw the ball on a couch in the officials' locker room, and the football was eventually recovered and given to McNally, who tried to get it back in the game but got denied because the ball didn't carry referee Walt Anderson's distinct markings. Anderson initialed each ball before the game. However, later investigators could not conclude whether the referee had even marked K-Ball #1 before the game. The NFL later fired Scott Miller for selling game-used footballs without the league's permission.

Kraft had had enough. He ordered Stacey James, the team's head of media relations, to write his counterpart Greg Aiello, the NFL's communications chief, to demand action.

"Once again, we have another LEAK (this one citing four sources close to the investigation)," James wrote. "What is unconscionable to me is that the league holds data that could very well exonerate us from any wrongdoing and completely dismiss the rampant reports and allegations of nefarious actions."[2]

Patriots attorney Robyn Glaser then forwarded James's letter to Jeff Pash. "We hereby DEMAND that the misinformation...be formally and publicly corrected by the league IMMEDIATELY."

Glaser had worked for the team for the past decade following a stint as a music industry attorney in Los Angeles. She was a born fighter and wore black fingernail polish that she covered only with boxing gloves during her strenuous daily workouts. Admittedly, Glaser, a Colby College graduate, had never watched an NFL game in its entirety before joining the Patriots, opting instead for reality shows like *Project Runway*.[3]

Glaser now found herself front and center in the biggest reality show in sports, one brimming with bold allegations of cheating and corruption, heavy drama, and deceit.

Pash responded to Glaser's demands by e-mail, telling her that he had no reason to believe the leaks came from the league office but that he'd pass on the concerns to Ted Wells. This weak response lit a fire under Glaser, who called it "disingenuous."

"Jeff, you need to step up," Glaser demanded. "It's been made resoundingly clear to us that your words are just a front."

The attorney's vitriol had no effect on Pash, who chided Glaser for sending such a "personal and accusatory note." The NFL executive insisted that his responses to her concerns were both candid and respectful.

"I work for the Patriots, as well as 31 other clubs and the Commissioner," he replied. "Sometimes that creates tension, as it apparently has here."

The tension was, in fact, palpable, and each camp was dug in. Through it all, Robert Kraft thought about the toll it was taking on his quarterback. Kraft's respect for Brady was greater than his admiration for any other player. He felt that any mother would be lucky to have a son like Tom, a guy who competed and worked hard for everything he had ever accomplished. The owner slammed the Wells Report in a lengthy statement upon its release, calling its findings "incomprehensible," and then put his own legal team to work on a rebuttal.

Within a week, the Patriots released their own Deflategate document titled *The Wells Report in Context* online. In it, the team questioned the NFL's decision not to notify the Patriots about concerns raised by the Ravens and the Colts prior to the Indianapolis game or take any preventative measures to ensure that the teams were using footballs with equal pressurization. Did the NFL willfully put the Colts at a disadvantage just so it could catch the Patriots in the act?

The document also stressed that the deflation of the Patriots' balls was due to the impact of the temperature and fully consistent with the Ideal Gas Law and pointed out that, according to the Wells Report, three of the four Colts balls tested at halftime were below league regulation. The report hammered the Wells Report line by line. The document called into question the league's financial dealings with Ted Wells and pointed out the fact that NFL executive David Gardi had jumped to conclusions when he fired off a letter to the team on January 19 that accused the Patriots of tampering with footballs without even considering any scientific explanation about ball deflation. *The Wells Report in Context* even analyzed the minute and forty seconds that McNally had spent in the bathroom with the bags of balls, arguing that it was the proper amount of time for a man to urinate and wash and then dry his hands.

The Wells Report in Context made a lot of sense to Patriots fans and even those reporters eager to tear down the mighty franchise. But the architects behind the document "jumped the shark" when they attempted to explain Jim McNally's use of the word *deflator*. The Patriots continued to add information to their website over time and, in June 2015, offered their own explanation for the juvenile banter between McNally and the friend he called "dorito dink," John Jastremski. According to the team, the word *deflator* referred to weight loss and not footballs.

"Mr. Jastremski would sometimes work out and bulk up," the annotation read. "He is a slender guy and his goal was to get to 200 pounds. Mr. McNally is a big fellow and had the opposite goal: to lose weight. 'Deflate' was a term they used to refer to losing weight."[4]

Even the most ardent Tom Brady supporters had a difficult time believing this explanation, while Patriots haters pounced on it. On Twitter, one critic called it a "my dog ate my homework" defense. Skepticism was widespread and deflected from the fact that, for the most part, the Patriots' rebuttal to the charges in the Wells Report was spot-on. During the off-season, the debate continued to play out in the court of public opinion and on just about every sports talk radio program in America. The divide was as easy to identify as that between Democratic blue and Republican red states. If you hated the Patriots, you were more inclined to believe every word of the Wells Report. If you were a Patriots fan, you put your trust and faith in the team and its quarterback.

Four bloggers from the popular Boston-based website Barstool Sports protested at NFL headquarters in New York. Website founder David Portnoy and three colleagues, all wearing Brady jerseys, first picketed outside, chanting "Free Brady, fire Goodell," and then handcuffed themselves together in the lobby. They were then handcuffed again, this time by New York City police officers, and escorted out of the building and into a squad car.

"This is the best day of my life, getting arrested for Tom Brady," one protester said, smiling.[5]

It was a theater of the absurd, but the protesters' sentiments were shared by fellow fans and former Patriots players.

Brady's longtime friend Matt Chatham voiced his outrage as well. Chatham by this time was long retired from the league after a stint with the New York Jets but had moved back to Boston and kept a high profile in New England as a television analyst. The former NFL linebacker had also made headlines in 2013 when he carried Boston Marathon bombing victim Heather Abbott to safety, away from the smoke and fire caused by the two pressure-cooker bombs that exploded near the finish line. Abbott lost her leg as a result of the terrorist attack, but she praised Chatham and his wife, Erin, for staying by her side during those chaotic hours that transformed the city. Chatham had earned the public's trust and now used the platform to defend his old teammate and friend.

"If manipulating fan indifference were the only thing at play here, Roger Goodell's NFL wouldn't be nearly as nefarious as it is,"

Chatham wrote in an article for his website footballbyfootball.com. "The real problem is illustrated in the clear disrespect Roger Goodell's league has for the intelligence of the American fan, seen this time in a statement released by the league outlining their rationale for punishing the Patriots."

The ex-player simply could not get past the very idea of the accusation.

"The football has to typically pass through multiple officials' hands every single play before it's set for snap," Chatham says. "There's no way around that. A scheme to significantly deflate footballs would be a lot of effort for something with a high likelihood to get caught right away. Basically it would just be dumb. People say a lot of things about Tom Brady and the Patriots. *But stupid isn't one of them.* Unfortunately, wanting scandal to be true—even the nonsensical ones—is a powerful public drug."

Even the commander in chief weighed in on the controversy. When the Super Bowl champions visited the White House in late April, President Barack Obama said, "That whole story got a little blown out of proportion. Even in the midst of a huge distraction during the biggest media circus of the sports year, they stayed focused...there's Belichick and Brady, the most successful coach and quarterback tandem perhaps in NFL history and there's the Patriot Way, a group that values teamwork and hard work above all else."[6]

Number 12 had attended the team's White House celebrations in the past but was markedly absent this time. Brady stayed away from Washington, but his other team was hard at work in the nation's capital.

Chapter Fifteen

TOM BRADY VS. THE NFL

DeMaurice Smith was ready to defend his union's highest-profile member. The NFLPA leader had begun work with the AFL-CIO on an amicus brief that they filed with the United States Court of Appeals for the Second Circuit. What began as a story about palace intrigue inside the NFL offices and Gillette Stadium had now evolved into a John Grisham–style legal thriller. In the fifteen-page document, the labor union argued that Brady's suspension should be vacated because Roger Goodell had "failed to follow basic procedural fairness and acted arbitrarily as an employer seeking to justify his own disciplinary decision rather than as a neutral arbitrator."[1] It was a fancy way of saying that Goodell had presided over a kangaroo court in which he served as judge, jury, and executioner.

Smith also worked the phones, connecting with several influential team owners including John Mara of the New York Giants.

"What are we doing?" Smith asked Mara. "If you wanna fine him [Brady], fine him. But now we're talking suspensions?"

Smith didn't believe Brady was guilty of any wrongdoing, but even if that was the case, it was a minor infraction at best and now it was being treated as a capital offense by Goodell and his minions.

He walked Mara through the case. "There are allegations that there were minute differences in a limited number of balls in the first half of a playoff game where in the second half, the opposing team got beat like a drum with balls that were properly inflated. Again, what are we doing?"

Mara and the other owners, except for Kraft, continued to back Goodell's decision.

"They were circling the wagons, which is easy to do because there's just one wagon, the NFL shield," Smith recalls. "When the NFL is conducting an investigation of any kind, they are incapable of giving an honest answer."

Smith then began ripping Roger Goodell in public.

"I think the Wells Report delivered exactly what the client [Goodell] wanted," he told ESPN. "This was no independent investigation. You can't really have credibility just because you slap the word *independent* on a piece of paper."[2]

Jeff Pash's involvement in the probe was a clear example of the skewed prism with which the investigation was conducted.

Smith also accused Goodell of looking the other way when it came to the transgressions and crimes of his bosses—the NFL owners.

"You have the case of Colts owner Jim Irsay, where someone [his onetime mistress] overdosed and died in his house," Smith argued. "You have the case of Cleveland Browns owner Jimmy Haslam, where the business he was connected with was found to be in violation of federal law. You have the case of the Minnesota Vikings owners, where a state court judge ruled that they had engaged in fraud. Somewhere in the middle of that is a huge yawning gap."

When asked if he trusted Roger Goodell, Smith said pointedly, "It's not my job to trust him. It's my job to represent our players."

Smith had been down this road before, not only in the Ray Rice case but during the Bountygate case in 2012, when four New Orleans Saints defensive players were suspended along with head coach Sean Payton and two assistant coaches for allegedly offering cash bonuses for injuring opposing players, including Hall of Fame quarterback Brett Favre. According to NFL investigators, Saints players earned one thousand dollars for causing an opposing player to be carted off the field and an additional five hundred if a player was knocked out of a game.

Still, the suspended players testified under oath that no such practice existed and the NFL could not prove that it did. Twenty hours of testimony and 50,000 documents revealed very little evidence tying the players to the bounty program. The suspensions were later overturned by Roger Goodell's former boss Paul Tagliabue, who handled the appeal.

"Goodell said they had videotaped evidence incriminating the players in Bountygate, but this proved to be untrue," said Smith. "They're not concerned with truth. The NFL lied and twisted facts to get the conclusion they wanted, and now they were doing it again to Tom."

Meanwhile, the case was adding a mountain of stress to Tom Brady's personal life. He was being flayed by the national media and torn apart by Goodell, the NFL's most powerful man. An asterisk had been placed next to his career accomplishments, and he was lumped into the group of superstar cheaters that included Barry Bonds, Alex Rodriguez, and Mark McGwire.

His mansion in Brookline, Massachusetts, became his bunker. Brady was rarely seen in public, and questions swirled in the tabloids about whether the unfolding drama had taken an irreparable toll on his marriage. The celebrity magazine *OK* reported that Gisele walked out on Tom after a bad fight. The former celebrity darlings were now rarely photographed or seen in public together.

And Brady's marriage wasn't the only relationship now called into question. Fans began to wonder if there was fission between the quarterback and Robert Kraft. The owner had been one of Brady's most vocal supporters throughout the Deflategate saga, so fans were surprised when Kraft made the announcement in San Francisco on May 19 that he would accept Goodell's discipline and would not appeal.

But no one was more shocked by Kraft's statement than Brady, who hadn't been given a heads-up by the owner. Maybe Kraft was adhering to his father's advice when Harry Kraft told him, "You have a wonderful way of not holding grudges that can hurt you. Stay that way and you'll live a happy life."

But Brady and the fans didn't see it that way. Number 12 had been the Patriots player most responsible for the team's success, both financially and on the field. Kraft had built a small city around his stadium called Patriot Place that included a hotel, restaurants, and retail shops. It's likely that none of that would have been possible without Brady.

Perhaps, Kraft had weighed his decision against his fellow owners' disdainful treatment of the late Raiders owner Al Davis, who had engaged in both a hot and cold war with the NFL for decades and thus was ostracized by the group of billionaire owners, who used every opportunity to punish him. Taking an Al Davis–like position was not a good long-term business strategy for Kraft or the New England Patriots. Later, when Cowboys owner Jerry Jones battled Roger Goodell over the six-game suspension of star running back Ezekiel Elliott for abusing an ex-girlfriend, Jones reportedly told the commissioner over the phone, "I'm gonna come after you with everything I have. If you think Bob Kraft came after you hard, Bob Kraft is a pussy compared to what I'm going to do."[3]

Patriots fans were looking for similar words of defiance from the owner, whom many now branded as a traitor. Despite currently running the winningest franchise in New England sports, Kraft was eviscerated by the members of Patriot Nation, who took to the airwaves to denounce the owner.

With Kraft laying down his arms, Brady and the NFLPA would have to fight the war on their own.

There would, however, be a short respite to all the talk of Deflategate when Robert Kraft hosted a lavish ceremony at his current Chestnut Hill mansion to present Brady and his teammates their Super Bowl rings.

"I've got all my rings," the quarterback excitedly told the owner. Kraft smiled.

Gisele Bündchen pointed to her purse. "I know, I've been carrying the rings. That's my job."[4]

Later inside a giant tent before the rings were handed out, Brady and Kraft shared a private moment together in the middle of the party.

"We're lucky," Kraft told his quarterback.

"I know, we sure are," Brady replied.

"And I'm lucky to have you in my life," the owner continued.

Brady pulled Kraft close and gave him a warm hug.

"I feel the same way. I love you so much."

The championship ring was smothered with 205 sparkling diamonds and was the biggest Super Bowl ring ever produced. The phrases "Do Your Job" and "We Are All Patriots" were engraved on the sides along with Kraft's signature.

Gisele pulled the rings commemorating her husband's three previous championship seasons from her purse, and Tom slipped them on his fingers in anticipation of the fourth.

Bow-covered boxes were handed to each player and coach by members of the five military branches, and then on a count of three, they were opened. Number 12 placed the newest bauble on his finger and flashed his bejeweled hands for the camera. It was a statement to the fans and more important to

Goodell. This was a moment and an honor that he could not take away.

The evening had gone a long way to repairing the relationship between Brady and Kraft. Number 12 would forgive the owner for his apparent lack of support, but he would not forget. More than a year later, during the 2017 regular season, Brady was asked by radio host Kirk Minihane if he was comfortable with the way Kraft had handled Deflategate. The quarterback offered no comment. It was a gesture that spoke volumes.

Brady's appeal to the NFL was set to be heard in late June 2015. DeMaurice Smith and his team had less than two months to prepare. The NFLPA lawyers would spend nearly every waking moment on the case, which meant that all would spend more time at the office and less time at home with their families. The late-night strategy sessions were a free-flowing forum for ideas and debate. Smith did not surround himself with yes-men or -women, nor did he demand that no one reach for a slice of pizza or a sandwich before he ate. He debated strategy with Heather McPhee and others and decided that the best course of action was to target directly the NFL's only perceived connection between the quarterback and the deflated footballs—the assumption that he was "generally aware" of alleged cheating by Patriots employees Jastremski and McNally. One major issue they would have to deal with was the fact that Tom Brady got rid of his Samsung phone and replaced it with a new iPhone 6 after his agent, Don Yee, had told him that the physical phone would not be subject to any investigation, only the records of calls and texts.

Once Smith and his team learned that Brady had destroyed the phone, they feared that the league and the media would scream cover-up.

"Gisele had been destroying her phone for years, ever since the phone-hacking scandal erupted in Britain," Heather McPhee explained. "She's an international supermodel and had knowledge of ways to protect herself from having her photos and conversations hacked by reporters and served up to the public. Tom did the same thing."

Much of the fear stemmed from the fallout of a 2005 investigation of a reporter for the Rupert Murdoch–owned tabloid *News of the World* and a private investigator who were arrested and later convicted for hacking phone conversations between Britain's Prince William and his brother, Prince Harry. Reporters were also known to have targeted politicians, movie stars, and even the mobile device of a thirteen-year-old kidnapping and murder victim.

Ironically, in the court battle that followed Brady's appeal, his personal e-mails, which were among 40,000 pages of documents submitted by the NFLPA, were revealed to the public. Among them were conversations between Brady and a childhood friend about comparisons to his longtime rival Peyton Manning.

"I've got another 7 or 8 years. He [Manning] has 2," Brady wrote. "That's the final chapter. Game on."[5]

It was now game on for Brady and his legal team. When number 12 arrived at NFL headquarters at 345 Park Avenue in New York on the morning of June 23, 2015, and stepped out of a black Chevy Suburban, he was smartly dressed in a dark suit but appeared gaunt, the weathered creases on his forehead now more visible. A couple of Patriots fans fought for the star quarterback's attention as he walked across the sidewalk. Brady smiled graciously, but Heather McPhee had her game face on. The hard-nosed attorney stiff-armed one autograph hound to clear a path so her client could enter the building quickly without being corralled by the throngs of media positioned outside.

Inside, Brady and the NFLPA team were led to the basement of the building, where the appeal would be heard. To McPhee, the move was a clear attempt at intimidation by the league.

"Their state-of-the-art conference room on the sixth floor

would have easily accommodated us, but instead they stuck us in a cramped basement room," McPhee recalled. "So it's hard not to read symbolism into the location they chose."

At six foot four, Brady looked like Gulliver in the land of Lilliputians as he attempted to navigate the tight space with his lanky frame.

After entering the cramped conference room, Commissioner Goodell addressed both sides.

"We all know why we're here this morning. This is in response to an appeal filed by Tom Brady," Goodell began. "I'm particularly interested in anything Tom has to say, and I look forward to hearing directly from him. . . . I will oversee this, but as you know, I'm not an attorney."[6]

Exactly, DeMaurice Smith thought to himself. *It's one of the main reasons why we asked you to recuse yourself from hearing the appeal, but you refused and here we are.*

Before anyone would hear from Tom Brady, lawyers on both sides had to set the stage. Opening statements for the NFLPA were presented by Jeffrey Kessler, a renowned labor lawyer hired by DeMaurice Smith to argue Brady's case. Kessler was a legendary courtroom brawler who had worked on the Ray Rice appeal, had helped establish NFL free agency, and represented Bill Belichick in 2000 when the coach sued the NFL and the Jets to break his contract to go to the Patriots. Kessler was fighting for New England once again, and this time he had plenty of ammunition to defend Brady, thanks to the meticulous case built by the NFLPA.

"You didn't have any witnesses yourselves," he addressed Goodell. "You are essentially relying on Wells's conclusions. I'm compelled to note at the beginning that the conclusion of the Wells Report, with respect to Mr. Brady, is that he was generally aware of something. It is our position that there is no policy, no precedent, no notice that has ever been given to a player in the NFL that they could be subject to any discipline...for being generally aware of something."[7]

Kessler in essence was accusing the NFL of making up the rules as it went along in the Deflategate case.

"It doesn't make sense for Brady to be involved with the inflation of footballs," Kessler argued, "as what he cares about it is how they feel in his hand, not how they are inflated." Brady's lawyer played word games here in an attempt to suggest that although number 12 liked a softer football, he had no knowledge of the exact air pressure of each ball.

He also said that punishing Tom was equivalent to censuring a player who may have been generally aware that another player was taking steroids but had nothing to do with supplying or injecting the performance-enhancing drug. In that situation, Kessler argued, the only person who could be punished was the player taking steroids, not someone who might be generally aware it was happening.

It was now Tom Brady's turn to tell his side of the story, and this time he attempted to remove any doubt that he was even generally aware of any scheme to deflate footballs.

"Have you ever specifically told anyone on the Patriots...that they should change the inflation level of the footballs after you've approved them?" asked Kessler.

"No, I would disapprove of that," Brady answered.

Kessler asked him if the issue of inflation ever came up as a factor when selecting his footballs.

"Never," the quarterback replied.

During cross-examination, Lorin Reisner, a partner of Ted Wells, questioned Brady about his cell phone.

"Were there any e-mails or texts that you were worried about which showed you knew about deflating or anything like that? Was there anything you were trying to hide or conceal in your mind?"

"Absolutely not," Brady replied.

The quarterback had provided the NFL phone records that showed he sent or received ninety-nine hundred text messages over an eighty-three-day period following the initial Deflategate reports. It is not clear what percentage of these text messages had focused on the growing crisis, but the level of activity was not deemed to be excessive, given the two-and-a-half-month timeline of texts.

Following Brady's testimony, the NFLPA called its expert witness, Edward Snyder, dean of the Yale School of Management, to debunk the scientific and statistical analysis used by Ted Wells to determine the cause of the ball deflation. Snyder, through the use of several slides, called the conclusions of the Wells Report nothing short of "improper."

When it came time to question Wells himself, Kessler asked the lead investigator why he was so quick to dismiss Brady's claim that he had nothing to do with any deflation of footballs before the AFC championship game. Wells went back to the quarterback's decision not to turn over his cell phone.

"I did reject it [Brady's testimony] based on my assessment of his credibility and his refusal or decision not to give me what I requested in terms of responsive documents," Wells testified. "I will say to Mr. Brady, in my almost forty years of practice, I think that was one of the most ill-advised decisions I have ever seen because it hurt how I viewed his credibility."

As Heather McPhee had predicted, Don Yee's ill-fated strategy not to cooperate with Wells had hurt his client. The investigation wasn't just professional for Ted Wells any longer. It had become personal. McPhee felt that Wells's objectivity was clouded by anger toward Yee and—by association—Brady.

Attorney Kessler believed that Ted Wells was also motivated by something else. He asked Wells about whether he viewed himself as an "independent investigator" while working under a retainer paid for by the NFL.

"I do the best job that I can," Wells replied.

The appeal hearing lasted ten long, grueling hours. And like Brady's Patriots teammates in the Super Bowl, his legal team felt it had left everything on the field. But with Roger Goodell in charge, the field was anything but level.

Five days after the hearing, the NFL announced that it would not reduce the quarterback's four-game suspension. Roger Goodell called Brady's smashing of his cell phone a deliberate act of destruction of potentially critical evidence that went beyond the mere failure to cooperate with the investigation. That news nugget was gobbled up by hungry reporters looking for a smoking gun against the superstar. Brady took to Facebook in an attempt to explain the destroyed cell phone.

"I replaced my broken Samsung phone with a new iPhone 6 AFTER my attorneys made it clear to the NFL that my actual phone device would not be subjected to investigation under any circumstances," Brady wrote. He went on to say that he was never made aware at any time during the investigation that failing to turn over his phone would cause trouble.

Brady was paying for his agent's mistake. As with the weird "deflator" explanation, even some of Tom's staunchest supporters had a hard time believing it.

DeMaurice Smith immediately filed a petition in federal court to vacate the NFL's arbitration decision.

Chapter Sixteen

HIGHS AND LOWS

The NFLPA wanted to argue Brady's case in front of a real judge and not someone who just believed he had the authority to act like one. The union filed a federal lawsuit in Minnesota, a state that had been friendly to players in the past, most notably Vikings star Adrian Peterson, who had recently won a lawsuit to vacate a suspension for abusing his child. But a judge there said it made no sense to hear Brady's case because he played in Massachusetts, the union had its headquarters in Washington, D.C., and the NFL league offices were located in New York. Since the league had also filed a lawsuit, the case would be heard in Manhattan in front of Judge Richard M. Berman of the United States District Court.

The two-hour hearing took place in August, and no cameras were allowed in the federal courtroom. Instead, sketch artist Jane Rosenberg was hired to draw up a visual representation of the proceedings. The artist quickly sketched the room with Brady sitting next to agent Don Yee in the second row. Rosenberg's image of number 12 looked more like Freddy Krueger, which turned into a nightmare for the artist when the sketch went viral and was mocked across the country. It was a light moment in the middle of a dark storm where Brady's legacy and his future were squarely on the line.

Attorney Jeffrey Kessler argued before Judge Berman that Goodell's power wasn't limitless and that there had to be a fair and consistent method to how the commissioner disciplined the players.

But Berman seemed more concerned with what he called the "quantum leap" between Wells and Goodell in their findings. Ted Wells said that Brady was "generally aware" of the ball deflation, while Roger Goodell stated in his ruling that the quarterback had been involved in a "scheme."

Berman pushed for a settlement between the two sides but was ready to make a ruling if a compromise couldn't be reached.

Meanwhile, Tom returned to training camp in Foxborough as he prepared for the 2015 regular season and waited for a deal to come. But there would be no settlement.

On September 3, 2015, Judge Berman erased Brady's four-game suspension in a stunning rebuke to Roger Goodell. In his filing, Berman wrote that Goodell "had dispensed his own brand of industrial justice" and found aspects of the NFL's decision "fundamentally unfair" to Brady.[1]

When word of Berman's decision reached the Patriots, the team immediately posted a photo of Brady with his fist raised in the air on its Twitter feed. It was just a picture. No words were necessary. Teammate Rob Gronkowski posted a photo of Brady riding the big tight end's back after a touchdown. Let's go!, Gronk wrote. This season to be one heck of another ride!

Another ride indeed. The Patriots started the 2015 season with ten straight wins before finishing with a 12–4 record. Along the way, they clinched their seventh-straight AFC East title, tying a league record. Brady played all sixteen regular-season games, passing for forty-seven hundred yards and thirty-six touchdowns with only seven interceptions.

Deflategate was now a painful but distant memory for the quarterback and his fans. But another tempest was forming on the horizon. Fans felt the first sting of disappointment in the AFC championship game against Peyton Manning and his new team, the Denver Broncos. Denver denied the Patriots the opportunity to repeat as world champions as the defense stopped a late Brady surge to win the game 20–18. To add salt to Patriots fans' wounds, the Broncos went on to win Super Bowl 50 against league MVP Cam Newton and the Carolina Panthers in San Francisco, Brady's hometown. The victory allowed Peyton Manning, who had struggled mightily through the season, the chance to ride off into the sunset of retirement under a flurry of orange and blue confetti.

A smiling Roger Goodell handed Manning the Lombardi Trophy on the podium. Just days before, the commissioner had told reporters during his annual Super Bowl news conference that the future looked bright and that there was lots of work to do. He talked about growing and improving the game. There was no mention of Brady or lawsuits, but Goodell had always vowed to appeal Judge Berman's decision. It seemed laughable now, a case of sour grapes to most fans and reporters alike. Brady had won the war. Or so they thought.

But DeMaurice Smith and Heather McPhee were worried. There was an old clause in the league's collective bargaining agreement with the players called Article 46, which allowed the commissioner the power to impose discipline and handle any appeal regarding matters relating to conduct detrimental to the integrity of the game. In short, the clause gave Goodell the authority to punish with impunity any player that crossed him. Smith detested Article 46, but for now it was the law of the NFL land, and that spelled bad news for Brady.

In April 2016, the United States Second Court of Appeals ruled to reinstate Tom's four-game suspension. The court stated that Roger Goodell "properly exercised his broad discretion under the collective bargaining agreement and that his procedural rulings were grounded in that agreement and did not deprive Brady of fundamental fairness." Article 46 had taken down number 12.

The sports world was stunned, and Patriots fans decried what they called the commissioner's witch hunt. Behind the scenes, Brady and DeMaurice Smith tried to negotiate a settlement with the NFL that would overturn the suspension and thus allow Tom to play the first four games of the upcoming 2016 regular season. The quarterback even offered to pay a $1 million fine, but Roger Goodell wanted more. He demanded that Brady state publicly that former Patriots equipment guys Jastremski and McNally had purposely tampered with footballs, even without his knowledge. Tom said no.

"There's no way I'm gonna ruin these guys for something I believe they didn't do," he told Smith.

For the first time since the start of the 2001 regular season, an able-bodied Tom Brady would not be taking his rightful place behind center for the New England Patriots. He'd missed the 2008 season with a torn ACL, and that had been among the most difficult and painful periods of his life.

The four-game suspension meant that Brady would have to forfeit $235,000 in salary, and, more devastating to the quarterback, he would be locked out of Gillette Stadium and not allowed to have contact with any member of the Patriots organization beginning on September 3. Brady had led the most successful franchise in the modern era of professional football, and now it would be as if he were persona non grata in Foxborough.

Close friends like Matt Chatham texted Brady to express their support and to see how he was holding up. Number 12 laughed off the concern and said he was fine. He wasn't. Tom Brady was reaching a breaking point.

He tried to appeal the decision, but the petition was denied by the United States Second Circuit Court of Appeals. Brady's only other option at that point was to take the fight all the way to the United States Supreme Court. This would be nothing short of a Hail Mary pass and would mean more time in law offices and in court and less time on the field. At his age, it was not a risk Brady was willing to take.

"I'm very grateful for the overwhelming support I've received from Mr. [Robert] Kraft, the Kraft family, and most of all, our fans," he wrote on Facebook. "It has been a challenging 18 months and I have made the difficult decision to no longer proceed with the legal process. I'm going to work hard to be the best player I can be for the New England Patriots and I look forward to having the opportunity to return to the field this fall."

In his 2017 interview with the authors of this book, Tom Brady maintained the moral high ground with regard to his suspension and those who had conspired against him. "I'm a positive person. I just let those things play out," he said before a short pause. "It was just a…I don't want to say anything negative about anyone at this point and I'm not gonna [and never] will. [I thought,] I'm just gonna focus on what I need to do, which was just to get ready to play. Things didn't work out the way that I wanted them to so I had to sit out the four games, but I tried to take advantage of [the suspension] and do things that I wouldn't normally get a chance to do like spending time with my family, my wife, and my parents. That was the best thing about it…just having more opportunities with them."[2]

Despite Brady's positive outlook, the punishment handed down by the league would have a lasting effect. Instead of discarding his suspension letter, he preserved it in a neat binder filled with anecdotes and memories of the 2016 regular season.[3]

Chapter Seventeen

ISOLATION

It was the final game of the 2016 preseason, and Tom Brady was out on the field. Normally, number 12 would watch a meaningless contest such as this one from the sidelines—resting both his body and his mind for the arduous sixteen-game regular season ahead. But this exhibition game was anything but normal. Brady had been splitting time with his young backup, Jimmy Garoppolo, in preparation for the first four games of the regular season, which the starting QB would have to sit out.

Brady played the entire first half of the preseason finale against the New York Giants, completing sixteen of twenty-six passes with a touchdown and an interception. For number 12, it was an uneven performance made even more curious because he was playing against the Giants' scrubs and not their starters. His timing was off with Edelman and the Patriots' newly acquired tight end, Martellus Bennett. Still, fans savored every moment, knowing it would be the last time they would see their beloved quarterback until early October.

The Deflategate suspension went into effect at 4 p.m. on Saturday, September 3, 2016.

At that moment, Brady became a ghost. He couldn't go near Gillette Stadium or communicate in any way with staff or any of his buddies on the team. Still, his presence was felt in Foxborough. The day after the suspension began, the team hung two gigantic Brady banners on the Gillette Stadium lighthouse that were visible from both inside and outside the stadium.

Tom would loom large over the field, but the Patriots were Garoppolo's team for now.

"Jimmy's done a great job of working hard for the two and a half years that he's been here and studying and improving every year in our system," offensive coordinator Josh McDaniels said during a Sunday conference call with reporters. "He's going to prepare hard this week and be ready to go in the game."[1]

From the outset, Bill Belichick tried pouring cold water on any potential quarterback controversy by declaring that the Patriots were Brady's team and that he would return to the starting lineup on October 3 when the suspension was over.

Still, fans couldn't help but think back to 2001, when Brady had replaced Bledsoe due to injury. Most assumed then that Bledsoe would get his job back when he was healthy, but that never happened and the rest is history. Could Brady fall victim to a situation similar to the one that had launched his own Hall of Fame career?

He had to stay focused and sharp.

"I really tried to train as if I was just playing from week to week," Brady recalled. "And I'm always working on my mechanics and on my pocket movement. By the time I got back to the practice field, I felt that I was kind of in sync. I was in my pads and helmet in [private practice sessions] and doing a lot of football drills, working on my mechanics with [former major league pitcher] Tom House, which was great, obviously working with Alex [Guerrero] a lot to keep my body just ready to go...so four weeks was about just as long as I could take."

It would take a small village to keep Brady in football condition.

Tom House helped the aging quarterback rediscover the accuracy in his long throws, while Guerrero focused on improving Brady's strength and flexibility.

He also needed someone to throw to, preferably a highly competent athlete doing highly athletic things on the other end of the simulation. Brady wanted a professional-quality wide receiver to run through his practice simulations with him. But he also understood these kinds of people weren't just to be found hanging out on any street corner in Massachusetts.

Speculation on how Brady would stay on top of his work was widely batted around throughout the summer of 2016, with much of the discussion centering on former teammates, retired guys like Troy Brown, Deion Branch, and Wes Welker. One of them would have to bunk at Camp Brady for the month to help keep number 12 on top of his game. The idea of it sounded reasonable enough, but the realities were quite different. Although Brown was still in tremendous shape, he was now forty-five years old. Branch and Welker both had growing families and lived far away, so the logistics of a monthlong man-camp did not work. But fortunately, there was an alternative nearby.

Ryan McManus was a team captain for Dartmouth College, and a two-time All–Ivy League player as both a wide receiver and kick returner. He was a smart, elusive, and productive player. With his five-eleven, 193-pound frame, he reminded Brady of the trio of New England slot receivers he'd had so much success with—Wes Welker, Julian Edelman, and Danny Amendola.

Brady's body guru Alex Guerrero reached out to McManus, and Team Brady had their man. For McManus, the September relationship just made sense.

"I played football at Dartmouth [in New Hampshire], and then was lucky enough to be invited to rookie mini-camp with the Patriots," he recalled. "They had twelve receivers on the roster prior to camp starting, and I had some things in my past, injury-wise, that I think maybe steered them away from not signing me. Either way, it was an awesome experience.

"I got a call from Alex [Guerrero], and he basically asked when I wanted to work out with Tom, just like that! And in my head I'm thinking, 'Wow, I'm dictating when Tom Brady is going to work out? That's pretty funny.' So I'm like, 'Whatever time you need me there, I'll be there.' That happened as simple as that."[2]

McManus showed up the first day at the soccer field at the Dexter Southfield School in Brookline, close to Brady's home, with a pair of gloves and cleats. He thought it was going to be a standard throwing session. But Brady and Guerrero showed up with a hockey bag full of stuff, including Tom's helmet, shoulder pads, jersey, and resistance bands. Brady was trying his best to replicate what he was missing in Foxborough, and his approach had changed drastically since his early years in the NFL.

"Those old throwing sessions...I was so young. You're just doing stuff to do it. You don't know if it's gonna pay off in a game," Brady said. "You don't know if exactly what you're doing is going to amount to anything. Now I just really want to get to the things I think are gonna be effective in the game and that I think will work. I just want to be more efficient with my time and my energy. It's just all about doing things that are realistic, and from a quarterback standpoint, [it's useful to work on] a lot of drops and pocket movements and running and throwing with accuracy and taking hits after the throws. I had people hitting me with bags, and [I was] just trying to stay sharp.

"I'm still trying to work on routes and throwing regimens now," he added. "It's not like it's ever a finished product. You're just continuing to try to get better and more consistent, more accurate and better at timing and better at anticipation, but the problem with football is that [the team] changes from year to year with different players that come in, so it's just [about] trying to get [them] up to speed."

As it turned out, it was McManus, the recent college graduate, who had to get up to speed with the gridiron great.

"I instantly felt like I was the most underdressed person at the party," McManus recalls.

"Nobody mentioned anything at first, but during one of the breaks he [Brady] pulled me aside and explained that he likes to wear exactly what he wears in the game. At that point, going forward, I knew I had to bring a helmet and shoulder pads to fit in that way, which was funny. That was the first little tidbit he passed along. He called it a 'TB nugget.' Practice how you're going to play."

On each occasion, Brady would do his warm-up—his stretching, and band resistance drills—with Guerrero, and then he and McManus would go into routes. Brady liked to work on each of a variety of routes, in no particular order. "With other quarterbacks I've worked with, it usually starts with the shorter stuff—the hitches, slants, and quick outs—and work your way up to the deeper routes. But with Tom, he wanted to treat it just like it was a game, mix it up between a short route and a long route, and then everything in between."

McManus would run the route, catch it, and then Brady would throw about seven more balls at the exact spot where the young receiver caught the first ball. Number 12 drilled in on his throws, consciously honing his techniques. Alex Guerrero would film every throw on an iPad, and then as McManus jogged back with the eight balls, Brady would be watching each throw in slow motion, going over it in meticulous detail, talking about the angle of his arm, or how close his chin was to his shoulder.

"As we worked, he definitely gave me a lot of tips in terms of the kinds of routes he wanted run, at what depth, and things like that," McManus said. "The first couple sessions, we were out on a soccer field, so it was kind of a best guess on depth and things like that because there weren't any lines. He was pretty specific in terms of the angle of the breaks, the distances, and things of that nature. But he always did it in a very constructive way—it wasn't like he was ragging on me. I was a kid trying to help him out, and help myself out and stay in shape. Through it all, he was super positive and super helpful. I really appreciated that."

During each passing drill, Brady shrugged off and avoided invisible defensive backs, playing the game both physically and mentally as best he could.

"We would rep a specific route or concept, and then we'd talk on my way back, giving me a little bit of a breather, and I needed it [laughing]. Brady would say, 'Such and such team, like the Jets, they like to do this a lot. This is the route we want for that.' Or he'd recall a certain touchdown he threw to Gronk or Julian or somebody and he'd say this is the *exact* route he threw and why he threw it. We weren't just running routes for the sake of running routes, we were working on specific things he uses in game."

One thing McManus paid close attention to were the digs and passes across the middle as well as Brady's orders to come back to the ball from different depths. What the young receiver could not know at the time was that Brady would return to these passing concepts later in the season when it mattered most.

"When we first started, I didn't really know what to expect…like how hard is this guy actually gonna throw it, how early, things like that. By the end I was pretty comfortable. Because I had some exposure to the organization…and what expectations there were. Definitely things got easier and more comfortable as the weeks went on," McManus recalls.

The training sessions had to be done under a veil of secrecy as Tom wanted to work out far away from the television cameras and the public.

"By the end, I think the last practice was the only one where we got caught. There was a lacrosse tournament that had just ended across the way. The field is right by the parking lot, so one kid came out and saw, and ten minutes later there are two hundred people—parents and kids—watching and cheering us on as we completed a pass on the air, which was certainly a new experience for me.…More than anything that stood out to me was Brady's focus and mind-set. He's a gamer and a competitor. How he talked about the game, how he approached something as simple as running routes…it became clear that his mentality was just a step above everybody else's. I remember thinking when I left after working with him for just a few weeks…I would never bet against this guy."

The stress of getting locked out of Gillette Stadium and being sequestered from his teammates paled in comparison to the growing concern Tom felt at the time for his family. His mother, Galynn, had breast cancer. When she was diagnosed during the summer of 2016, the cancer was at Stage 2, which meant that it was still contained to her breast but was fast growing. Doctors told Galynn and Tom Sr. that the only way to survive was to be as aggressive as the cancer itself. This meant that Tom's mother would have to put her body through five months of painful chemotherapy and radiation. Galynn also underwent two lumpectomies amid a number of surgeries.

"Hearing about it for the first time that my wife of many years, I could lose her…" Brady Sr. told the NFL Network's Andrea Kremer. "I'm not ready to lose her."[3]

Neither was their son. Number 12 had experienced loss before when Dick Rehbein died prior to his sophomore season and ascension to greatness. He'd also lost another mentor, College of San Mateo head coach Tom Martinez, who died on his sixty-sixth birthday in 2012. Martinez had tutored Brady on his throwing mechanics since high school. While quarterbacking the Patriots, Brady reached out to Martinez after every game to discuss and dissect each throw. On occasion, Brady would fly the coach to Boston and spend days with him looking for ways to improve his game. The coach had been in failing health for years as he battled diabetes and cancer before suffering a fatal heart attack during dialysis treatment. The loss of Martinez dealt a crushing blow to the quarterback. Even four years after the coach's passing, Brady was still profoundly impacted by his influence and heartbroken by his absence. So much so that on February 21, 2016, the anniversary of his death, number 12 remembered his coach in a Facebook post. "Tom [Martinez] made everyone around him a better person," Brady wrote. "Thank you for being the ultimate example Tom. I'd be nowhere without your voice in my ear all these years."[4]

Still, no one had a greater influence over Brady than his parents, especially Galynn. As Tom Sr. observed, "He never says Hi Dad [on television]. It's always Hi Mom."

Tom and his mother remained close throughout the ordeal although they were coasts apart.

"We FaceTimed a lot," Galynn said. "Losing my hair was tough for me. I'd have my bandana on and he [Tom] would say, 'Oh, Mom, you look so beautiful, so beautiful.'"

It was torture for Brady not to be in California with his mother and not to have both of his parents in the stands for regular-season games upon his return. But number 12 told his mother that she'd be ready and in better health for the Super Bowl. It was both a premonition and a promise. Tom Sr. and Galynn charted out her chemotherapy and saw that the treatments would end two weeks before the championship in Houston, Texas, and their son planned on playing in that game.

The quarterback absorbed the anguish and pain he felt about his mother's cancer and turned it into fuel for his return to the lineup.

"With my mom, it's very emotional in my family all the time," Brady revealed. "I grew up with three sisters, so, it's just that I have had the best support from them for such a long period of time, and that has never changed. I just love them so much. I love my sisters, my parents, my wife, and my kids. When your family is good, life is good. I just gotta eliminate all the other BS. You know, I really don't give a shit about many other things except my family, my teammates and coaches, and playing hard. That's where my mind was at."

While Tom was ordered to stay away from professional football, he could still attend college games. Number 12 was welcomed with open arms at the Big House in Ann Arbor, Michigan, in late September, where he served as honorary captain for the Wolverines in their showdown against Colorado. It was the first time that he had stepped onto the field at Michigan Stadium since 1999. Brady tossed the football with his son Jack, watched the team through warm-ups, and played catch with head coach Jim Harbaugh before approaching midfield for the ceremonial coin toss. Tom had been estranged from the Michigan program for years until Harbaugh worked hard to make amends on behalf of the university. Before the game, Brady thanked him by addressing his players.

"It was a chilling speech. It made the hair on the back of your neck stand up," one player said, while another added, "It made me realize maybe the greatest quarterback of all time was saying that I represented him. That got me in the mind-set that I wanted to go out and play even better than he [Brady] ever did."[5]

Michigan went on to beat the Colorado Buffaloes 45–28.

Lingering rumors about Brady's troubled marriage were also put to rest at this time. He and wife Gisele took a romantic getaway to Positano, Italy, where they were photographed kissing on lounge chairs and even sunbathing nude. The photos sparked some laughter back in New England, but they were harmless compared to the collective panic Patriots fans experienced while watching a video of the quarterback jumping off a cliff into the water during a family vacation to Costa Rica after the 2014 Super Bowl.

Tom Brady looked happy and rested and no one doubted that he'd be ready to return to the Patriots huddle. Most important, he didn't doubt himself.

"Getting back into the building and getting back to work, it was really like I never left," Brady recalled. "I was part of all the OTAs [organized team activities] and training camp, and by the time I came back the guys were working hard. They were in a routine and I just didn't want to screw it up. I just wanted to come in there and do my job the best way that I could. The practices were all the same that I had experienced and all the routines were very much the same. It was more about *me* getting into *their* rhythm. They hadn't had me around or heard my voice in a while, but I just felt like I was fresh and ready to go."

PART IV

Chapter Eighteen

THE RETURN

October 9, 2016—FirstEnergy Stadium, Cleveland

Brady arrived at FirstEnergy Stadium wearing a sharp suit and was all business. His passing sessions with McManus, his ban from talking to his teammates, and his agonizing wait were finally over.

It was business as usual for his teammates, too, as they had been trained to overcome the absence of their undisputed leader.

"Coach [Belichick] kind of stayed to character—the whole next-man-up kind of mentality," safety and team cocaptain Devin McCourty said. "With Tom not in the captain's meetings, we just kind of moved on. We knew he'd be back. We didn't really address it or think twice about it. It is what it is. We all know what he means to this team, so we knew when he got back he'd fall right in line. Because of his professionalism and leadership, we knew he'd come back blazing and ready to go."

And with that, it was time for Brady to get back to doing what he did best: leading his team and lighting up opposing defenses.

While number 12 and the rest of the team were mum on the suspension, defensive lineman Jabaal Sheard sent a not-so-subtle message to the league as he arrived at the stadium: he wore a Brady jersey backward, so the "12" and "Brady" were visible to everyone who saw him coming.

Robert Kraft and son Jonathan were pleased to see the team rally around their suspended quarterback. They felt that each player had a responsibility not to let Tom down during his absence. While some sports reporters predicted that Brady would return to the lineup with his team in a big hole, the players refused to make it part of the ongoing story line. The Patriots went 3–1 under backup quarterbacks Jimmy Garoppolo and Jacoby Brissett.

"Jonathan and I watched the preparation and the practice," Robert Kraft explained. "The preparation was all done within itself. It wasn't to do anything fancy. It was just basics. The team went out and executed."[1]

Within the confines of Gillette Stadium, everyone from the owners to the coaches to the players believed that Brady got screwed by the NFL, but they were no longer willing to discuss it publicly.

"Right now we're focused on Cleveland," Belichick said in his league-mandated weekly press conference. "Can't do anything about what was or wasn't in the last four weeks. We're into Cleveland week, and that's where all our focus is. Not worried about last week. Not worried about next week. Not worried about last year. Worried about this week against Cleveland. That's it. Period. This week. Cleveland. We're focused on Cleveland this week. Period. Cleveland."

Pressed as to how it would be to see number 12 back under center, Belichick snapped, "[I] feel like we need to go out to Cleveland and play well in order to win. That's what we're going to try to do.

"We'll do the same thing we do every week. There's always players that fall into that category [of coming back after an absence], whatever the position is," he added. "We'll take it day by day.... We go out there and practice, we make the corrections, we come back in, go over some new stuff.... That's what we do."

Rob Gronkowski toed the line, too, almost.

"No matter who is at quarterback, you've always got to prepare the same," he told the press corps before the Cleveland game. "The demeanor has been the same throughout the building. We've got to prepare every single week to the max. So, it's just like any other week—"

He paused. And then added, "except Tom's back at quarterback, baby!"

Other players joked about Brady's absence and made light of his return.

"He looked good, man," Matthew Slater told the *Boston Globe*. "Good hair. Good physique. Stylish, per usual."[2]

Amendola described the quarterback as "tanned, happy, and pumped."

"We're excited to have our friend back," he said. "He's a great football player.... Obviously everyone is psyched, for sure."

Walking from the team bus into the stadium, Brady was stoic. He focused directly ahead with an intimidating thousand-yard stare. One fan referenced his Michigan roots, saying, "Go, Blue." Another said, "Go, Browns." He didn't flinch at either remark. He may not have let on that it was anything other than just another NFL game, but inside the fire burned.

"We all knew what Tom had gone through over the last two years, but it wasn't one of those huge rallying cries like, 'Do this for Tom!'" McCourty said. "But I do think each player thought Tom having to deal with all of that was crazy, so guys partly wanted it for him, but also for the rest of the 2016 team because of how tight we were as a group. We were all very close, enjoyed our time together.[3]

"Starting with the four-game suspension, a lot of people didn't give us a chance to do well at the beginning part of the season," he added. "For Tom, it was great to see us have his back while he was out, but when he was back in there it wasn't just 'Do this for Tom.' It was 'Let's do this for this team because this team is truly special.'"

Robert Kraft echoed that statement. "Every negative experience has some positives, if you have the right people. Deflategate created a sense of team and togetherness. They [the NFL] thought they were weakening us, but instead, they really made the team stronger."

While Brady and the organization downplayed the "redemption" angle to almost comical levels, Tom's inner circle wasn't shy about letting the world know that TB12 was on a mission.

"I think Deflategate hurt Tommy a lot more than he'll let anyone know," Tom's Michigan teammate and close friend Aaron Shea told ESPN. "We barely talked about the details other than a lot of f-bombs going back and forth. But now you've pissed off the GOAT [greatest of all time]. I grew up in Illinois, and if you got under Michael Jordan's skin, he would score 50 or 60 on you. This is only going to make Tom better. It's going to hurt the other 31 teams because Tom is healthy, he didn't have to take any hits the first four games, and now he's angry."[4]

Those were the words Patriots fans wanted to hear. Those were the words being thrown around daily on the sports radio shows in Boston. *They hate us 'cause they ain't us.* Redemption.

Shea took it even further.

"I want him to stick it to Roger Goodell so bad," he said. "At the end of the year, I want him up there holding that Lombardi Trophy and taking it from Roger Goodell. Then I'd tell Tom, 'That's it, man, you couldn't go out any better than that.'"

Brady is the godfather to Shea's son, and the candid interview was as close as anyone in the media got to hearing Tom's true feelings about the whole Deflategate fiasco and his suspension.

Asked if he thought number 12 was out for revenge, Shea an-

Tom Brady fought for respect and playing time while sharing quarterback duties with Drew Henson at the University of Michigan. *(University of Michigan Photography)*

Brady was selected by the New England Patriots with the 199th pick of the sixth round in the 2000 NFL draft. *(University of Michigan Photography)*

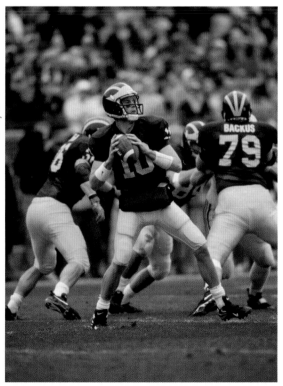

Brady seen here enjoying some downtime at a Boston area indoor race car venue before his first Super Bowl season in 2001. Left to right: Debra Nugent, former Patriots defensive lineman David Nugent, Brady's sister Nancy, former Patriots linebacker Matt Chatham, Brady's sister Julie (wearing helmet), Brady, and Brady's mother, Galynn. *(Courtesy of Matt Chatham)*

NFL owners believed coach Bill Belichick was not punished harshly enough after "Spygate," which then set the stage for "Deflategate." *(Casey Sherman)*

Despite the growing Deflategate storm, Brady led the Patriots to a fourth Super Bowl win against the Seattle Seahawks in 2015. *(Dave Wedge)*

National Football League Players Association attorney Heather McPhee was part of Brady's legal team and led the star quarterback into NFL headquarters in New York City for his June 2015 suspension appeal hearing. *(Associated Press)*

DeMaurice Smith believes NFL commissioner Roger Goodell's quest for power led to the league's aggressive investigation of number 12. *(Associated Press)*

Following a four-game suspension, Brady led the Patriots to a Super Bowl LI victory against the Atlanta Falcons at NRG Stadium in Houston, Texas, on February 5, 2017. *(Courtesy of New England Patriots)*

Tom Brady faced a formidable Falcons team in Super Bowl LI without his prime target, Rob Gronkowski, who was injured midseason. *(Casey Sherman)*

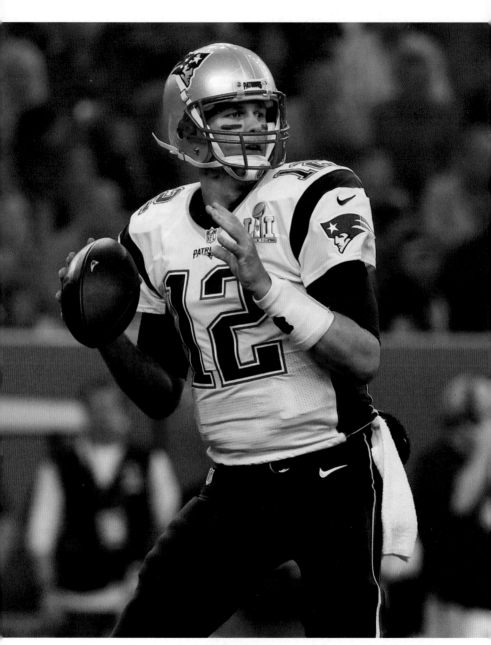

Down 28–3 in the third quarter, Brady mounted the greatest comeback in Super Bowl history. *(Courtesy of New England Patriots)*

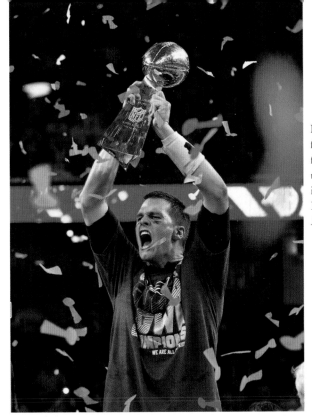

Number 12 became the first quarterback to win five Super Bowls after the miraculous victory in overtime against the Falcons. *(Courtesy of New England Patriots)*

Patriots owner Robert Kraft, joined by his son Jonathan, hoists the Lombardi Trophy as NFL commissioner Roger Goodell stands by his side. *(Courtesy of New England Patriots)*

Brady reflects on an arduous yet satisfying championship season at his locker at NRG Stadium on February 5, 2017. *(Courtesy of New England Patriots)*

The NFL's greatest quarterback and the league's greatest coach share a special moment at the trophy presentation ceremony at NRG Stadium on February 5, 2017. *(Courtesy of New England Patriots)*

swered, "One hundred percent. He'll never tell anyone that, but we're all human. You want to stick it to someone who stuck it to you. Deflategate was a witch hunt for Goodell and all the other owners who wanted to slow the Patriots down. And now everyone in the NFL knows Tom is back and fired up. If there's one guy in the history of sports who didn't need to cheat, it's Tommy Brady."

In Cleveland, the Patriots were supposed to be in enemy territory, but Brady's return felt like a home game at Gillette Stadium as swarms of fans arrived from New England.

Patriots fans entered the stadium early to see Brady in warm-ups while reporters and photographers charted his every move.

Signs were hung in the end zones supporting Brady, much to the chagrin of the Browns. One sign read, THE RETURN OF THE GOAT, with a picture of Tom. #FREEBRADY was printed in bold letters on another.

The Krafts could not believe the thunderous chants for their star quarterback—chants that started long before kickoff and were repeated louder and louder throughout the game.

"It was really unbelievable," Robert Kraft told the authors of this book. "The chanting of his name. We sat in Foxboro on those metal benches and went through those tough seasons. To go to a visiting stadium and like forty-five minutes before the game to hear the crowd yelling Brady's name. It was really remarkable."

About an hour before kickoff, Brady walked from the locker room through the tunnel and onto the field, flanked by Jimmy Garoppolo. He jogged the length of the field and stopped in the far end zone and pumped his fist wildly toward an army of Patriots fans.

"Let's go!!!" he shouted. The crowd went crazy.

No one expected any rust to collect on Tom Brady, including the team's owner.

"He's a nice guy, but you won't meet anyone who's more competitive than he is," Kraft said. "He does his work and goes home and watches film at home. I think Gisele has the potential to be an expert on film viewing. He was ready for that day."

Ted Karras saw this firsthand. Like Brady, the rookie offensive lineman from the University of Illinois had been drafted in the sixth round and had fought hard to make the squad. Karras hailed from a long line of NFL talent. His grandfather, Ted Karras Sr., won an NFL championship as a member of the 1963 Chicago Bears, while his dad, Ted Karras Jr., played defensive tackle at Northwestern University and was a member of the 1987 Washington Redskins squad that won the Super Bowl in a season shortened by a players' strike.

And his great-uncle was Alex Karras, the four-time Pro Bowler with the Detroit Lions who had also once been suspended by the league. Karras would have the last laugh on the field and on the screen in comedies like *Porky's* and *Victor/Victoria*. In the acting world, he was perhaps best known for his starring role in the family sitcom *Webster* and his turn as Mongo, an outlaw who punched out a horse in the Mel Brooks classic *Blazing Saddles*.

With such an impressive NFL pedigree, it's not surprising that Belichick took a flyer on the six-four, three-hundred-pound lineman.

Karras was a Belichick kind of guy. The young lineman not only made the team in 2016, but he played in all sixteen regular-season games and the playoffs, mostly on special teams. In Cleveland, he waited in the tunnel with the rest of the team, listening to the "Brady, Brady" chants, when the quarterback approached him.

"It was the first time I really saw Tom Brady in action," Karras recalled. "He head-butted me before the game. I'm a role player and so I felt pretty good about that."

The Patriots won the coin toss and deferred, as they almost always do. The New England defense forced the Browns into a quick three-and-out series and a punt.

Brady took the field in a calm and deliberate manner.

"I wasn't really nervous," he recalled. "It's just about experience and playing 250-plus games. You're excited and certainly anxious to get out there and start playing, but once you get out there, it's just football. Getting the first few snaps out of the way is always good. We had a really great plan and we executed it very well."[5]

Number 12 buttoned his chin strap and trotted out to the huddle at the Patriots' 20-yard line, as his fans cheered wildly in the stands. Even some Browns fans clapped, recognizing the historical significance of this upcoming series.

Tom strode into the huddle and called his first play of the season. He got under center, took the snap—his first live play since the previous season ended in the AFC title game in Denver—and fired a perfect strike to Edelman, who rumbled to the 30 for a first down.

Finding Edelman first was fitting as it spoke to their mutual trust and close friendship. Like Brady, Edelman was a product of Northern California. He grew up in Redwood City, just thirteen miles away from Brady's hometown of San Mateo. His dad ran a small business and dedicated most of his free time to coaching his kids on the football field. Like Brady, Julian had and maintains a strong relationship with his father, Frank. But he wasn't coddled at home or on the gridiron. When Edelman was just twelve years old, his father imparted this advice about facing a tough opponent: "When you get them down, you break their fucking neck." These were tough words for a preteen to hear, but they resonated with the boy, who played like a hulking linebacker despite his small frame. Edelman was a seventh-round draft pick for the Patriots in 2009 and was used originally as a kick returner despite having played quarterback in college. He was an afterthought in the receiver corps until Coach Belichick parted ways with Wes Welker, one of the team's biggest stars, in 2013. Edelman filled Welker's role in the slot and developed into one of the most beloved members of the Patriots and a close friend to Tom. Brady's return in the Cleveland game had special meaning for Edelman.

"The moment was exciting," Edelman told the authors of this book. "Your quarterback hasn't been out there for four weeks and you now get to have him. It's always gonna be exciting. He had a great game and that tells you he had a great week of practice. He was just being Tom out there."[6]

The chains moved and Brady and his squad marched up to the line of scrimmage again.

He took his second snap, made a quick read, and threw another perfect pass over the middle to Gronkowski, who took it nineteen yards to the Patriots' 49. Next, running back LeGarrette Blount took a handoff and rocketed through a gaping hole for thirteen yards. Next was a short pass for two yards to Martellus Bennett.

Brady was in the groove.

After a short incompletion to running back James White, Brady took a shotgun snap and hit Gronkowski over the middle again, this time for a thirty-four-yard completion that moved the Patriots to the Browns' 2. Two plays later, Blount found the end zone. It was a classic Tom Brady drive, executed with surgical precision, going eighty yards in eight plays in just 3:13.

Number 12 torched the Browns all afternoon, racking up gaudy stats: twenty-eight for forty, for 406 yards and three touchdowns. A signature moment came in the third quarter when Brady called his own number on a third and four from the Patriots' 31-yard line. He rambled for four hard-fought yards and took a hard smack from beefy defensive end Emmanuel Ogbah.

Brady popped up quickly and emphatically made the first-down signal with his arm, firing up Patriots fans again.

When the thrashing was over, New England had posted a 33–13 win, a score that would suggest the game was closer than it actually was. The league was on notice.

"I mean, it's Tom Brady, so you don't expect anything less," Edelman told reporters in the locker room postgame.

"He was fired up, we were fired up to have him back out there, and we were just trying to make plays for him," added Bennett, who caught three scores.[7]

The media had a field day with the gridiron beatdown and Brady's near-perfect performance. Pundits used all sorts of superlatives for the game and seized on the redemption narrative. Some were already calling the season Brady's scorched-earth tour. Others called it the revenge tour. But, per usual, for number 12, the game wasn't a perfect effort.

"I think there was plenty of rust out there," he said in his postgame press conference.

"[We] got the WD-40 out for him," Bennett said.

"He didn't look rusty to me," new Patriots receiver Chris Hogan observed.

"Me, neither," said Gronkowski. The all-world tight end was among those who discussed the importance of Brady's return.

"It's super great," Gronkowski told reporters. "He's our leader. He's our guy. He came out here on fire, and we did what we had to do all week as an offense."

Tom joked about his first-down run during his postgame press conference and was sure to thank the fans who traveled to Cleveland for the game.

"We've got amazing fans," he said. "I think we've got the best fans in the world. They showed up today and it was great to hear them."

But what he wouldn't discuss was his suspension, nor would he be lured into answering questions about how it felt to be back after missing four games.

"This isn't a time for me to reflect," he said. "I'm happy we won today. I'm happy we win every time we play. I have a job to do and there's no point in looking back, whether we won Super Bowls, or lost championship games, or the last four weeks. None of it matters. [I] Just go out and do the best I can do every week.... It's fun to come out and play, and fun to win. That's the most important thing."

Pressed by reporters for comment on the four weeks he spent away from the team, he added, "I've just moved on, man."

And move on he did.

Chapter Nineteen

ROLLING

Like a classically trained pianist who can sit down at any piano in any concert hall anywhere in the world and just play, Tom Brady's preparation and wealth of football knowledge allowed him to pick up right where he'd left off the season before.

"Twenty sixteen, in general it was a really good season in that I felt like I, at this point in my career I know what I'm about to experience," Tom told the authors. "I know what I'm seeing. I just gotta trust my eyes and try to make good decisions and play fast."

After Brady torched the Browns, pundits predicted—and opponents feared—a repeat of the 2007 season, when the Patriots were under fire for Spygate and went on a record-shattering rampage. With Hall of Fame receiver Randy Moss on board, an emerging Wes Welker, a running game anchored by thousand-yard rusher Laurence Maroney, and a stacked defense, the Pats blew out team after team that season, embarrassing many.

Number 12 threw fifty touchdowns against only eight interceptions. The fifty-score season was an NFL record that stood for five years until rival Peyton Manning broke it in his first and most productive season with the Broncos. Moss caught ninety-eight passes for nearly fifteen hundred yards and an NFL record twenty-three touchdowns. Welker hauled in 112 balls for almost twelve hundred yards and eight scores. The team scored an astounding 589 points while going undefeated in the regular season, a feat that had not been accomplished since the Miami Dolphins went 14–0 in 1972.

The Patriots scored over fifty points twice, over forty points twice, and over thirty points eight times, meaning they didn't score under thirty several times that season. Brady's season was among the best on record as he completed 398 of 578 passes for 4,806 yards. His 117.2 passer rating that year was second best in league history.

Coach Belichick was criticized throughout the year for keeping his quarterback and all other starters in games long after the score was well out of hand. Brady and his teammates took offense to the criticism publicly. This was not Pop Warner, high school, or even college. It was professional sports, where men are paid big money to perform at the highest level. In other words, this is what they were paid to do.

They may not have invoked the Spygate scandal publicly as a driving force in their evisceration of the league that year, but it was there.

"We're not trying to win 42–28, we're trying to kill people, we're trying to blow them out if we can," Brady said on his weekly interview on WEEI radio in Boston late in the 2007 season.[1]

But then, he caught himself and provided some balance and measured perspective.

"You want to build momentum for each week, you don't want to be up, 42–7 or 35–7, and all of a sudden you look up and it's 35–21," he said. "We don't want to be part of that, you don't want to go into next week realizing that for the last 18 minutes of the game your team didn't play well, or didn't play up to its capabilities. You gave other teams momentum for the next time they play you, or you gave another team a reason not to be intimidated."[2]

The 2016 New England Patriots team heard comparisons to

the 2007 team, both praiseworthy and critical in the wake of the Browns blowout.

"Our expectation was to come out here, perform as a team and win," Coach Belichick told reporters after the Cleveland game. "I'm talking about the whole team. That includes everybody. What else would we come out here for? I think Tom works hard. He's always worked hard. I don't think there's any question about that. I think there are a lot of things he needs to work on. There are a lot of things we all need to work on as a football team. There are things we need to improve on. That's all of us—players, coaches, everybody."[3]

It was strictly business, not personal, according to the coach and his quarterback. But those who covered the team on a daily basis believed differently.

"Don't buy it. This *is* personal for Brady," *Boston Globe* Patriots beat writer Chris Gasper opined. "What he loves to do was taken away from him. Those he loves were saddened and stressed out by seeing his reputation tarnished and his name soiled. Despite his unflappable demeanor, Brady also suffered signs of stress from the air pressure imbroglio. As the legal walls closed in on him after the vacation of his suspension was overturned by a federal appeals court, Brady was forced to accept and serve a ridiculous punishment. Welcome back, Tom."[4]

Brady and Belichick may have wanted the hype to just disappear, but it only got more intense the following week as number 12 made his return to Gillette Stadium to face the 2–3 Bengals. Tickets for the mid-October game were the most expensive NFL ticket of the season and were going for more than seven hundred dollars apiece on resale websites. In addition to Brady, another key member of the team, linebacker Rob Ninkovich, was also making a return to Foxborough after being suspended four games for a banned-substance violation.

As Brady waited to make his grand entrance, a video montage

of his greatest moments played on the Jumbotrons to the tune of Skylar Grey's "I'm Coming Home." Patriots great Troy Brown also stood sentry in front of the locker room doors. Wearing sunglasses and a dark suit and flashing one of his three Super Bowl rings, Brown appeared on the stadium big screens, whipping the crowd into a frenzy. Was this a football game or was it WrestleMania? The team knew what their fans wanted so they gave it to them.

Brown opened the doors and there stood Brady, without his helmet on. He led his team out of the locker room and down the stadium hall to the tunnel flanked by fullback James Devlin and Julian Edelman. He was the only player without his helmet on. Just before he led his team onto the field, he turned to Edelman, shouted, "Let's go," and slapped him five.

Brady took off running as Ozzy Osbourne's "Crazy Train" blared from the stadium speakers. A unit of colonial reenactors fired their muskets in the end zone. Fireworks shot out of a huge replica of the Patriots' "Flying Elvis" logo that encased the tunnel. Tom ran to the 50, stopped, walked over to the coaches, and grabbed a drink from a Gatorade cup and pulled on his helmet. As he threw warm-up tosses, the cameras never left him and projected his every move to the crowd. The applause he received when the lineups were announced and his name was called was thunderous.

Brady put on another near-perfect display, lighting up the Bengals defense for 376 yards and three touchdowns while completing twenty-nine of thirty-five passes.

In two games, he had thrown six touchdowns and zero interceptions.

The next week was supposed to be a potential AFC championship game preview as New England traveled to Pittsburgh, but the game lost some of its luster because quarterback Ben Roethlisberger was scratched from the lineup with a knee injury, replaced by backup Landry Jones.

Jones and the Steelers were overmatched. New England won 27–16.

Tom Brady continued his torrid march with the Buffalo Bills next on his hit list. Once again, he led the Patriots to a lopsided victory, 41–25, in which he threw for 315 yards and four touchdowns. The offense was executing near to perfection and the defense was also jelling, but the unit was about to get shaken up.

Jamie Collins, a 2013 second-round pick out of the University of Southern Mississippi, had become a leader on the defense. He had freakish athletic ability, as evidenced by his jaw-dropping leap over the offensive line to block a crucial extra point against the Colts in 2015. He had a breakout year in 2014, leading the team with 199 tackles and recording four sacks and two interceptions, and was integral to the win over the Seahawks in Super Bowl XLIX. He was named to the Pro Bowl a year later, recording five and a half sacks and eighty-nine tackles on the season despite missing four games due to an undisclosed illness.

In 2016, Collins appeared to be playing well, registering forty-three tackles over the first six games with a sack and two interceptions. But he was replaced on run packages and played only about half of the snaps in the Bills game. The next day—on Halloween—he was traded to the lowly Browns for a compensatory third-round pick.

The move stunned Collins's teammates and had some fans questioning why Belichick would shuttle away one of his most athletic players from a championship-caliber team, which had already taken a hit with the off-season trade of another defensive star—Chandler Jones—who'd been hospitalized for a hallucinogenic reaction to synthetic marijuana.

Others shook their heads and repeated the mantra they'd been repeating for the past seventeen years: *In Bill [Belichick] we trust.*

The trade, however, was not without good reason. Collins's rookie contract was up and he'd be a free agent at the end of the season, and there were reports that he was seeking a huge deal similar to the six-year, $114 million package the Broncos had showered on linebacker and Super Bowl MVP Von Miller. News also surfaced that Collins was upset over being told he'd be a part-time player because of his deficiencies against the run. Other reports accused him of freelancing and not following designed play calls and of butting heads with coaches.

In his weekly radio appearance on Westwood One, Brady called it a "tough day" because of the trade and heaped praise upon Collins.[5]

"It's always tough to hear news like that with a teammate that I've played with and been in so many battles with," he said. "Jamie is a great player for our team and I'm sure he'll be a great player for the Cleveland Browns. . . . I'm always sad when we lose a player that I like and someone that I respect like Jamie. It's a tough day, but it's part of the NFL, this business. Coach Belichick makes these decisions and we as players still have to go out and do our job."

It was the bye week, so sports reporters and talk show hosts had fourteen days to tear apart the trade. Belichick said little about it and refused to get into specifics about the factors that led to his decision.

"In the end, we did what we thought was best for the football team," he said flatly on his weekly appearance on WEEI radio. "There are a lot of things to take into consideration. I'm sure we could bring up a lot of points to talk about, but in the end, that's really the bottom line."

The criticism only intensified the following week when the Patriots lost their nationally televised Super Bowl rematch with the Seahawks at home 31–24, the only regular-season game attended by Brady's father. Seattle quarterback Russell Wilson outplayed Brady this time, racking up 348 yards passing and three touchdowns. For the first time since his return, number 12 threw no touchdowns and tossed an interception. The Patriots defense, meanwhile, gave up season highs in points, yards, and first downs. It was a bad performance that once again called into question the coach's decision to trade Collins.

"It's time to start worrying about the Patriots defense," shouted a *Washington Post* headline.[6]

Worse than the regular-season loss to the Seahawks and even the trade of Jamie Collins was the loss of Brady's biggest and most reliable big play target, Rob Gronkowski. The tight end suffered a brutal hit by Seattle defender Earl Thomas and then was knocked out of a game with the Jets two weeks later with a back injury. Team doctors determined that he needed back surgery to repair a ruptured disk. He was out for the season just as he was reaching peak form. Gronkowski's motor had begun to run upon Brady's return but now he was done. The tight end finished with twenty-five catches for 540 yards and three touchdowns in a season cut short by injury. Once again, the loss had many questioning whether the Patriots could make a serious run at another world championship.

But Brady's "revenge tour" kept rolling. New England beat the Jets twice and also rang up victories against the Rams, Ravens, Dolphins, and the Broncos in Denver. The Broncos were fighting for a playoff spot at 8–6, and the game was vitally important for the Patriots as they were battling with the Steelers for the best record in the AFC and home field advantage throughout the playoffs. Mile High Stadium had always posed trouble for Tom, and he played his worst game of the season, but still managed to come away with the victory.

Brady threw for less than two hundred yards with no touchdowns, was sacked twice, and fumbled twice. With a performance like that, a team generally loses. But the Patriots defense was now fully recovered from the Collins trade. In fact, the squad was playing better than ever before. Defenders sacked quarterback Trevor Siemian four times and held Denver to just a field goal in the 16–3 win.

The final assault on the league came in week fifteen, when the Patriots crushed the Jets once more, 41–3, led by Brady's three touchdown passes and a pair of scores by Blount. Jets quarterback Ryan Fitzpatrick was sacked twice and harassed all day by defensive stalwarts Trey Flowers, Chris Long, Alan Branch, and Jabaal Sheard. Fitzpatrick also threw two costly interceptions to cornerback Malcolm Butler. The Patriots defense was now giving up the fewest average points in the NFL.

Despite missing four games, Brady finished the regular season with 3,554 passing yards, twenty-eight touchdowns, and only two interceptions. It was the best touchdown-to-interception ratio in league history. And he was thirty-nine years old.

Chapter Twenty

FREIGHT TRAIN

The competition for 2016 league MVP was coming down to Brady and Atlanta Falcons star quarterback Matt Ryan. Both players were worthy of the honor.

Ryan had thrown for nearly five thousand yards with thirty-eight touchdown passes against only seven interceptions. The Falcons QB was playing the best football of his career, and he and All-Pro receiver Julio Jones were the most feared tandem in the league, the season's version of Brady and Randy Moss.

Debate was white-hot over which player should be named the NFL's most valuable player.

Brady critics argued that he shouldn't be eligible because of the suspension, while supporters predicted that the brilliance of his twelve-game run would never be duplicated. The argument raged on into the playoffs as the Falcons and the Patriots each had first-round byes. While the Patriots waited to see who they would play in the divisional round, a mini-distraction arose as offensive co-ordinator Josh McDaniels and defensive guru Matt Patricia both surfaced as candidates for several head-coaching vacancies.

McDaniels had already tried his hand at head coaching—

unsuccessfully—when he left the Patriots in 2009 to helm the Broncos. The son of Ohio coaching legend Thom McDaniels, Josh grew up in Canton, Ohio—the home of the football Hall of Fame—and attended John Carroll University, where he played wide receiver. His quarterback on that team was Nick Caserio, while other teammates included future Bills linebacker London Fletcher and Chargers general manager Brian Polian.

Both McDaniels and Caserio joined the Patriots coaching staff in 2001. McDaniels started as a personnel assistant and was promoted to defensive assistant and then to quarterbacks coach, where he developed a close rapport and friendship with Brady. McDaniels was on the staff for all five championships and was the architect of the record-breaking 2007 offense. He was lured away from the Patriots after helping guide the Patriots and backup quarterback Matt Cassel to an 11–5 record after Tom went down with a torn ACL in the first game.

McDaniels signed a four-year, $8 million deal with the Broncos and came in with much fanfare as the replacement to Denver legend Mike Shanahan. Jay Cutler was the quarterback for the Broncos, but as soon as McDaniels arrived trade rumors swirled, including one that involved a swap with the Patriots for Cassel. The team pulled the trigger on a different deal, though, one that sent Cutler to the Bears and made Kyle Orton Denver's starting quarterback.

The season started well as McDaniels's team won six straight, including an overtime victory over Belichick and the Patriots. The Broncos cooled, however, and ended the season 8–8, missing the playoffs. In 2010, McDaniels's first head-coaching experiment ended when he went 3–9 to start the season and was fired in December. The poor record was only part of the reason for his firing.

Another factor was a mini-Spygate incident in which Broncos assistant Steve Scarnecchia, the son of Patriots offensive line guru Dante Scarnecchia, was caught illegally taping a 49ers pregame walk-through in London. Scarnecchia was fired and investigated by the league for the taping. McDaniels was hit with a $50,000 fine for failing to report the incident to the league, and the Broncos were also fined $50,000 for the violations.

He sat out the remainder of the season and was hired as the offensive coordinator for the St. Louis Rams but was let go in 2012 and returned to the Patriots.

His handling of Brady, not to mention the rotating cast of receivers and running backs in 2016, made him the envy of the league. Still, there were no indications that he seriously considered leaving. The rumors persisted, however, providing a minor distraction as the Patriots prepared for the Dolphins, Raiders, or Texans in the divisional round.

The Steelers beat the Dolphins and went on to play the red-hot Kansas City Chiefs, while the Houston Texans beat the Raiders, who were forced to turn to the untested Connor Cook after losing star quarterback Derek Carr and backup Matt McGloin to injuries. Cook made his first career start in the playoffs, which christened him the first quarterback in modern history to do so. The Texans, even without injured sack master J. J. Watt, proved too much for the injury-depleted Raiders and cruised to a 27–14 victory, punching their ticket to Foxborough.

Over in the NFC, the Falcons, too, were awaiting their divisional-round foe, while many were closely watching the Giants. New York snuck up on the league in 2007 and 2011, had beaten the favored Patriots in those Super Bowls, and many were wondering if a third rematch might be in store. Some fans lusted for another shot at the Giants, which they saw as the ultimate redemption, but others shuddered at the thought of dropping a third Super Bowl to Eli Manning's team.

Those dreams and concerns both ended wild card weekend when the Giants, who no longer had the guidance of former coach Tom Coughlin, were demolished by Aaron Rodgers and the Packers. The Seahawks, meanwhile, crushed the Lions and earned a date with Atlanta.

A week later, Matt Ryan embarrassed the Seahawks' "Legion of Boom" defense, racking up 338 yards and three touchdowns as he led his team to a 36–20 victory.

Brady was good but not great as he threw two interceptions against Houston, as many as he had all regular season. He also tossed two touchdowns, but the offense was carried by the reemergence of running back Dion Lewis, who became the first player in NFL playoff history to score touchdowns rushing, receiving, and kick returning. In the end, the Patriots claimed an easy 34–16 win that sent them to their sixth-straight AFC championship game, an NFL record.

That same weekend, Ben Roethlisberger and the Steelers narrowly defeated the Chiefs, 18–16, setting up New England's third AFC title game against Pittsburgh and Brady's second against Roethlisberger. The Steelers had gone 11–5 in the regular season, including a 27–16 loss at home in week seven to the Patriots without their starting QB, and looked solid in their playoff victories over the Dolphins and the Chiefs.

Clouds hung over Gillette Stadium for the AFC championship game and it was a chilly 41 degrees. Weather played no factor as the Steelers once again proved no match for Brady and the Patriots. The revenge tour was in its second-to-last stage as a number 12 was near perfect, connecting on thirty-two of forty-two passes for 384 yards and three touchdowns, including a back-breaking thirty-four-yard flea-flicker bomb to receiver Chris Hogan, who had played college lacrosse for Penn State, in the second quarter. It was the kind of play that tore the heart out of an opponent.

Roethlisberger was mediocre and the Patriots tallied four unanswered scores in the second half. The Steelers fumbled on their own 26 and Roethlisberger threw an ill-timed interception, while the stout New England defense shut down Pittsburgh all day. When the clock ticked to zero, the scoreboard read Patriots 36, Steelers 17, and New England was on its way to Houston for a league-record ninth Super Bowl.

The win also marked Tom's league-record seventh conference title. It was also the seventh for Belichick, who passed the Dolphins' Don Shula for the most conference championships by a head coach in NFL history.

By the time the game ended, the Patriots already knew their opponent. Earlier in the day, Matt Ryan and the Falcons had beaten Aaron Rodgers and the Packers at the Georgia Dome by a lopsided score of 44–21. Ryan had been even better than Brady in his championship, throwing for 392 yards and four touchdowns.

And with that, the heavyweight matchup was set. Super Bowl week would have all the traditional hype, but the story line was already clear: Would Tom Brady get his ultimate revenge against Roger Goodell and the NFL? Or would his scorched-earth season end in bitter disappointment? To no one's surprise, the team refused to talk about it, except in vague terms. As he tends to do, Belichick ignored the questions completely and focused solely on the X's and O's and an opponent that he knew had one of the most prolific and difficult-to-contain offenses in the history of the sport.

Matt Ryan was a touchdown machine, Atlanta's running backs were the most productive in the league, the defense was young, fast yet hungry, and receiver Julio Jones was simply embarrassing defensive backs and tearing the top off of the league's best defenses week after week.

Ryan was enjoying the best season of his career, but there were still those who doubted whether he had the heart and mettle of a true champion. His previous playoff record was a dismal 1–4 and he still had much to prove to fans in Atlanta and around the league.

A former number three overall pick in the NFL draft out of Boston College, Ryan had a stellar regular season in 2016, with a nearly 70 percent pass completion percentage and the fifth-highest quarterback rating in history. The Falcons signal caller's regular season was one for the record books and stood among the best quarterback seasons in league history, alongside Brady's performance in 2007, Aaron Rodgers's in 2011, and Peyton Manning's in 2004. His statistics were that good.

The Falcons won eleven games to clinch the NFC's second seed as Ryan and his star-studded receiving corps continued their winning ways throughout December and January.

Atlanta rolled through the playoffs, racking up record-smashing stats as Ryan went a stunning fifty-three for seventy-five for 730 yards with seven touchdowns and no interceptions.

Bill Belichick raved about how good Ryan and the Falcons were.

"One guy can't stop them and we can't just stop one guy," the coach said at his first press conference at NRG Stadium in Houston. "They have too many great players...they create a lot of problems for a defense. We're going to have to play good team defense...I'm sure we're going to have to make some in-game adjustments and figure out some things as we go. They're tough. They're averaging forty points in the playoffs, highest-scoring team in the league through a sixteen-game regular season, which, that says a lot right there....They're really good and they're consistent. They move the ball and hang up a lot of points every week. It's obviously the biggest challenge of the year...best offensive team that we've faced. We'll have our hands full, we know that....It's a very difficult offense to stop."

With all that in mind, Belichick didn't seem to care about some tweet two years ago about deflated balls. He didn't seem to care about Roger Goodell. And he certainly didn't seem to care about the reporters' questions regarding his coaching legacy.

"I really don't think about any of that," he said. "I just try and think about how we can prepare, compete, and perform our best Sunday night against the Falcons. That's a thing for you to write about. I'm just trying to get ready to coach the game and our players are getting ready to play it. We want to go out there and compete on Sunday night. All the rest of it is what it is."[1]

The coach then heaped praise on the Falcons, as he's known to do about every opponent, but in this case, the numbers he threw out along with the facts about Atlanta's dominance raised questions as to why the Patriots were favored in the game.

For many professional athletes, the limelight and the pressure can get to be overwhelming. They make mistakes. They say the wrong thing. They get heated, frustrated, and angry. Brady had been careful to avoid falling down the Deflategate well as reporters hounded him throughout the season about his suspension. Now number 12 was back at the Super Bowl podium and he wasn't going to be distracted by the redemption narrative. At least he wouldn't admit that he was.

"I'm focused on this game and the importance to our team. We've worked really hard to get to this point, and the attention should be on this game, and it's been a fun week to prepare for a great opponent. It's going to be a great game," he said in his first Super Bowl week press conference.

He was asked about his mother and the adversity he had faced throughout the season.

"It's personal with my family and I'm just hoping everyone's here on Sunday to share in a great experience," he said. "But, it's just been a tough year. Every family goes through different things and my family's always been a great support system for me, and hopefully we can make everyone happy on Sunday."

Brady also showed respect for the fans who stuck by him.

"It's great for your team, but there's also a lot of people that made an investment in you. They spent their time and energy on their weekend. They've worked their tails off all week for those two days and when Sunday comes on and they can do anything and they choose to watch the Patriots," he said. "They made an investment in us and we want to reward that. We want our fans to know that all the time they spent cheering for us has paid off."

In one of his last public comments before the game, Belichick struck an ominous tone. For those expecting Tom and company to cruise to victory and cement his legacy, the veteran coach reminded the world that the Falcons were not to be taken lightly.

"One thing about this game is you're playing against a great team...and the Falcons are a great team," he said. "Certainly we don't want to play this game from behind you know, 24–0 or 24–3 or something like that, you know where Green Bay ended up last week. We've got to avoid that. It'll be a long night if we don't."[2]

He didn't know just how prophetic those words would be.

Chapter Twenty-one

THE TIES THAT BIND

As scheduled, Galynn Brady successfully completed her chemotherapy and radiation two weeks before the Super Bowl, and as her son promised, the Patriots would be playing for the world championship in Houston, Texas.

However, there were complications stemming from her medical treatment, and Galynn developed pneumonia followed by a severe case of shingles. Her doctors questioned whether it was a good idea for her to make the trip from California. But she was determined. The tickets were purchased, the hotel booked, and twenty-four hours before the scheduled flight, doctors finally cleared her for takeoff.

"I put my [surgical] mask on, got on the airplane, and decided to go," she recalled.[1] "I wanted to be there for Tommy and I wanted to be with our family. Everyone was going to the Super Bowl and I didn't want to miss that."

Galynn's battle with cancer was not made public, but there was a rumor circulating among those covering the game that she was sick.

Asked at a press conference a few days before the game if his mother would be attending, Tom told reporters, "I hope so. I don't know. I'm planning for it, but we'll have to play it by ear."

He said she needed medical clearance to fly because of her condition but wouldn't discuss any more of the personal details.

"Um, my mom has been dealing with some health issues. Those are personal things that our family is dealing with," he said. "I think there are a lot of things that change your perspective on football over the years. When you come in the league and you're twenty-three years old, it's everything. It's still incredibly important because it's my job, but you know my family and the relationships I have are ultimately the most important thing. . . . This year has just been a very challenging year, but a great year. We're at this great point, and we just have to go finish the job."

On this day, he embraced the non-football questions and elaborated on what his mind-set had been for the season and gave a glimpse into just how he was able to put aside the noise and focus on football at such a high level. So many other players of his caliber have crumbled under the pressure at some point or another in their careers—whether due to injury, off-the-field drama, contract problems, diminished performance, or other adversity.

"As a football player, a lot of different things come at you at different times," he said. "When I'm dealing with football, that's where my focus needs to be, and I think over the years you just learn about compartmentalization and what your life has to be because you can't bring things from the outside to your job because everyone is counting on you."

Brady also gave some rare insight into his family life and talked about Gisele's role in keeping their busy household running every day while he focused on the day-to-day rigors of an NFL season.

"My wife does everything for the kids in the morning. I'm out of the door at six o'clock. When you do that for five months it gets tiring for them," he told reporters. "You owe so much to your family and your wife and your spouse or people who support you because they're bearing the burden at home for us to live our dreams. Our dream is so important, but it's not their dream. They're sacrificing a lot of their lives for what we do, and you want to be able to reward them as well. That's what makes it such a special day."

It was a glimpse into the quarterback's personal life, one that he might not have divulged as a younger man. But this was an older, wiser Brady and one who had become extremely adept at controlling his own messaging rather than letting the tabloids or the sports media craft his image. He'd taken to social media more and more over the previous couple of seasons, even hiring a new social media coordinator to oversee his brand.

The result was a more personal touch. Pictures with Gisele and his kids. Snarky memes taunting opponents after victories. Inspiring messages to his fans. Giveaways. Much like the Players' Tribune has allowed players to deliver their messages directly to the fans without the interference of a reporter, columnist, or talking head, Brady harnessed the power of social media—and Facebook in particular—to humanize himself as much as possible without violating the integrity of the so-called Patriot Way.

It was a fine line he walked to create some hype for himself and the Patriots without crossing over into trash talk or creating distractions that would raise Belichick's scorn.

The morning of the Super Bowl was a perfect example. With Brady having answered a few questions about his mother's health situation, he posted a picture on Instagram and Facebook of he and his father kissing her on the cheek.

"Sandwich kiss for mom at Picture Day!!! Go Pats!!!!"

The picture received 453,000 likes and 22,000 comments.

Also that day, Galynn's daughter-in-law Gisele, the most famous supermodel in the world, treated her to a personal makeup session.

Number 12 had also been very outspoken about his father in the days leading up to the game. During one news conference, he

filled up with tears while calling his dad his hero. But in the context of what was going on with Galynn at the time, it was clear
Tom was not just giving lip service to a man who had been a great
father. He was paying tribute to his dad for being the man his
mom needed during the fight of her life.

Tom Sr. also fought for his son. By the time of the Super Bowl,
he was still wounded by what felt like a smear campaign against
his son and was furious when critics tried to diminish his accomplishments.

"When it happens to your son, it's a whole different context,"
the elder Brady told KRON radio in San Francisco. "Or your
daughter or any one of your kids, and I think any parent kind of
understands that. They'd rather take the slings and arrows in the
heart than have their kids take it....For what the league did to
him and what Roger Goodell constantly lied about is beyond rep-
rehensible as far as I'm concerned."

Brady Sr. continued his rant. "[Goodell] went on a witch hunt
and went in way over his head and had to lie his way out in numerous ways, and the reality is that Tommy never got suspended
for deflating footballs. He got suspended because the court said
that he could—Roger Goodell—could do anything he wanted to
do to any player for any reason whatsoever. That's what happened. The NFL admitted they had no evidence on him."

Unsurprisingly, the comments went viral as they showed just
how personally the whole scandal was taken by the Brady family,
despite Tom's consistent public refusal to discuss the situation. Internally, the team was not happy that Brady's dad had gone rogue
and poked Goodell in the eye and stoked the Deflategate flames
just days before the Super Bowl. Tom, as usual, was diplomatic in
discussing his father's comments.

"I've banned my dad from talking, so he's no longer available to
the media," Brady joked on his contracted weekly appearance on
the *Kirk & Callahan Show* on Boston's WEEI 93.7 FM. "I love my

dad. As any parent knows how much you love your kids. My dad has been my best friend my entire life. He's always been my number one supporter. Hopefully he's at the game cheering me on. He's a great man and I love him to death. He's taught me everything about life. Certainly about how to be a father because he's been the best one a son could ever ask for. I try to pass those things on to my kids because he was so supportive of not only me but my three sisters [who] were all great athletes in their own right. My mom.... They're still married after close to forty-six years. I've been very, very fortunate."

Brady told the radio hosts that he was focused on his family's love and not Goodell's so-called witch hunt.

It was a communications strategy that came from the top of the organization, from Belichick specifically. One of the signs hanging in the tunnel in the bowels of Gillette Stadium sums it up with the words *Ignore the Noise.*

The team had grown into as cohesive and committed a unit as Belichick had ever coached. Players didn't directly address Deflategate or the suspension often, but internally there was no denying it was a motivating factor. The Patriots took it as a personal affront that anyone would claim their 2014 title was somehow tainted because of suspicion of underinflated balls.

The 2016 team was filled with a healthy mix of seasoned veterans, young and hungry players overlooked by many teams, and a variety of journeymen and castoffs. They "ignored the noise" and embraced how Brady always put the team first, despite his high-profile celebrity persona and daily media demands.

From the locker room attendant right up to Robert Kraft, the organization kept its egos in check and the thirst for redemption to themselves. But they were united for one sole mission: victory.

Just a few days before the Super Bowl, Ernie Adams, the team's research director, tripped while trying to avoid a kickoff during practice in Foxborough and hit his head. Adams, a respected and trusted adviser within the organization and close friend of Belichick, was taken away on a golf cart and received several stitches. Shortly after getting sewn up, Adams made his way back onto the Foxborough practice field. His toughness galvanized the team.

"We've all been knocked down out there one way or another, but that was unexpected and a little bit scary," Belichick recalled. "[But] you're not keeping Ernie out of the Super Bowl."[2]

It was a small symbol of the fight inside every member of the organization, a spirit that was infectious all season and only grew as the team prepared for the Super Bowl.

Meanwhile, NRG Stadium's parking lot swarmed with fans of both teams dressed in Patriots red, white, and blue, and Falcons red and black. The stadium was draped with billboard-sized banners of Ryan and Brady, signifying the matchup of the reigning league MVP and the greatest quarterback in league history. The banners, flowing next to the massive Super Bowl LI logo, raised the prospect of whether this day was going to be a passing of the torch, or another historic performance by the best ever to play.

A Patriots win would also make real the dream that had been dancing in the heads of Brady fans for some time, the moment when Roger Goodell would be forced to hand the Lombardi Trophy to number 12.

The commissioner stayed clear of Brady and Gillette Stadium throughout the playoffs, opting to attend matchups in other cities instead. Goodell watched games in Atlanta two weeks in a row. During games in Foxborough, the Patriots faithful serenaded themselves with chants of "Where is Roger?"

Goodell was pressed on this topic during his Super Bowl LI press conference days before the big game, when *Boston Globe* columnist Dan Shaughnessy took dead aim at the commissioner.

"You've not been in Foxborough for two years since the Deflategate investigation, your explanation strains all credibility that you needed to be in Atlanta two weeks in a row," Shaughnessy told him. "It appears that you're avoiding Foxborough. The Patriots are in this game and back home where I live it feels like there's still a war between the Patriots, their fans, and you. How would you characterize the situation and is it not awkward?"[3]

Goodell smiled uncomfortably at the podium before offering his response.

"Ah, I would tell you that it's not awkward at all for me. We have a job to do...there was a violation, we applied a process and discipline and we came to a conclusion that was supported by the facts and by the courts....If I'm invited back to Foxborough, I'll come."

For some Boston sportswriters, it was Goodell's equivalent of President Nixon's "I'm not a crook" speech. They analyzed every syllable to exploit any inconsistencies.

Boston Herald reporter Jeff Howe tweeted, Goodell was misleading when he said, "If I'm invited back to Foxboro, I'll come." Goodell makes the choice which playoff games to attend.

Sports Illustrated legal analyst Michael McCann also piled on with this tweet, Goodell again says the courts "supported the facts" in Deflategate. That's not what the courts supported. True, he's not a lawyer but still.

The commissioner also gave a rare interview to sports talk show host Colin Cowherd. The host asked Goodell if he would feel uncomfortable handing the Lombardi Trophy to Brady if the Patriots emerged victorious. "Not for a second," he replied. "Tom Brady is one of the all-time greats. It would be an honor."[4]

No one in New England believed a word.

Back in Boston, David Portnoy and his Barstool Sports minions had concocted a slogan to counter the commissioner and any other Brady critics: *They hate us 'cause they ain't us.* It was a rallying cry of cockiness and bravado that simultaneously slapped down critics and played up an us-against-the-world mentality. Like-minded Brady supporters also descended on Roger Goodell's $6.5

million summer home in Scarborough, Maine. One fan nailed several deflated footballs to a telephone near Goodell's estate, while another hired a local pilot to fly a banner over the house that read, "Comm. Goodell Jet home to N.Y." The aerial prank was in retaliation for a similar stunt in the skies over Gillette Stadium when a Jets fan paid for an airplane banner reading "Cheaters Look Up." The harassment got so bad that Goodell asked Scarborough police to step up patrols around his home.

The commissioner and his family appeared to be thin-skinned in response to the ribbing, and it was a trait that would continue even after Deflategate. In the fall of 2017, Goodell's wife, Jane Skinner Goodell, would be caught and exposed by the *Wall Street Journal* for setting up a fake Twitter account to defend her husband against criticism for his response to a campaign by players to kneel during the national anthem. The protests sent television ratings plummeting, and the commissioner's wife said she took the deceptive action out of frustration and love for her husband.

Brady carried the love and support of fans with him as he arrived at the stadium from the Marriott Hotel on the team bus. As always, he looked as though he had stepped out of a *GQ* ad, wearing his black Beats headphones, a slim-fitting gray and black checkered suit with a white pocket square, a white shirt with a gold collar bar, and a black tie.

Chris Long was nearby, sporting a black Grateful Dead tour shirt and sunglasses, his long brown hair pulled back in a man bun. Martellus Bennett, who had become a fan favorite as the season wore on, walked next to Long wearing a red and blue checkered flannel over a hoodie, a trio of thick gold chains swinging from his neck and his own set of Beats on his head.

Running backs Blount and White strode in together solemnly, the former in a maroon suit with a white collared shirt and the latter in a gray and white suit with a floral-patterned shirt and black tie. None were smiling, and all looked like they were ready for a fight.

Inside the stadium, NFLPA chief DeMaurice Smith was finally nearing the finish line of another long Super Bowl week, which is generally an exhausting one for Smith as he and his team manage about 250 player appearances at a variety of events, while every NFLPA sponsor is there. The NFLPA also hosts its own party on Thursday night, followed by an event for its members on Friday. And Saturday is the NFL's gala, where Smith is called upon to work the room.

He saw Goodell only briefly that week and only caught a couple glimpses of Brady at Media Day. He had seen Tom work the media in the past but noticed a change in tone this time.

"Whether it was explicit or not, it felt different because of what everyone on the union side and the player side had gone through that season with [Tom's] discipline. Obviously, [the feeling] was there," Smith remembered. "And also the fact that you've got a thirty-nine-year-old quarterback playing in the game."

Smith generally doesn't root for either team and actually rarely has time to watch any of the game as he's too busy running from suite to suite to schmooze with sponsors, players past and present, league officials, and friends. Most of all, he just hopes that none of his players get hurt.

As the fans streamed into the seating area, Smith made his way to the NFLPA suite alongside an entourage of friends and family. In the group was a close friend from his days at Riverdale Baptist High School in Maryland and a pair of homicide detectives whom Smith worked with for years while a federal prosecutor. Also sharing the suite was Smith's wife, Karen, and their two children, Elizabeth, then nineteen, and Alex, seventeen.

Down on the field, the two teams stretched, eyeballed one another, and went through the normal pregame routines while fans at the stadium buzzed with anticipation. Cameras flashed. Stadium crews prepared staging for the halftime show by Lady Gaga. The sidelines were packed with celebrities like actor Mark Wahlberg, rappers T.I. and Lil Jon, Usher, former Houston Rocket Yao Ming, comedian Rob Riggle, Olympian Simone Biles, New York Yankee Alex Rodriguez, members of the cast of *Hamilton*, and singer Harry Connick Jr.

Ernie Adams, who just days earlier was reeling from a head injury sustained during practice, watched Falcons receiver Julio Jones very closely, looking for something—anything—to gain even a minuscule edge for his secondary. The All-Pro receiver had battled an ankle sprain late in the season that limited his cutting to the left, so Adams was watching him to see if there was any sign that his quickness in that direction was diminished. If it was, it meant the Pats' defensive backs could possibly cheat a little bit or perhaps jump some routes. Belichick and his staff knew that if they could somehow limit Jones's touches or yards, then they'd have a shot at slowing down the Falcons juggernaut.

But after watching him in warm-ups, Adams determined that Jones's foot looked fine. That determination meant there was only one option: play Jones straight up and hope your defensive backs could make a play or two to keep his catches down, especially the deep ones.

Frustrated with his findings, Adams returned to the locker room to brief Coach Belichick and defensive coordinator Matt Patricia so they could adjust their strategy and prepare for the full strength of the Falcons' air assault. It wouldn't take long for the cornerbacks, safeties, the coaches, their teammates, and the entire world to see the awesome power of the Falcons offense on the sports world's biggest stage.

PART V

Chapter Twenty-two

THE LOCKER ROOM

February 5, 2017—NRG Stadium, Houston, Texas

Tom Brady and Robert Kraft had a long-running pregame ritual. Before each game, the owner and his quarterback got together alone somewhere away from the team and had a one-on-one talk before the Patriots took the field. Brady always felt a closeness to Kraft, despite moments of real friction over Deflategate, and the owner cared deeply for him. It's a relationship that started that day before Brady's rookie season when he told the billionaire team owner that drafting him was the best decision the team had ever made.

Their pregame discussions sometimes included a quick chat about the opponent or the game plan. Usually they ended with Brady assuring his owner, "We're going to kick some ass today." And he always said it with confidence and a steely stare, never leaving any doubt that he would do everything possible to carry through on that promise.

On other occasions, the talks were more personal. But never before any game did they have a talk as frank and personal as the one they had before the Super Bowl against the Falcons.

Brady's mother had not been able to attend any games during the season, and Tom Sr. had made it only to the Sunday night game against Seattle, a nail-biting loss.

"I'm glad Mom's here tonight," Tom told Kraft. "But I feel bad Myra can't be here for this one."

"They're both here," Kraft said of Galynn and his deceased wife. He paused. The rumble of the pregame ceremonies echoed through the cavernous bowels of NRG Stadium.

The owner looked his quarterback squarely in the eyes. He saw grit, determination, and that fire that he recognized whenever Brady's back was against the wall or whenever these biggest of moments were at hand.

"Let's win this one for Mom," Kraft said. "Let's dedicate it to Mom."

Brady welled up with tears as he fought back the emotion of the moment, struggling to maintain his focus and composure. He leaned forward and gave Kraft a bear hug and kissed him on the cheek.

"Let's go," he said.

They released their embrace, gave each other another nod, and number 12 turned back toward his troops. While he had always been able to compartmentalize the chaos around him, it was undeniable that his mother remained on his mind.

While his father was Tom's most vocal supporter and protector, Galynn Brady had always been the family's calming force. Now that calm was shaken by the turbulence of a deadly disease.

As Brady walked back to his locker, he passed the running backs, including James White. A former fourth-round pick out of Wisconsin, White had celebrated his twenty-fifth birthday just a few days earlier.

White grew up in Fort Lauderdale, Florida. His father was a police officer and his mother a probation officer. The rules were strict in the White home for James and his older brother, Tyrone.

Because both parents were in law enforcement, they knew all the pitfalls that trapped so many young men in Miami Dade County and put far too many on the path to prison rather than college.

"There were a lot of rules. They were tough on us," White told the authors of this book. "They tried to keep us on the right path. They shaped me and my brother into who we are."[1]

Athletics also ran in the family. James's father, Tyrone White Sr., was a wide receiver at Missouri Valley College before transferring to Florida A&M. James's uncle played for the University of Minnesota.

James White had a regular season with the Patriots under his belt and was adjusting well to NFL life, including splitting time with a talented backfield that also included Dion Lewis and LeGarrette Blount. While Blount had rushed for eleven hundred yards and eighteen touchdowns and was generally the featured back, White had emerged during the season as a reliable weapon as he got more touches due to the absence of Lewis, who spent the first half of the season rehabbing from a 2015 ACL injury.

"I don't necessarily see it as fighting for playing time. I see it as just competing," White said. "I think it's always good to have multiple guys in the backfield. It makes the offense more versatile. It wears the defense down when you can bring a fresh guy in. Guys that can do different things...or two people out on the field at the same time. It keeps the defense off-balance. I like it. It keeps guys fresh. I think it just makes the team overall better."[2]

Splitting time was nothing new for White. In fact it was something he'd been used to his whole playing career. At Fort Lauderdale's St. Thomas Aquinas High School, he was a standout back on a national championship team that also featured Cincinnati Bengals back Giovani Bernard. During his senior year in high school, White rushed for over a thousand yards and twenty touchdowns, earning him his nickname Sweet Feet.

At Wisconsin, he was in a world-class Badgers backfield that included three other NFL talents: John Clay, who played for the Pittsburgh Steelers; Monte Ball, who played for the Broncos and Patriots; and Los Angeles Chargers star Melvin Gordon. During White's freshman year, he rushed for nearly eleven hundred yards and fourteen touchdowns on a Badgers squad that was ranked number five in the nation and lost in the Rose Bowl to undefeated Texas Christian University, which was led by Bengals quarterback Andy Dalton.

When White was a senior, he ran for 1,444 yards and eighteen touchdowns and started to show his receiving prowess, making thirty-nine catches out of the backfield for three hundred yards and two scores. It was this versatility that caught Coach Belichick's attention and led him to draft White in the fourth round.

And that versatility was also a big reason why the Patriots were in Houston and why White was certain his number was going to be called quite a bit by number 12 on this night.

"I knew I had the ability to make some plays," White recalled. "I knew I'd have my part and I was ready for it. I was excited to go out there and have the opportunity to play on such a big stage with my teammates. That's what you work all year for—to have that moment—so I wanted to leave it all out there on the field and just find a way to help my team get a win."

White's parents were at the game, as they always were, and he was able to spend some quality time with them in Houston during Super Bowl week. As with all players at the Super Bowl, it's a difficult balance to enjoy all the hoopla while maintaining focus. But as this was the Patriots' seventh Super Bowl with Brady and Belichick, and White's second, he was far from a wide-eyed rookie, and as he laced up at his locker, he knew what it was going to take to beat the Falcons.

"They play a lot of man-to-man coverage, and I just wanted to win my matchups," White said. "And I wanted to be open if they played zone, and find a spot in the zone so if Tom looked in my direction I was in the right spot. Just try to pay attention to details...I just wanted to be a viable option. If the ball was handed to me, I just wanted to make sure I did the right thing with it."

After three years playing with Brady, White had a great feel for the quarterback, and like all players who thrived in the Patriots offense over the course of the team's unprecedented run, he knew that he had to out-study, out-work, and out-perform the opponent every chance he got.

"Ever since I stepped foot in the building, ever since my rookie year, you could see how hard the guy [Brady] works on and off the field," White said. "It rubs off on everybody else. He's a competitor. He competes in practice. He competes in every moment. He makes everybody on the team better. He heightens your awareness.

"You just want to go out there and be great," he continued. "He's the greatest quarterback of all time. I'm definitely glad he's on our team...just a fearless guy. Great teammate. There's nothing more you can ask for from him."

As White sat at his locker getting ready, he thought about the turbulent regular season. He knew the suspension had taken its toll on his quarterback, but also that he was never one to let emotion get in the way of business.

Sitting at his nearby locker, Brady was a portrait of intensity, focus, and calm. It was an icy demeanor all his teammates knew well. Tom wouldn't say it, but this was the biggest game of his career. His personal legacy was on the line. He had been pilloried in the press, accused of being a fake, a phony, and a cheater. Other players, most of whom he had abused on the field repeatedly, took cheap shots at him on social media and in the press. His blood boiled inside, but outside, he was measured and calculated. He was also challenged by his coach.

"Tom, we've been to six Super Bowls together and we've never scored a point in the first quarter. Can we get that done?" Belichick asked.[3]

Brady nodded.

Brian Flores, the Patriots' linebackers coach, was hopeful. *Man, we're going to score thirty points in the first quarter,* he thought to himself.[4]

In the tunnel before taking the field, team cocaptain and special teams All-Pro Matthew Slater gathered with Dion Lewis, Julian Edelman, Danny Amendola, James White, and safety Patrick Chung. The six key players clutched hands as Slater spoke. He looked each of them in the eyes as he reminded them all of how they wound up there, about to play in the Super Bowl.

"Fellas, as we go out here, man, I want you all to think about the story, man, your story. D-Lew [Lewis]. Traded. Cut. J-Dub [White]. Couldn't even get on the field your rookie year. Dola [Amendola]. Walk-on. You [Edelman]. No position. PC [Chung]. Had to go to another team, come back. Now you're one of the best safeties in the league. Remember the journey, fellas. It all led to this."

"Playmakers, on three. One...two...three."[5] The six turned and sprinted toward their destiny on the NRG stadium gridiron.

The team was led onto the field by a staffer waving a massive red, white, and blue flag with a simple message, the word *One* and the Patriots logo. Pyrotechnics fired into the air and the team's Pat Patriot mascot sprinted out of the tunnel, fist raised high. Behind him was Brady, followed closely by Edelman, who was sporting a thick, black, bushy playoff beard, center David Andrews, and Amendola.

As number 12 led his teammates onto the Super Bowl gridiron for a record seventh time, he sprinted side by side with his two backups, Jacoby Brissett and Jimmy Garoppolo, end zone to end zone, screaming and shouting, "Let's go!"

When Brady reached the far end zone, he pumped his fist in the air and leaped and shouted some more, pointing up to the

Pats fans in the corner section. Brady had been booed loudly at this exact moment a year earlier at Levi's Stadium in Santa Clara, California—the home of the 49ers—as the Patriots' rival Denver Broncos and Peyton Manning took the field against Cam Newton and the Carolina Panthers for Super Bowl 50. It happened during a special ceremony to honor all the previous Super Bowl MVPs. Brady smiled through it, but deep down he was hurt by the negative reception in what was essentially his hometown.

But now the roar of the crowd was deafening one year later in Houston as rabid Patriots fans thirsty for redemption shouted their approval, eager to support their team and their quarterback in his quest for gridiron immortality.

Country music superstar Luke Bryan sang the anthem a cappella, standing on the NFL logo at the center of the field flanked by a military color guard, overlooking a massive American flag unfurled and stretched between the 35-yard lines. Brady, as he always does, listened intently, his head bowed, gently swaying back and forth.

Chris Long, with black war paint smeared down his face and his mane flowing out of a Patriots wave cap, held his hand over his heart as he looked straight ahead. The injured Gronkowski stood nearby, in street clothes, in a similar pose. Matt Ryan stared across from the opposite sideline, himself a picture of calm resolve.

Number 12 mouthed the final few lines of the anthem along with Bryan before a spine-tingling stadium flyover by the U.S. Air Force Thunderbirds sent the crowd into a patriotic frenzy. Former president George H. W. Bush, a longtime Houston resident, was escorted onto the field after the anthem in a wheelchair, along with his wife, Barbara, to assist with the coin toss. The ninety-two-year-old former president had recently been released from Houston Methodist Hospital, where he had been treated for pneumonia. He received a thunderous ovation, in stark contrast to newly sworn-in Vice President Mike Pence, who was roundly booed when he was shown on the stadium big screen.

The former president's appearance made for some emotional—and funny—tweets.

Having George H. W. Bush appear was such a special moment, Coach Belichick almost had a facial expression, joked author and *National Review* correspondent Jim Geraghty.

The Patriots captains called heads. President Bush flipped the coin into the air. It landed on the turf and head referee Kent Payne announced it was tails. The Falcons deferred and gave the opening kickoff to the Patriots.

On the sideline, Brady pulled on his helmet, buttoned his chin strap, and clapped his hands. This was the moment he had been anticipating for many, many months. And now it was here.

Chapter Twenty-three

FIRE AND ICE

FIRST QUARTER

As Brady prepared for his first offensive series, he may have been reminded of the genesis of Deflategate. Breaking: A league source tells me the NFL is investigating the possibility the Patriots deflated footballs Sunday night. More to come, Kravitz had tweeted at 12:55 a.m. on January 19, 2015. It seemed mundane to many, but it was that last line that raised red flags: *more to come.*

Brady's mother's cancer and that tweet were likely somewhere kicking around in the back of his mind, but flashes from thousands of cell phone cameras filled the stadium as Atlanta Falcons kicker Matt Bosher ran up to the ball and kicked off on the opening play of Super Bowl LI.

The ball sailed into the end zone, and Brady and his offense took the field. The next sixty minutes of football would further determine his place in history.

Tom's first snap from scrimmage was an incomplete pass. He

dropped back and cycled his eyes through his reads. First, he passed on what he saw in a hitch route by rookie receiver Malcolm Mitchell to his right, and then skipped over a Chris Hogan post route that would need more time to develop. Finally, he came back to his left to deliver an accurate enough but slightly high throw to Julian Edelman on a low crossing route into tight coverage that ideally would have arrived a second sooner. For any other quarterback, this wasn't a bad play. But for the master of both timing and accuracy it was anything but masterful.

And it was also the start of one of the worst halves Tom and the Patriots ever played.

Now second down and ten yards to go from the New England 25-yard line, the towering Martellus Bennett ran a vertical clearout route to Brady's left with Edelman catching a delayed low crossing route behind the path left by the big tight end. This route forces the beefier linebacker nearest Edelman to try to stay with the speedy wideout as he runs all the way across the formation. Brady feasted on the scenario, hitting Edelman with a nine-yard completion.

On third and one, Brady hurried the offense to the line, trying to snap the ball quickly before the defense could get set. The direct run by LeGarrette Blount wasn't blocked or run particularly well, with the quick tempo seeming to harm the offensive line more than help them. In the rush, the big guys up front weren't able to locate Falcons middle linebacker Deion Jones in the blocking scheme as he knifed through the line, stopping the play for no gain and a forced punt.

It was a rough start as they went three and out and had to punt, giving the ball away to NFL MVP Matt Ryan and the league's top-scoring offense.

Ryan's first pass was a beautifully executed thirty-seven-yard dart to Devonta Freeman. But the Patriots defense pulled it together and forced Atlanta to punt from their own 40-yard line.

Falcons punter Matt Bosher had only kicked twice the previous game in a 44–21 thrashing of the Green Bay Packers in the NFC championship game. But he showed no signs of rust as he got off a soaring boot that pinned New England on its own 10-yard line.

The teams would continue to feel each other out, like boxers stalking each other across the ring in the first round, trading short drives that ended with punts.

On Brady's second drive, Josh McDaniels opted to get the ball quickly into one of the Patriots' top playmaker's hands, calling a speed reverse to Julian Edelman that netted just two yards. On second down, Edelman was double-teamed, leaving Amendola with single coverage in the slot. Amendola is a master at deception, using his hips to trick defenders as to where his route might go. He ran a "bow route," named for its curved shape, and the idea behind it is to initially widen the defensive back through the initial release from the line of scrimmage, displace him from the path of the arc, and then "bow" the route back to the vacancy. Amendola darted to the outside, then deftly bent back to the slot, just as Tom's laser arrived for a thirteen-yard gain.

This was a perfect execution of the offense and what the Patriots' fans had waited for.

The Krafts liked what they were seeing now from their quarterback and his receiving corps.

"On most other teams, the receivers are all very competitive, but Danny, Julian, and Chris Hogan all supported each other," Jonathan Kraft pointed out to the authors. "Brady spreads it around, too. On another team, a receiver might take offense to that, but what receiver is going to go talk shit to Brady?"[1]

Robert Kraft agreed with his son's assessment. "Usually the number one receiver, if there is one, is selfish. If they don't get the ball in the first quarter, they get upset. This is a very unselfish group."

Game on.

On the very next snap, Brady completed the first of what would be many deep outside comeback routes, this one to Hogan for fifteen yards. When the ball left Tom's hand, the defensive back's coverage was skintight, as if he were the receiver's shadow. Hogan employed a technique known as "getting friendly" at the top of the route—a move in which the receiver comes back toward the quarterback instead of running away from the passer or stopping and waiting for the ball to arrive. Another subtle layer to Brady's brilliance on the play was that there was a zone defender to Hogan's side who could have gotten underneath the route to make it a much harder throw. But Tom sold the play-action run fake, which froze that extra defender. When he turned from his fake and saw the linebacker had bit to play the run, it was just a matter of getting the ball to Hogan before the defensive back could get out of his break. It was football as art.

Over the next several plays, the Patriots dutifully moved the ball into Falcons territory. But a devastating sack from Falcons defensive end Courtney Upshaw powering through offensive right guard Shaq Mason thwarted Brady's momentum.

On third and eighteen, number 12 held the ball for over six seconds in a well-protected pocket, hoping for something to develop downfield with a chance of stealing a long conversion. Nothing materialized, and he was forced to take a one-yard sack to end the series, triggering another Ryan Allen punt.

Glimpses of the revenge tour Patriots offense ripping through an overmatched Falcons defense appeared briefly on the second New England series, but those hopes faded fast. Fortunately, the Patriots defense did their job again, eventually forcing Atlanta into another punt, bringing about the third Patriots offensive series of the Super Bowl with 1:36 remaining in the first quarter.

Brady started the drive by targeting Edelman once again on a nifty double-cut out route. The play was another example of the subtleties of high-level route running, and Edelman was one of the league's best. His first juke turned the defensive back's hips away from where Edelman knew he was inevitably taking the route: back to the sideline. The slot receiver darted back toward the sideline, leaving the defensive back doing a full 180 to recover. The window created by that turn was all Brady needed to deliver a thirteen-yard precision pass to kick off the series.

Next came a nice seven-yard run up the middle by the power back Blount, the first taste of running game success for New England. Another short run for Blount ended the first quarter, leaving the Patriots with third and one to keep the drive going. And then came one of those captivating plays that reminded the millions of NFL fans watching around the world that Brady was here to do something special.

SECOND QUARTER

With Gronkowski out for the game with his season-ending back injury, it was abundantly clear through the first quarter of the game that Edelman was going to be a priority target, especially in critical situations. Edelman's prescribed job was to run a short crossing route, moving from the offense's left to its right. Not surprisingly, he received tight man-to-man coverage, but the gauntlet of linebackers in the area directly in front of Brady at first-down depth shut down the idea of any attempt to his close friend Edelman as the play was designed.

But great quarterbacking isn't just throwing. Sometimes, it means being a musical conductor on the field.

With tight coverage all over the field and solid pass protection extending his pocket, Tom calmly improvised. He looked to Edelman, who had run his assigned route to no avail, and then motioned upfield with his left hand. Edelman took the cue and wheeled upfield, changing his horizontal route into a vertical one. The defensive back overplayed the short route, leaving only a deep safety in the middle of the field to contend with. Julian found the space and Tom delivered a perfect ball to cap off the improvised route, and the Patriots had their biggest offensive play of the day— a twenty-seven-yard completion down to the Falcons' 33-yard line.

The play showed the synergy between Brady and Edelman— a critical creative connection made possible on the fly because of the thousands of practice reps the two had between them. The quarterback and his receiver had spent countless hours training in Foxborough as well as in Los Angeles and Montana, where Brady had homes.

"You have a clock in your head [judging down and distance] and I know what Tom likes and what he expects us to do," Edelman explained to the authors. "I peeked over and saw that he was moving around the pocket, so I decided to take off deep and we were able to connect."

Under ordinary circumstances, a play of that level could deflate or at least slow down a defense. Brady and company would usually follow up that sort of backbreaking play with another strike or two in the red zone and seven points. Instead, the best New England offensive play of the game to that point was immediately followed by a crushing turnover as Blount fumbled on the ensuing snap.

As so often is the case in the game of football, that turnover ended up being a particularly punishing gut punch. Not only did it thwart the Patriots' first legitimate chance at getting on the scoreboard, but the Falcons turned it into seven points themselves with a drive the length of the field, ending in a five-yard Devonta Freeman touchdown scamper.

With an opportunity now for the Patriots offense to answer this early-game adversity, they once again failed. A quick three-and-out series led to another punt. New England fans and sports pundits were suddenly questioning the critics who had downplayed Atlanta's speedy defense. The paper matchup said the Patriots should have no problem moving the ball against this Falcons D, but three series into the game and it was the New England offense that was looking overmatched.

Brady was being hurried, receivers were being jammed and knocked off their routes, the running game was stuck in neutral, and the whole offensive timing was a mess. There was no rhythm, no flow. It wasn't quite the punishing defensive blitzkrieg that the New York Giants inflicted on the Patriots in the 2007 and 2011 Super Bowls, which had the quarterback running for his life, but it was equally effective.

On the other side of the ball, Matt "Matty Ice" Ryan was looking every bit the league MVP that he was. Questions about his ability to perform on the biggest stage were far from anyone's mind as he had continued his torrid playoff run.

Atlanta began its next series with solid field position at its own 38-yard line. And in nearly the same brief time the New England offense had just been on the field, the Patriots defense surrendered a fast, five-play scoring drive for another Falcons touchdown, increasing the Atlanta lead to 14–0 on a nineteen-yard touchdown catch by tight end Austin Hooper. Again, the Falcons were making it look easy.

The Patriots defense was being exposed while Tom Brady was not only out of sync but truly struggling. Some would say it looked like maybe—just maybe—Father Time had finally caught up to the thirty-nine-year-old quarterback and that we were all witnessing his last stand. Was Tom Brady getting *old* right before our eyes?

The Super Bowl was not following the Patriots' script, while the Falcons played with an edge and a purpose.

Brady and the Patriots offense got the ball back again, but what followed was as ugly an offensive series as you'll ever see from a New England team—although that truth was somewhat concealed by the two separate defensive penalties that artificially extended the drive. There was a pass drop. There was spotty protection, prompting multiple "just get rid of it" throws by Tom. There were poorly executed run plays. And then, there was perhaps the worst play the legendary quarterback had made in his storied Super Bowl history.

Aligned in shotgun formation with a three-wide-receiver set to his left, Brady took the snap. The edges of the protection closed in on him immediately, the rush advancing quickly. Danny Amendola was the inside receiver in the bunch, and he ran a quick angle route—first out and then back to the inside. Defensive back Robert Alford was sagging in his coverage and swooped in as Amendola broke back to the middle of the field.

Television announcer Joe Buck recognized something at that moment that Brady had not. "The Falcons overload the right side of the Patriots offense," Buck told a nationwide audience.

Tom never saw the hidden defensive back in the chaos of the routes crossing one another. He threw a missile into the traffic that hit Alford square in the numbers. Alford had nothing but grass in front of him.

There was only one Patriots player left to stop him and it was Brady. The quarterback chased after Alford and attempted an awkward diving tackle. The Falcons player flew past him and dashed for the end zone as Brady flopped to the turf.

"He's gone," Joe Buck shouted. "There are no flags and the Falcons add to their lead."

Brady rose to his feet, took his helmet off, and walked off the field in disgust. It was all slipping away. The legend looked old and tired. For sports fans and journalists alike, it was similar to watching Muhammad Ali getting battered around the ring by a younger, stronger George Foreman in the opening rounds of their epic fight in Zaire, in 1974. Atlanta was now up 21–0 in a game the Patriots were favored to win by three points.

"Trouble now," Bill Belichick announced to his assistants' headsets. The head coach's words came as no surprise, as everyone could see what was happening on the field. The key now was not to allow panic to set in.

The pick six felt like a backbreaker. Falcons fans and Brady haters alike celebrated the images of Tom flailing for Alford's feet and tumbling to the ground helplessly with a pained look on his face.

How's your day going, Tom Brady? #SB51, Bleacher Report tweeted with close-up pictures of the quarterback's distressed face.

Fox Sports reporter Seth Kaplan referred to the creepy, Frankenstein-like courtroom drawing of Tom that became a meme of its own during the Deflategate proceedings, tweeting, This is the worst Brady has looked since that courtroom sketch.

The frustration Patriots fans felt was only exacerbated by the legions cheering Brady's collapse, mocking him for Deflategate, and reveling in New England's failures in a game most experts had predicted they would win.

If Brady's path to redemption was to end with a Super Bowl trophy in Houston, then it had taken a nightmarish turn.

On the Falcons' sidelines, there was smiling, showboating, and gloating.

"They ain't ever met nothing like this," Falcons receiver Mohamed Sanu said, his cockiness backed up by the scoreboard.

But at least one player was wary that no lead was safe with Brady on the other sideline. Third-year receiver Taylor Gabriel had seen this movie before, and sought to temper his teammate's bravado.

"It's Tom Brady, though," Gabriel said, ominously.

"I know. I know. I'm never comfortable," Sanu conceded. "We about to put up forty-something on they ass. What I'm saying is, they ain't never seen anything like this."[2]

Brady's first play after the crushing interception is one that could easily have been forgotten in a game that would be filled with memorable moments. But it's one that, had it gone another way, probably would have destroyed any possibility of what was to come.

On the play, Brady's arm reared back for a deep throw to his left, but he was hit just as he threw. The ball fluttered uncontrollably over the line of scrimmage. Martellus Bennett was running a crossing route from the right side of the formation and wasn't the intended target on the play, but luckily wound up in the perfect position to snatch the ball out of the air and prevent another catastrophic turnover. In retrospect, Bennett's tremendous awareness and hustle on that play was the team's first step in trying to turn the game around. It was a must-make play in a game that would soon be filled with them.

Bill Belichick had spent his entire tenure in New England preaching the importance of making seemingly innocuous plays. The so-called little things were so clearly critical that none of the memorable plays can happen without them. Bennett's play was an example of that ethos.

Still, while the catch may have saved the game for the moment, things didn't immediately get better for the Patriots. On the next down, Edelman extended to Tom's left and Amendola lined up in the slot right. Brady had good protection, and as the routes crossed twenty yards downfield, Edelman's defender was perfectly shielded from the route.

The shifty slot receiver popped out on the other side, but the quarterback overthrew him for another incompletion. It was a huge missed opportunity at the time, as it would have likely been a touchdown because the defender was so far behind as the routes crossed. There was nothing but green pasture in front of Edelman. It was a beautiful call by McDaniels but turned into just another gaffe by the struggling Brady.

The next play featured some coaching-clinic pocket movement as Brady delivered a laser beam to James White on the outside, resulting in a big twenty-eight-yard gain. Tom ran through every eligible receiver in his route progression to get back to White, dancing gently in the pocket the whole time, his eyes focused downfield.

A couple plays later, Brady hit White again but unfortunately failed to see a wide-open Hogan downfield.

As the clock ticked away in the first half, Bennett was called for a holding penalty, negating a big screen play to White that had taken the ball down to the Falcons' 3-yard line. The penalty put New England into playing for a field goal mode on second down and twenty yards to go with just twelve seconds left.

Another screen pass, this time to Bennett, failed, so the Patriots called a quick time-out to try to score some points before the game truly got away. Stephen Gostkowski kicked a forty-one-yarder through the uprights to put New England on the board finally. While the points would ultimately prove to be crucial, at the time, Patriots fans in attendance and across the world groaned in frustration that a field goal was all the great Tom Brady could muster.

The team staggered into the locker room at halftime. Lady Gaga's bass-heavy music boomed in the cavernous catacombs underneath NRG Stadium. Brady felt like he had been through the meat grinder. But, as he had his entire career—even in the darkest moments of Deflategate—he kept his composure and his focus on the task at hand.

They could still come back. No team before the Patriots in Super Bowl LXIX two years earlier had ever come back from a ten-point deficit. But history wasn't on their side. A comeback from eighteen points down was extremely rare during the regular season and had never happened in a Super Bowl.

Still, in the stadium, at Super Bowl parties outside of New England, and on social media, millions, predictably, were now dancing on Tom's grave and writing him off. It was hard not to, as the Patriots were on the wrong side of a 21–3 drubbing and showed few signs of life. Twitter trolls lambasted Brady and his struggling squad, all but declaring the game over.

Author and podcaster Peter Shankman, a New Yorker who attended Boston University, tweeted to his 175,000 followers:

People angry right now:

1) Patriots fans

2) Advertisers who bought ads in the second half. #SuperBowl.

The Sunday Night NFL official Twitter account tweeted out a picture of Tom on the bench, his head bowed in dejection, with the words Not great, Tom. #SB51

Breaking Bad actor Bryan Cranston kept the cyber-trolling going, tweeting to his two million followers, Lady Gaga covered more ground on the field than the Patriots. #SuperBowl.

Chapter Twenty-four

THEY WILL FIGHT THEIR ASSES OFF!

HALFTIME

During the extended halftime of Super Bowl LI, Bill Belichick was concerned about the lopsided score, but he didn't think it was indicative of the play on the field. He noted that his team had actually held the ball for more than eighteen minutes of the first half, as compared to Atlanta's eleven.

"I felt like we had control of the game. We didn't have control of the score," Belichick said later.[1]

He even told his offensive coordinator as much. "We'll be okay. Our guys believe. They will fight their ass off," Belichick said to McDaniels.[2]

He then turned to his players.

"Let's just play one play at a time," Belichick told his men. "We can't worry about things we can't control. Let's worry about what we can control."

At that moment an unlikely leader emerged with a rallying cry.

"This is going to be the best comeback of all time," free safety Duron Harmon shouted across the locker room.

Harmon was another classic Belichick guy. Picked up in the third round of the 2013 draft, he was one of two Rutgers University defensive backs selected by the Patriots that year, joining Logan Ryan. The pair had up-and-down moments throughout their first few seasons, and Belichick's affinity for Rutgers players became a kind of running joke on sports talk radio in Boston.

Harmon was having the last laugh, however, as he emerged as a solid role player and, more importantly, a quiet leader on the defense in 2016. In the divisional round against the Texans, he picked off Brock Osweiler and took it back thirty-one yards. His versatility at safety and cornerback also allowed more freedom for safety Devin McCourty to roam.

No one laughed. No one blinked an eye, especially Brady. His mother was sick and his legacy and reputation were on the line. Although he was considered a future first ballot Hall of Famer, some critics still called him a cheater. Journalists across the country had placed an asterisk next to his name in spite of his many accomplishments.

Those closest to him knew just how much it hurt him to be portrayed as a cheater and a liar. It flew in the face of everything he was and strived to be. But the quarterback had to block it all out now.

"It was all out of my mind. I wasn't thinking like way down the road or all these different things. I was just thinking about how can we get back in the game?" Brady would later recall. "It's one play at a time. It sounds so cliché but that's the way you are. That's the reality. You can't score twenty-five points in one drive. We did a great job in all three phases coming together as a team and that's what Super Bowls are all about. You're playing the best teams on the biggest stage and you know you gotta get the job done."[3]

While the players in that locker room were aware a comeback

of this magnitude would be nothing short of a sports miracle, in Belichick's world, there was only one path to victory: do your job.

"We have to keep doing what we're doing, play like we know how to play and don't think about what happened," he reinforced firmly. "They have to score a lot more points to keep us down."[4]

Edelman understood Belichick's words.

"A lot of the things that were happening in the first half, that was just us beating ourselves," he would recall. "We were in the red area twice and we had a fumble and we threw an interception, but it wasn't like we weren't moving the ball. We just had to really soak in what we said we had to do and we couldn't make any more mistakes. Our coaches did a really good job of keeping us in the moment and keeping us focused on each play instead of thinking about the big picture. Instead we focused on doing our job on each play."[5]

Chris Long, son of Raiders Hall of Famer and longtime Patriots tormentor Howie Long, was one of those Belichick players who needed a shot on a new team to prove he still had worth. A blue-chip recruit out of Santa Monica, California, with football in his blood, he played at the University of Virginia and had a stellar college career, coming in tenth in the 2007 Heisman Trophy voting, even earning one first-place vote, but losing to Tim Tebow.

Long was drafted second overall in the 2008 draft by the St. Louis Rams right after the Dolphins took University of Michigan offensive tackle Jake Long (no relation). The player selected with the third pick right after Chris Long? Matt Ryan out of Boston College, the quarterback who was now toying with him and his Patriots teammates.

Chris Long put up solid numbers with the Rams, leading the team in sacks and quarterback pressures for several seasons. In 2014, his time in St. Louis came to an end after he suffered a serious ankle injury that required surgery.

Belichick picked him up as a free agent in March 2016, signing him to a classic Patriots one-year deal for $2 million. There were questions about whether the then-thirty-one-year-old had anything left in the tank. The short-term deal not only gave Long a chance to play with a contender, but it was also a chance to prove he wasn't finished. A great year with New England would mean a long playoff run, a shot at a title, and a chance at one final lucrative contract.

He came into training camp and made the most of his stay. Belichick praised his work ethic and effort throughout the season, and Long became an important role player on the defense that had helped propel the Patriots to this moment.

In the locker room at halftime, Long's ears perked up at Harmon's declaration. He would later say that Harmon's words shook the team out of its funk at the exact right moment.

"We were down," he recalled. "I think most of us believed, but some of us had some doubts. It's natural to have some doubts. We're only human."[6]

With Harmon's words in their heads, Brady and the Patriots made the walk back to the tunnel to head back out onto the field.

"Halftime on the sideline, us being together as a team knowing we're not quitting. We just gotta play better. It's not really the plays, it's more the feeling and how proud I am that our team never gave in to any adversity," Brady would remember vividly.[7]

"The vets did a great job of leading by example. No one panicked," first-year receiver Malcolm Mitchell told the authors of this book. "They didn't have to say anything to me. You could see from how they handled themselves, their posture, how confident they were in the team's ability to respond."[8]

On the sidelines, the coaches tried to keep the players focused, reminding them that they were well prepared and that there was still plenty of time to mount a comeback.

"Trust the system," the team was told. "Do your job."

It was gut-check time and the moment they had been working toward since the summer.

The Patriots had famously trained all season by running up a steep hill behind Gillette Stadium in Foxborough. It was a brutal practice drill but one designed specifically for this time and place. The players were well conditioned in part because of the uphill practice running.

"Do you believe we're going to win?" McDaniels said to Lewis, White, and Blount.

"Yes," they collectively responded, nodding their heads.

"I do, too," McDaniels said. "Let's just play our best half. I don't want anyone to do anything they can't do. Don't try and make it all up in one play. Just play each play by itself."[9]

THIRD QUARTER

Because the Falcons had deferred after winning the coin toss at the opening of the game, Matt Ryan and company got the ball first after a Gostkowski kickoff. New England's defense had a tall order to keep the red-hot Atlanta quarterback from marching down and putting the nail in their collective coffin once and for all. A comeback from 21–3 was a big enough task. Allowing the Falcons to extend their lead to 28–3 would be a disaster.

Unsettled Patriots fans settled in for the second half. If this was indeed Brady's final stand, they would continue to watch to the bitter end, as they were committed to their quarterback.

The defense was stout, though, and forced the Falcons into a rare three-and-out.

It was now Brady's turn. Number 12 jogged onto the field, hoping to get something going. But despite the locker room confidence and his determined focus, the offense was still out of sync.

On first down, Tom looked off the middle-of-the-field safety by keeping his eyes and shoulders to the right side, and then whipped back left and threw a perfect ball into tight solo coverage to Chris Hogan on the outside. Hogan had begun aligned to Brady's left in the slot, but Tom motioned White out of the backfield beyond Hogan's alignment. The down safety adjusted with the motion, giving Brady the information he wanted: man-to-man coverage across the board with a deep middle-of-the-field safety.

The coverage was tight—too tight it turned out—and although Tom threw a perfect ball, it was punched out from Hogan's hands. It was the perfect throw in a competitive situation that showed Brady was back on his mark and still trusted his receivers to fight on.

The throw wasn't rewarded with a completion, but it foreshadowed a litany of high-level passes to come. And as Belichick had so often said, you have to make catches in competitive situations to win the big games. You can't just catch the wide-open ones. One glance at the Super Bowls they lost to the Giants would prove as much. Those victories were sealed for the Giants on two huge catches on jump balls. The Patriots needed some huge catches of their own. Despite the incompletion, it was clear that one thing was certain: Brady was unafraid and was going to put the ball in competitive spaces to help his team crawl back to life.

Second down was a negative gain, a two-yard loss on a screen to Amendola. As a mild solace, Tom delivered a dart to give the play a chance, but it was poorly blocked. On third down, Edelman dropped a perfectly placed crossing route with catch-and-run potential that would've likely earned a first down. All in all, Brady had just thrown three perfect balls and the offense had nothing more than another three-and-out and a loss of two yards on the possession to show for it.

"Guys, at some point we all gotta just start making the plays," Tom shouted to his struggling teammates as he walked back to the sidelines. He gathered with his receiving corps on the bench.

"We just needed to execute one drive, and after that drive we'll come to the sidelines and we'll talk about the next drive," he later said.

The discouraging series at this point amounted to a significant emotional weight for the players in the game. Nothing had gone the Patriots' way in the first half. When New England did finally get their way to start the second half—a quick defensive stop, a nice special teams return to midfield—only to do nothing with the opportunity, it triggered a collective groan from Patriots fans throughout the stadium that was sensed by the players down on the field.

While the Patriots continued to chip away, their fans saw their Super Bowl dreams slipping away. The game was all but over. And it was about to get even worse.

Matt Ryan and his squad got the ball back and promptly marched eight plays for eighty-five yards and a touchdown that chewed up nearly four and a half minutes of the third quarter.

The score was 28–3. The rout was on.

Chapter Twenty-five

NO ROOM FOR ERROR

The biggest deficit Brady had ever erased in his career was a twenty-four-point hole in a 2013 home game against the Broncos. No Patriots team in history had ever come back from twenty-five.

Yet the Patriots sideline remained eerily calm. There was no throwing of helmets or pointing of fingers. They still knew that if there was one player in the world who could lead them back, it was number 12.

"Look, there's no room for error now," McCourty told his defensive teammates.

There were others who believed, too, like Tom's dad.

"This is gonna be the greatest comeback ever," Tom Sr. texted to his family group chat. "I gotta believe. And I believe."[1]

High above the field in the owner's luxury suite, Robert and Jonathan Kraft felt sickened. They were trying to figure out what the hell was going on with their team. How could a Belichick-coached squad fail this badly in the franchise's seventh Super Bowl? Yet, like Tom Brady Sr. and the players on the field, the Krafts did not abandon all hope.

"Think he's giving up at 28–3?" Jonathan asked his dad about their quarterback.

The elder Kraft was stoic and contemplated the possibilities. Before he could answer, Jonathan said what they were both thinking: "No fucking way."[2]

Twitter and a host of NFL players watching from their couches certainly gave the Patriots zero shot at a comeback.

This game is a classic case of one team playing on 'All Madden' & the other team playing on 'Rookie,' tweeted Seahawks center Justin Britt.

I repeat DEFENSE WINS CHAMPIONSHIPS #SB51, tweeted Giants defensive end Justin Tuck, who had tortured Brady in the 2011 Super Bowl won by New York.

Another celebrity who was quick to give up on the Patriots was Boston-bred actor Mark Wahlberg, a so-called Patriots superfan and friend of both Brady and the Kraft family. After the score hit 28–3, it seems Wahlberg had witnessed enough and could stomach no more. He left NRG Stadium with his wife and two sons. His abrupt exit was captured on video and immediately went viral.

"Diehard" Patriots fan Mark Wahlberg left Super Bowl LI early, NFL Memes tweeted out to 426,000 followers.

Wahlberg's surrender to the moment was symbolic. It was difficult for any New England fan to watch the bloodletting. It was a car crash, but in this instance, you wanted to look away. This was even the case for Brady's close friends. The quarterback had made cameos in Wahlberg films and TV shows, including *Entourage* and *Ted 2*, the latter of which involved a raunchy scene in which Wahlberg and his come-to-life teddy bear Ted try unsuccessfully to steal the quarterback's sperm. When Deflategate broke, Wahlberg told *US Weekly* that he texted Tom to offer up support.

"I sent him a message—saying from a guy who's been there, [not to] worry about it," said Wahlberg, who has faced sharp criticism over the years for committing a racially motivated hate crime that he served prison time for as a teenager. "'Keep your head up. It will all blow over.'"[3]

Wahlberg did not have his friend's back on this day, but Brady's teammates did.

"Let's go, baby," Edelman said to Tom. "Going to be a hell of a story."

Brady nodded silently. His jawline was rigid. No one liked a challenge more than Tom Brady, and now he had the biggest one of his career. His flawless fourth-quarter comeback in the 2001 Super Bowl in New Orleans over Kurt Warner and "The Greatest Show on Turf" had planted the seeds for his legacy and put him in the conversation for great clutch quarterbacks. At the time, though, it was considered to be just a fluke performance from a new young quarterback who looked like he had some potential.

His next two Super Bowl victories in 2003 and 2004—and the accompanying playoff masterpieces along those journeys—built on his growing legend. As the years went on and he and Belichick racked up record-breaking season after record-breaking season, his legacy continued to grow. The 2007 perfect regular season and his fifty touchdowns that season showed he was among the best ever. His Super Bowl losses in '07 and '11 gave critics ammunition to knock him down a peg.

Deflategate gave them more gunpowder.

Now what lay in front of him was the opportunity to orchestrate the greatest comeback in Super Bowl history and lay waste to the critics once and for all.

"Let's go now. Let's start showing some fight!" Brady shouted to his teammates on the sidelines with just 8:31 to go in the third quarter and the scoreboard showing the lopsided 28–3 tally. "We've got to play harder, tougher. Harder, tougher, everything."

In the next series, Brady began to make his move. He took what the Falcons gave him and made them pay. A twelve-yard pass to

White was followed by a short run from Dion Lewis. And then on a huge third and three Brady tossed a screen to Edelman, who faked an end around and tossed a deep bomb to Lewis that fell just beyond the outstretched arms of the running back, landing incomplete.

But this game was not going to be won on trick plays.

Groans from Patriots fans could be heard from Foxborough to Houston. TVs switched off. Twitter again sounded Brady's death knell. This one was over. The fat lady was singing.

It was fourth down and the Patriots were at their own 46-yard line. There was nothing left to lose. Punting it away would have been delaying the inevitable by giving it back to Ryan for the chance to put the game completely out of reach.

So Belichick and McDaniels made the call to go for it. A do-or-die fourth down in the most difficult of circumstances.

Like other all-time sports legends such as Michael Jordan, Babe Ruth, and even Tom's hero, Joe Montana, Brady had displayed the ability to perform at his highest level when it mattered most. Not only that, but perhaps more so than any other athlete in history he seemed able to simplify each of these huge moments and treat it as if it were just any other play.

Out of the shotgun formation, he dropped back and fired a pass in the flat to Amendola, who scrambled seventeen yards for one of the biggest first downs in Patriots history. Brady had made the throw thousands of times before.

The drive was alive. A two-yard pass to Amendola. An incompletion to Edelman. And then, on third and eight, Brady bounced in the pocket, saw no one to pass to, and rambled up the middle of the field, tucking the ball and picking up fifteen yards for another big first down.

In spite of Blount's costly fumble in the first half, Belichick stuck with the veteran workhorse. The former Oregon Duck running back rambled off consecutive carries of four, nine, and finally a more modest two yards. Fans perhaps were wondering why the Patriots were running the ball when the clock was their primary enemy at this point in the game, but it was a strategic decision that paid dividends. What it did was show the Falcons they weren't going to just fling the ball all over the field and instead would continue to pound the ball. This decision helped to tire out the Falcons defense.

The final Blount run made it second and goal at the 5-yard line. New England then substituted out the big back for the more versatile pass catcher White. With the shifty running back aligned to Brady's left alongside him in the shotgun, White bolted on the snap of the ball into the flats and caught a quick dump-off pass. He immediately slammed on the brakes, sensing the tackler behind him was ripe to overrun the route. The would-be tackler whiffed, allowing White the space he needed to dive into the end zone.

"Good job, good job," McDaniels said to the young back as he came off the field.

"When White scored that first touchdown late in the third quarter, it was one of those bizarre football crowd reactions that is hard to forget," Matt Chatham, who was in attendance, later recalled. "It definitely wasn't an explosion of cheering and applause—more like a nervous release of pent-up energy. Patriots fans were well represented in the Super Bowl crowd that day, but they had barely anything to cheer about up to that point. I'm not so sure there were that many people letting themselves think 'maybe' at that point. They were more just glad to finally have something to express some happiness about."

There was only two minutes left in the third quarter when Gostkowski came out and missed the easy extra point as the ball clanged off the upright.

Stephen Gostkowski didn't have his best year kicking in 2016, but he still had one of the strongest legs in the league. He had missed just three extra points during the regular season but shanked one the previous week in the AFC championship game against the Steelers. This one was much worse.

Esquire writer Luke O'Neil, who covered the team all season and wrote a scathing piece three days before the Super Bowl about Brady's support of Trump and how it challenged his fandom, was at the game wavering between doing his job and rooting for the team he'd loved since he was a toddler. He spent the game searching for places to smoke cigarettes so he could calm his frayed nerves.

O'Neil had created a private Facebook group a few years earlier dedicated to jaded Patriots fans who were homegrown Boston friends of his. The group was originally named for former player Brandon Spikes and referenced an XXX-rated scandal the former linebacker was involved in. Over the seasons, the name changed, but the tone remained the same: this group lived and died with their team, even when their loyalty was challenged by the likes of Deflategate and the team principals' open support of President Trump.

During the first three quarters, the group chats wavered between apathy over the blowout and near happiness as some posted that the team got what it deserved because of its support for the divisive Trump. After the missed PAT, O'Neil posted, simply, "Over." The schizophrenic thread's mood shifted with each nail-biting play and was a microcosm of the national social media conversation as this game morphed from boring blowout to perhaps the greatest game ever played.

Patriots hopefuls did the math and determined that should the team even be able to mount a serious comeback, the missed extra point would almost certainly be catastrophic.

That gaffe aside, the defense had to stand up strong again.

Now trailing 28–9, New England tried a surprise onside kick, but it failed miserably. The kick went eleven yards and was recovered by the Falcons' LaRoy Reynolds, an undrafted free agent

special teamer out of the University of Virginia who was in his
first year with Atlanta. Causing additional pain, the Patriots were
called for illegally touching the kick before it went the required ten
yards, giving the Falcons an extra five yards.

It was yet another sign of hopelessness and frustration as Matt
Ryan and company took over at the New England 41-yard line
with an eighteen-point lead and just two minutes left in the third
quarter. It was easy to assume they would march down the field
and at the very least extend their lead with a field goal.

And it felt even more certain when Ryan took the snap on first
down and fired a laser to receiver Austin Hooper for a nine-yard
gain.

But the defense would have something to say about the outcome of this series.

"No more mistakes. No more 'my bad.' Everything gotta be
perfect," linebacker Dont'a Hightower growled.[4]

The dreadlocked defender had become the unquestioned
leader of the Patriots defense and was known for big plays in
big games. During the Super Bowl against the Seahawks, it was
Hightower's shoulder tackle on Marshawn Lynch that had led to
Malcolm Butler's game-winning interception on the next play.

It was time for Hightower and his unit to step up once more.

On second down with one yard to go for the Falcons, Patriots
defensive end Trey Flowers shot the gap and took down running
back Tevin Coleman for a one-yard loss. That negative gain was
compounded by a ten-yard holding penalty that pushed Atlanta
back to the 41-yard line and out of field goal range. New England
took the penalty, setting up another second-down situation. Atlanta would need to march eleven yards for a first down. On the
following play, Ryan's pass was incomplete, bringing up a critical
third down.

The NFL MVP took the shotgun snap and gazed downfield. He
had no idea that a freight train was heading his way. Patriots line-

backer Kyle Van Noy, a midseason pickup from the Detroit Lions, broke through the line and smothered Ryan, slamming him to the turf.

Like many New England players, Van Noy was another castoff who had struggled in Detroit before getting traded to New England for some late-round draft picks. Born in Reno, Nevada, Van Noy was an All-American linebacker at Brigham Young University who was taken in the second round by the Lions in 2014.

He spent two seasons in the Motor City. The first season, he was hampered by an abdominal injury but was a role player who saw action in eight games. In 2016, he started seven games and made thirty-nine tackles but was still considered to be a disappointment.

The new Detroit general manager in 2016 was Bob Quinn, a longtime Patriots scout who got his start in pro football under Belichick. When Quinn's former boss and mentor called looking for a linebacker, Van Noy was made available. Belichick got him and a seventh-round pick for a sixth-round pick. It was a steal, as Van Noy stepped right into the Patriots rotation in late October of 2016 and was a key part of the defense that helped the team win fourteen regular-season games. It was another classic Belichick move. He was the high priest of finding diamonds in the rough and giving struggling players new life.

The Van Noy sack now stands as one of the most crucial in Patriots history, but it didn't go as expected for the big defender. He had originally intended to go for the football and try to knock it out of Ryan's grip, but the quarterback protected it well so the defensive end crashed into Ryan with all of his 245 pounds.

The tackle on Ryan pushed the Falcons back to their 49-yard line and out of field goal range. Atlanta's players were exhausted now. New England had watched the Falcons punch themselves out while the Patriots players had plenty left in them when they needed it. The countless hours of sweat and grit running up that steep hill in Foxborough all season now made perfect sense.

"I think it was a huge factor in our ability to play longer and harder when it counted most," offensive line coach Dante Scarnecchia said later of the hill-running practice.[5]

The third quarter was coming to a close and the Patriots were down 28–9, but they were still showing a willingness to fight.

Robert Kraft looked at his son as they surveyed the situation once again.

"Do you think we'll win?" the elder Kraft asked.

Jonathan Kraft thought a beat and considered the score.

"It's possible, but not probable," he said.

Chapter Twenty-six

UNSUNG HEROES

FOURTH QUARTER

As Tom Brady got the ball to begin the fourth quarter of Super Bowl LI, the offense found itself pinned at its own 13-yard line with the clock reading 14:51. Statisticians declared the probability of the Patriots' mounting a comeback to win the game at less than 0.4 percent.

The drive starter for New England's offense came with one of Brady's best throws of the game, a sneaky fifteen-yard completion to rookie wide receiver Malcolm Mitchell. It was the first of several key catches down the stretch for the wiry, six-foot-one Mitchell.

A graduate of the University of Georgia who grew up in Valdosta, Georgia, Mitchell was a two-way player and was second on the Bulldogs in receptions and receiving yards his sophomore year. But a nasty ACL injury suffered against Clemson in the first game of his junior season put him out for the season. He won comeback player of the year the following season, and had a stellar senior campaign, leading the team in receptions with fifty-eight, for 867 yards. Despite being named an All-American, the injuries pushed him down the draft boards.

He was another typical Belichick "character guy" whom the coach had his eye on and was happy to snatch in the fourth round. Mitchell was a team captain, almost a prerequisite for a Belichick draft pick, and had an inspiring story of perseverance and overcoming obstacles. His mother, Pratina Woods, had survived breast cancer when he was young and struggled in a bad marriage.

When he was just ten years old, she moved Malcolm, his sister, and his brother from Tampa to Georgia to get away from her abusive husband. The family lived with her mother, with Malcolm relegated to an air mattress on the floor as his mom tried to find a job. She landed one at a call center and in 2005 got a homeowners' loan through a nonprofit after several previous rejections, and she and her children moved into a small single-family home in Valdosta.

It was a pivotal moment for the young family, and for Malcolm, as he drew life lessons from his mother's struggles and accomplishments in the face of tall odds. But injuries and family issues were not the only challenges Mitchell had to overcome. When he got to college, he could barely read. Yet again, instead of hiding from his problem, he faced it head-on. Malcolm joined a local women's book club. He was the only male and he was the youngest by twenty years. He patiently learned to read novels like *Gone Girl*, by Gillian Flynn, and *Me Before You*, by Jojo Moyes, and has attributed the book club to changing his life. His off-the-field accomplishments earned him the David Jacobs Award his senior year, an award given annually to the player who best portrays courage, spirit, character, and determination. He became so enamored of reading that he even published his own children's book in 2016 called *The Magician's Hat*, which promotes the joys of reading.

When Mitchell arrived at Patriots training camp that previous summer, he was ready to study and worked hard to grasp the team's complex, timing-based offense. Brady liked what he saw in Malcolm. The receiver had big hands, which allowed him to gain yards after the catch because he could grab the ball in stride and never slow down. A receiver's success with the Patriots was determined solely on his connection with Brady. If the quarterback trusted you, you could expect big numbers. If he didn't trust you, you were cast away to the wideout's version of Siberia.

Brady trusted Malcolm Mitchell. The rookie had a decent regular season, catching thirty-two passes for 401 yards and four touchdowns, and was a viable fourth or fifth option in the Patriots' loaded receiving corps.

That vote of confidence was exactly why Mitchell's number was now being called over and over by Brady in the fourth quarter. Their first connection of the game came on a deep comeback route where Mitchell only gained separation for the blink of an eye as he broke back to the sideline at the top of the route—the precise moment when the ball was delivered low and to the outside, where only Mitchell could possibly catch it. The killer combination of the timing of Tom's release, the velocity of the ball racing into the tiny window before the defender could turn, and the pinpoint placement of a ball that traveled over thirty-six yards in the air was awe-inspiring. Brady was playing to perfection and Mitchell was ready.

"There are some days in practice you don't catch a pass from Tom at all. That doesn't mean you don't try your best," Mitchell recalled. "So in the game, if one drive you don't get a ball, it really doesn't matter. You have another drive coming up and maybe you do get a ball. You just want to make sure you're prepared for whatever opportunity that comes from him. That's how I think about it."[1]

The next play was a seven-yard strike again to Mitchell that moved the ball to the Patriots' 35-yard line. Next, James White picked up the first down, bursting through the line for six yards. The offense was finally getting its groove back.

But was it too late?

On first and ten, Brady saw Edelman streaking and lofted a bomb. It was the kind of play that Tom loved to go for—a home run that would leave the defense reeling. But this one was a swing and a miss. It went incomplete.

On second down, Brady went back to the reliable rookie, hitting Mitchell for eighteen yards that took the offense into Atlanta territory.

"That was all repetition, practice—you've already run it enough with Tom," Mitchell said, reflecting on the drive. "We'd been doing that all year, honestly, so even though it's a big situation, it feels like a routine route."

The Patriots had moved the chains to Atlanta's 41-yard line and a first down. Number 12 kept pushing. For the first time in Super Bowl LI, the game was slowing down for the legendary quarterback. He could see the entire field. James White ran a simple short hitch route, turning back inside to Brady. The quarterback spotted defensive back Robert Alford's break on the play and fired the ball to the outside, beyond Alford's reach. The ball was surgically placed in a spot about two feet off the ground just millimeters away from Alford's extended arms but within White's grasp. Brady couldn't have located the football any better than he did.

The game clock now read 12:24.

After an incomplete pass to Amendola, Brady went back to his second tight-end option, Martellus Bennett, with a twenty-five-yard inside fade that once again featured coverage tighter than Lady Gaga's halftime outfit. But Brady dropped the tip of the ball into a small hole where only Bennett, with his six-foot-six frame, could reach it. The defender simply had no chance.

It was first and goal from the Atlanta 7-yard line. But the Falcons refused to make it easy.

Brady took the snap and was sacked by Grady Jarrett under the crushing weight of a powerful three-man rush. A six-foot, three-hundred-pound defensive end out of Clemson, Jarrett was only a second-year pro but was playing with reckless abandon, not unlike the way Michael Strahan, Justin Tuck, Jason Pierre-Paul, and the rest of the Giants defensive corps did in those infamous Giants Super Bowl victories in 2007 and 2011 that had left Tom battered and bruised.

Jarrett was in Brady's face all day, causing mayhem, disrupting his rhythm, and making life hell for the offensive line. The Falcons defense was not supposed to be the strength of this team, but their speed, power, discipline, and intensity had been more than the Patriots could handle up to now.

The protection on the sack was solid, but at a pivotal moment Jarrett just made a great move in a three-man rush, pursued Brady into a vulnerable area of the pocket, and took him down. It was Jarrett's second sack of the night, with the first coming on another big play—a third and eighteen at the Atlanta 48-yard line back in the first quarter when the game was scoreless.

While Jarrett made a fantastic play, it was also a subtle mistake by Brady. Had he stayed put or slid to his right, he would have seen the routes he was seeking had actually opened up. Number 12 is generally considered one of the best in the business at pocket movement and manipulation, but on that play he made an error that cost him a dangerously big hit and a missed opportunity at a touchdown throw. It could have been catastrophic, but they were still alive, albeit five yards back to the 12-yard line.

A pass to White only netted two yards, and on third down Jarrett made his monstrous presence felt again, this time beating right guard Shaq Mason on a tremendous one-on-one interior swim move, propelling himself over, around, and through the Patriots protection. Brady lost another five yards, pushing the Patriots back to the 15-yard line.

Gostkowski completed the drive with a 33-yard field goal that seemed like a hollow victory, even though it closed the gap to

28–12. With just 9:44 left on the clock, the deficit seemed insurmountable.

Before Brady could get the ball back, New England's defense needed a swift series to prevent the Falcons from draining too much of the game clock. Despite the fact that the Patriots had all three of their time-outs left, a couple of successful first downs by Matt Ryan and this Super Bowl would be over.

After a Gostkowski kickoff, Ryan took over at the Atlanta 27-yard line with just 9:40 on the clock. The Falcons called a run on first down and Tevin Coleman sprinted for a quick eight-yard gain before getting brought down by Trey Flowers and safety Logan Ryan.

The clock wound down to 8:31.

By this time, Falcons owner Arthur Blank, the billionaire founder of Home Depot, was on the sidelines. He came down when the score was 28–3 to celebrate with his team. The seventy-four-year-old owner had set the Internet afire following his team's win in the NFC title game when he danced with his players during their locker room celebration. He looked even more joyful when his team was up by twenty-five against the Patriots as he watched giddily on the field with his wife, Angela Macuga. Robert Kraft, who could see his fellow owner smiling on the Atlanta sidelines, respected Blank immensely and didn't think he was showboating with his sudden appearance on the field.

"That being said, he had reason to gloat," the Patriots owner said.

It's not something Kraft would have done, and he thought his friend was making a big mistake. Kraft had been in this situation many times before. Nothing was settled until the game clock hit zero. There was still too much time left before the confetti cannons fired.

Blank, wearing a black pinstriped suit and a red, white, and black tie with the Falcons logo, had purchased the team in 2002, and this was the team's first Super Bowl appearance under his ownership. Atlanta had been to the Super Bowl only once before, in the 1998 season, losing to John Elway, Terrell Davis, and the Broncos.

The Falcons owner was now poised to deliver the franchise's first Lombardi Trophy and the city's second-ever world championship following the Braves' 1995 World Series title.

But while Blank envisioned a victory parade, Robert Kraft continued to study the game clock.

There was still time.

Falcons head coach Dan Quinn and his offensive coordinator, Kyle Shanahan, son of three-time Super Bowl–winning coach Mike Shanahan, discussed what to call next. Shanahan was just twenty-seven when he was named receivers coach for the Houston Texans in 2006, making him the youngest position coach in the league at the time. He later coached for the Redskins and Browns before landing in Atlanta in 2015 with a reputation as an innovative offensive mind who was unafraid to throw the ball all over the field. With an explosive tandem like Ryan and Julio Jones, he had two of the league's best. He and Quinn had trusted their star quarterback all season to make big plays in important moments. They lived and died on Ryan's arm and Jones's freakish athleticism.

Quinn was also young at just forty-six and had coached on staffs under some of the league's best over his sixteen years in the NFL, including Steve Mariucci for the 49ers, Nick Saban with the Dolphins, and Jim Mora and Pete Carroll with the Seahawks. He was on the sidelines when Seattle lost to the Patriots in Super Bowl XLIX. He was determined not to let the game slip away from him as Pete Carroll had done.

Quinn and Shanahan reviewed their call sheets. They knew a big play could return the momentum to their favor and keep Brady on the sidelines for at least another couple of minutes.

On third down, with just one yard to go and only 8:31 left in the game, Matt Ryan lined up in the shotgun once again, signaling to the Patriots and the world that he was going to throw.

Hightower was lined up to the far left of the Patriots' defensive line. The ball was snapped and Ryan started to drop back as he looked downfield. Receiver Aldrick Robinson was wide open. So was Jones across the middle.

But Hightower blew past Falcons running back Devonta Freeman. The overmatched back whiffed on his attempt to block Hightower, and the speedy linebacker accelerated and smashed into Ryan cleanly just as the quarterback prepared to unload what surely would have been a first-down completion, if not a touchdown. Hightower swatted at the ball and it came loose.

The linebacker and Ryan crashed to the turf. So did the ball. Quick-thinking Patriots lineman Alan Branch was right there and pounced on it.

Brady looked up at the giant stadium screen.

"Our ball!" he shouted. He turned toward his offense and shouted it again: "Our ball!" It was the Falcons' first turnover of the postseason. Matt Ryan was stunned.

New England now had possession of the ball at the Atlanta 25-yard line.

"The back had me. He didn't see me 'cause I was outside," Hightower told teammate Rob Ninkovich on the sidelines after the big play. "So he looked, and went."[2]

Just as with his big play on the Seahawks' final series in Super Bowl XLIX, Dont'a Hightower's heroic play on Ryan had a seismic impact. The momentum had swung violently in favor of the Patriots for the first time in the game. Now it was the Falcons who were back on their collective heels. Owner Arthur Blank shook his head and looked down at the turf, his dark eyes vacant. The NFL MVP walked wearily toward the Falcons' bench. Just minutes before, Ryan was the odds-on favorite to earn Super Bowl most valuable player honors. Now he appeared lost as Tom Brady trotted back onto the field.

Chapter Twenty-seven

THE STEEP CLIMB

There was now just 8:24 left on the clock in the fourth quarter, and it was first and ten and the Falcons pass rush sent another message to number 12. If he was going to bring his team back, he would have to earn every yard. Dwight Freeney, a veteran defensive end who won a title with the Colts ten years earlier, had haunted Brady for years. The quarterback called him "a machine." Now the machine was lined up on the opposite side of the ball wearing a Falcons helmet. Brady placed his hands under center, took the snap, and dropped back, faking a handoff to Blount, who sprinted up the middle through the offensive line. As the quarterback continued stepping back, Freeney rushed the line, beating left tackle Nate Solder around the outside, and pounced on Brady's back as he attempted to step up in the pocket. Tom protected the ball but went down with a thud to the turf under the 270-pound crafty veteran. The play lost five yards, but perhaps more importantly, it shaved another forty seconds off the clock.

After the Freeney sack, the margin of error dropped to zero.

"Over," an exasperated Luke O'Neil posted again to his Facebook group.

"I stopped watching," one group member admitted. "Should I start watching again?"

The superstitious bunch of wisecracking Patriots fans leaped on their friend.

"No. Don't change anything you're doing," one posted.

Patriots fans across the country went through similar exercises. People who had switched seats at the beginning of the fourth quarter went back to their original seats. Fans who had taken off baseball caps put them back on. Nothing brings out hardcore OCD more than a nail-biting sports comeback attempt, especially when a Boston team is involved.

Brady pulled himself off the turf and walked angrily back to the huddle.

"Let's fuckin' go!" he shouted. He breathed deeply, trying to regain his composure. He called the next play and got under center. It was second down and a long fifteen yards ahead for a first down.

The ball was snapped at the Atlanta 30-yard line.

Brady spotted James White open in the flat and hit him with a strike for four yards. Falcons defender Keanu Neal brought the shifty back down as the clock ticked to 7:03.

It was third and eleven. A field goal was not an option. Number 12 got into the shotgun, flanked by White. Hogan, Amendola, Edelman, and Mitchell lined up in spread formation. Mitchell ran a fast comeback route and nearly broke cornerback C. J. Goodwin's ankles when he got to the first-down marker as he quickly cut back to face his quarterback. Goodwin tried to stay with the route but fell just as Brady's powerful spiral landed squarely in Mitchell's hands.

First down.

Next, number 12 hit Amendola for eight yards to bring the ball down to the Atlanta 6-yard line. There were just six minutes to play.

They were in the hurry-up offense and lined up quickly with

five receivers wide. As Brady so often does, he noticed something he liked before the snap and gestured to Amendola to widen his split to be farther away from the formation.

As the receiver adjusted his alignment slightly, he recognized that he would receive off and inside coverage from the defensive back across from him. Without the shift, there was ambiguity on the coverage, but the defensive back barely moved with Amendola's slight shift, alerting Brady that coverage on any out route was likely to be taken with inside leverage. In other words, the defensive back could never get to a perfectly delivered ball low and to the outside at this down and distance. This subtle recognition is what the experts like to call football IQ.

The play unfolded precisely as number 12 imagined it would. He took the snap out of the shotgun and Amendola ran an out route. Brady placed the ball precisely where it needed to be as Amendola cut at the goal line. It was a perfectly thrown ball that Amendola hauled in as he crossed the goal line.

Up in the luxury box, Gisele Bündchen jumped up and down clapping for her husband. Robert Kraft high-fived his friends. He wore a wide smile. Jonathan Kraft exhaled but still wasn't smiling.

It was at this moment that fans rooting for and against the Patriots realized they were witnessing something special, perhaps even historic.

Twitter erupted, with Brady's opponents heaping praise on the quarterback.

Lol. Because Tom Brady is Tom Brady, tweeted Ravens defensive back Brandon Boykin.

Too much time for #12, offered Minnesota Vikings offensive guard Jeremiah Sirles.

WOW. Never count Brady out. EVER, Dolphins defensive end Andre Branch added.

Number 12 immediately held up two fingers, signaling that they were going for the two-point conversion to bring the game—

amazingly—to a one-score affair. What had seemed impossible just minutes ago was now very real.

With the score 28–18 and just under six minutes left on the clock, Josh McDaniels looked at the two-point conversion options on his play sheet and called "Ride 34 Direct," a direct snap to a running back who runs through the middle of an offensive line using a zone blocking scheme. It was a play the Patriots had used thirteen years earlier against the Carolina Panthers in Super Bowl XXXVIII in the same exact stadium, then called Reliant Stadium.

Against the Falcons, the play made perfect sense once again. James White lined up to Brady's left while slot receivers were aligned on each side and Martellus Bennett was posted a step behind the offensive line. White went in motion and settled to Brady's left, slightly in front of his quarterback. Just as it happened in 2004, the snap came from center David Andrews and White snatched it out of midair. Brady leaped to simulate an errant snap and White plummeted into the end zone.

The score was now 28–20.

"Hey, this could get interesting," referee Carl Cheffers said to linesman Kent Payne.

"Now we've got a ball game, folks!" announcer Scott Zolak screamed on the Patriots radio broadcast.

The Patriots still needed a gargantuan defensive stand against the league's top-ranked offense.

With just 5:56 remaining, the Falcons were prepared for an on-side kick and lined up with their best ballhandlers—the "hands team"—within ten yards of the Patriots kick line. Belichick and special teams coach Joe Judge talked it over with defensive coordinator Matt Patricia and decided that the defense deserved a shot at winning this game, rather than risk giving Matt Ryan the ball back just a couple tosses away from field goal range.

Gostkowski booted the kickoff down to the Atlanta 3-yard line and the returner took it back seven yards. Matt Ryan and Julio Jones had one more shot to knock out Brady and the Patriots.

Now it was Falcons fans who were praying for a miracle. Owner Arthur Blank remained on the sidelines, exposed and stoic as he awaited the fate of his franchise.

Matt Ryan appeared to be returning to form now. On his first play from scrimmage, he hit Devonta Freeman with a short slant that the speedy back took for thirty-nine yards before he was hauled down by Patriots rookie linebacker Elandon Roberts.

The clock ticked down to 5:18.

The next play went nowhere, but on second down and nine yards to go, the Patriots' valiant comeback attempt seemed to be wiped out in one nightmarish play that hearkened back to their two soul-crushing Super Bowl losses to the Giants.

Ryan stood in the shotgun as Julio Jones jogged in motion behind the line and set up to his quarterback's right. Everyone in the stadium knew that a pass to Jones was likely. He'd been pretty quiet for most of the game, but his specialty was big plays and this was the time for one. His coaches and his quarterback felt he was due.

The Patriots got a good rush and the pocket started to collapse. But Ryan stepped up and started running toward the line of scrimmage. Just before he got to the line, he cocked back his million-dollar arm and let one fly downfield. Jones was double-covered. Cornerback Eric Rowe leaped and swatted at the ball but missed as it sailed just over his fingertips and into Jones's outstretched hands. Duron Harmon, who had rallied the troops at halftime, provided safety help over the top but couldn't get to Jones in time to disrupt the catch.

The Falcons' star receiver grabbed the ball tightly with both hands as he fell toward the sidelines. Somehow, he was able to touch both toes to the turf and hold on to the ball in bounds. It was as athletic a catch as you'd ever see and it was a bitter case of déjà vu for Tom, the Patriots, and their fans.

@juliojones_11 you ridiculous bruh, not human, alien...tweeted Saints receiver Mark Ingram.

Brady and most of the Patriots players on the bench watched the replay on the Jumbotron and waved their hands to signal no catch. Then they watched again and again. And reality set in that Jones had come down with the ball. Blount sat with his mouth agape, looking up at the replay.

Tom shook his head in frustration. The entire Patriots team was stunned when the play was confirmed by the referees.

"Hey, you a bad man!" Sanu told Jones back in the Falcons huddle.

"That's an amazing catch," Blount told James White on the sidelines, shaking his head. "Every Super Bowl we play in...there's always that one catch."

The Falcons were now on the Patriots' 22-yard line and the clock was down to 4:40. Three run plays and a field goal and Arthur Blank would have his Lombardi Trophy and his parade.

On first down, Freeman took the handoff and was stuck hard by McCourty for a loss of a yard.

"It was a blitz call," McCourty explained to the authors of this book. "This was one of our more aggressive run blitzes, but it was made for this situation. We hadn't run it yet in that game."[1]

The Falcons may have been trying to run out the clock, but this was a critical negative gain that showed them how difficult it was going to be to move the ball on the ground.

On second down and eleven, Ryan took the shotgun snap and started to get set in the pocket. Trey Flowers busted through the middle of the line and steamrolled center Alex Mack, badly beating him and sacking the league's MVP.

The Patriots used their first time-out as the sack pushed the Falcons back to the New England 35-yard line and right on the edge of field goal range. From there, it would have been a long fifty-two-yarder to seal the game.

On the next play, third and twenty-three, the Falcons again went back to the air, rather than opt for a short run to keep the clock moving and shorten up a field goal attempt as much as possible. Ryan hit receiver Mohamed Sanu for nine yards, but Chris Long drew a crucial holding call on lineman Jake Matthews. The penalty pushed Atlanta back ten more yards to the New England 45-yard line.

They were now well out of field goal range.

Atlanta was facing third down and thirty-three to go for a first down.

Matt Ryan took the shotgun snap and fired a short pass toward receiver Taylor Gabriel, who was blanketed by Malcolm Butler, and the pass fell incomplete.

"It was obviously a unique situation for us as a defense to be down so many points," McCourty recalled. "I thought Hightower said it best when Atlanta scored in the third quarter to make it 28–3: 'We gotta play perfect.' When he said it, I echoed it to the rest of the guys because it was just true.

"It was cool to see our defense…not really panic or think they had to do something they hadn't done before," he continued. "We knew we didn't have to get interceptions or a bunch of craziness that wasn't really likely. Guys just had to lock in and do their job perfectly and execute. That was really the difference—no need for a panic mentality, we didn't have to create a new defense to have a chance."

McCourty understood the hole the team had put itself in and also knew that the only way to climb back to the surface was to take each play one at a time.

"Bill [Belichick] always talks about 'If everybody does the right thing, it doesn't have to be perfect,'" he added. "But because of the situation we couldn't afford any mistakes. We had to play perfect to just give ourselves a chance to win. So that's what the second half defensively turned into for us."

His defense having done its job, on the sidelines Brady was poised and smiling. He even winked at a teammate. This was a position he had been in before. This was TB12 time.

Up in the owner's box, Robert Kraft checked his son's pulse once again.

"Well?" the elder Kraft asked. "What do you think?"

Jonathan didn't blink.

"Probable," he said.

The Falcons were forced to punt. It was a thirty-six-yard boot to Edelman that pinned the Patriots at their own 9-yard line. They needed to go ninety-one yards in three and a half minutes with two time-outs. And then they would need another two-point conversion—just to force overtime.

"Let's go score and win this thing, baby," Edelman told Tom as the two strapped up and headed back onto the field.

"Let's go win it all," Tom replied.

"For your mom. For your mom, bro," Edelman said.

Galynn Brady had found the game almost impossible to watch. When the Patriots fell behind 28–3, she told her husband that she wanted to go home. She was heartbroken for her son. But little did she know that her strength and courage had not only inspired her son but his teammates as well.

Hearing Edelman's words, Tom nodded sternly as he went back to work.

Chapter Twenty-eight

YOU GOTTA BELIEVE

A determining moment in history is sometimes unrecognizable as it is unfolding. Such was the case as Tom Brady opened the next drive with back-to-back incomplete passes to White and Chris Hogan, the first a result of pressure as number 12 was hit just as he released the ball. The Hogan play was a deep 50–50 fade pass that fell incomplete.

Just like that, the Patriots found themselves in yet another critical situation. It was third and ten and hope was diminishing.

But Brady went back to one of his favorite plays, a sixteen-yard deep out route that Hogan caught for a first down. It was an exceptional clothesline throw that would probably deserve more mention if the world hadn't seen him do it so many times before. Ryan sat helplessly and nervously on the sidelines, relegated now to spectator.

Next came an incompletion on first down to Edelman, followed by a gutsy, clutch Malcolm Mitchell catch down the sideline to Brady's left, where Mitchell actually stumbled to a knee and then recovered to make the improbable grab. It was a big-time play from a young player who was quickly earning Tom's trust.

"What a half he's had," Joe Buck exclaimed to the national audience watching on television. Still, Mitchell wished he'd stayed on his feet for that one.

"Well the route sucked," he later recalled of the play. "But just from practicing and understanding coverages and being in sync [with Tom], I knew from the snap that he'd probably come my way because I was singled up. That's really what made me hop up off the ground so fast. Because at that point I hadn't really seen the ball. I just felt like he was going to throw it my way anyhow."[1]

The ball was now at the New England 25-yard line with 2:34 left in the game. On first and ten, Tom dropped back and threw an ill-advised pass toward Edelman, who was swarmed by Falcons defenders. What transpired next is forever part of Boston sports lore, and while it doesn't completely erase the pain of the Tyree helmet catch and later the Mario Manningham miracle catch against the Patriots in Super Bowl XLVI, it makes them a bit easier to swallow for New England fans.

Atlanta's Robert Alford leaped to intercept the ball but instead volleyed it with two hands into the air. Edelman and Falcons defenders Ricardo Allen and Keanu Neal all leaped simultaneously toward the pigskin as it fell toward the turf. The ball bobbled before it rested on Allen's arm and then Alford's shoe. Somehow Edelman managed to grab it with his fingertips just a millimeter before it touched the turf.

"I got it. I caught it. I caught it," Edelman said as he leaped up from the field with the ball. "I caught it. I swear to god."

Alford and Edelman watched the replay together on the field.

"Look at it. I caught it," Edelman said confidently. He was right.

Joe Buck called the catch incredible, while Jonathan Kraft was convinced that the play was the result of skill and focus, not luck. Edelman later told *Tonight Show* host Jimmy Fallon just the opposite. He admitted the catch was about "seventy percent luck."

Lucky or not, Atlanta challenged the ruling on the field.

The play was agonizingly reviewed, but it was incontrovertible. It was not only a catch, but perhaps the greatest one in franchise history.

"I didn't run my best route on that play," Edelman admitted later. "I was always told not to quit on a play especially in the moment that we were in there. A tipped ball over the middle, it's gonna be one of those things where you gotta fight to the very end."

The Patriots had a first down at the Atlanta 41-yard line with just 2:03 on the game clock.

On the sidelines, Ernie Adams was already thinking ahead. "We're still in a go-for-two mode, if we score again, when we score again," he said.[2]

On the next play, number 12 made one of his finest throws of the game, launching a heat-seeking missile over the middle that hit Amendola in stride for a twenty-yard pickup to the Falcons 21.

After the two-minute warning, James White's number was called on three consecutive plays: uncovered out of the backfield for a thirteen-yard completion, a quick seam route catch from the backfield for another seven, and finally a one-yard touchdown plunge through the right side of the Patriots' offensive line.

Still, all the defensive stops, the circus catches, and the statistics would mean nothing unless the Patriots converted on the two-point conversion. In typical Patriots fashion, Belichick was fully prepared for this moment. Normally, the team will include a pair of two-point conversion plays on its game call sheet. But for some reason, Belichick asked his coaches to have an extra one or two ready to go. They pulled out one of the spares, which was de-signed for Danny Amendola, known as the best "trash runner and catcher" on the team. The receiver would have to make the catch in traffic and then turn toward daylight.

"And now the biggest two-point attempt in the history of the Patriots franchise," Buck announced.

Brady lined up under center with five wideouts. Amendola started in motion from Tom's left toward the center just as the ball was snapped. He got into an open space and Brady hit him with a quick screen. Amendola followed Edelman and Hogan, who were running in front of him as lead blockers. The Falcons defenders were pushed just far enough away to allow Amendola to get the ball over the goal line. He spun and fell backward into the end zone as the refs signaled the successful conversion. There was a flag on the play, but it was against Atlanta. Dwight Freeney had jumped offside before the snap in a bid to get to Brady. The play stood.

"Nice job, 'Dola!" Edelman shouted.

The blocking by Julian and Chris Hogan was also key on that play.

"You may not be getting the ball every play but you still gotta go out and do your job," Edelman explained. "Blocking is a huge part of the conversation in our receiver room at Gillette Stadium, and we take great pride in it, especially the moment we were in at the time. You gotta do everything you can to execute, and we did that."

"This is a tie game!" Joe Buck shouted on the national television broadcast.

"I cannot believe what I'm witnessing!" Scott Zolak shrieked on the radio.

"It was all about details," Mitchell recalled of the comeback. "I think we were at a critical point where everything needed to be executed right—maybe not perfectly—but almost perfect. So it really just came down to doing your assignment, doing your job with one hundred ten percent effort to just help the team any way you could."

There were just fifty-two seconds left on the game clock, and Matt Ryan and the Atlanta Falcons had one final shot to end the fourth-quarter nightmare for their fans while the Patriots defense would be called upon once more to shut them down.

The league MVP looked shell-shocked during the Falcons' final possession. If Tom Brady was dialed in, Matt Ryan was tuned out. He had no mental control over the game and was relying solely on muscle memory now.

Flustered, he mustered a mere sixteen yards on four plays before the Falcons punted away as time ran out in regulation.

The Super Bowl was headed to overtime for the first time in history.

Chapter Twenty-nine

REDEMPTION

OVERTIME

New England Patriots captains Matthew Slater, Dont'a Hightower, and Devin McCourty walked together toward the middle of the field for a coin toss that would determine who would get the ball first in the overtime period. Ryan walked out by himself. It was, again, a symbolic visual. The Falcons quarterback looked alone, abandoned as Atlanta's ship continued to take on water.

A win for either team might have been only just a coin toss away, but the result almost seemed predetermined.

Matthew Slater made the call.

"Heads," he said.

The referee flipped the coin. Heads it was.

Slater signaled that the Patriots wanted to receive the kickoff. Ryan didn't look surprised. He looked like someone who was accepting his fate.

Jonathan Kraft saw that his team had won the coin toss. He had come full circle and knew, like everyone watching, what was about to come when Tom Brady took the field in overtime.

"Game over," he said to his father.

"Let's go score and win this thing, baby," Edelman said to his quarterback.

"Let's go!" Brady shouted.

The Patriots started overtime with the ball on their own 25-yard line. The drive began with five straight completions as Brady spread the ball around to four different receivers.

Six yards to White. Fourteen to Amendola. Hogan for eighteen.

"We have a lot of targets and we have the best distributor of the football in the history of the game," Edelman said. "It's tough on a defense when we're all doing our job."[1]

For Brady, it was no longer a game. It was art, and he was painting the field with the brushstrokes reserved only for a master of the craft.

When asked by the authors of this book which throw stood out most, it was impossible for Brady to pick just one.

"There were so many plays in that game, when you look back on it, it was a game of inches," he recalled. "Julian's catch, Hogan's catch. Malcolm Mitchell's slipping on a route and getting up and catching it on a second and long. They all make a difference."

He then added, "I threw the ball to Danny on our sideline. I just kinda dropped it on over his shoulder. It was a twelve-, fourteen-yard gain. Danny and I have worked on that together so many times. I threw another to Jules [Julian Edelman] on this crossing route in overtime and really kind of threaded the needle. I threw one to Hoags [Hogan] on the left sideline where the DB tried to get his hand in. Those were all important. The [offense] was pretty incredible, blocking, throwing, run after the catch. It's a lot of hard work and it pays off."

The silent, vacant stares and dour faces that were on the

Patriots sideline after Julio Jones's miracle catch had shifted across the field to the Falcons players.

There was now intensity and restrained excitement on the Patriots' sideline.

Brady completed another short pass to White but it resulted in a three-yard loss. Unfazed, the quarterback went to the air again, hitting Edelman fifteen yards downfield. It was surgical. White then chewed up ten more yards on an end sweep. No Patriots fan had expected him to have such a big game, but there he was competing for the game's most valuable player honors.

Number 2 for Atlanta nervously stalked the sidelines wearing a baseball cap, arms folded, waiting for more bad news while New England's number 12 marched his team down to the Falcons' 15-yard line. Brady fired a pass to Bennett that was nearly caught, but defensive pass interference was called on linebacker De'Vondre Campbell.

The Patriots were awarded a first down and goal to go at the Falcons' 2-yard line.

NFL security had summoned the Krafts to come down to the field to prepare for the postgame ceremonies. But the father and son were staying put. Like the rest of New England, they were superstitious about these things. They weren't changing a thing until the game was officially over. They had never gone down onto the field early for any of the other six Super Bowls, win or lose, and they weren't starting now.

After an incomplete pass to Bennett, the call was made to give the ball to White on a toss play to the right side of the offense. He had already scored twice, in addition to the crucial two-point conversion, and racked up 110 yards receiving on a Super Bowl record fourteen catches. For this play, Belichick's decision to have extra two-point conversion plays available was prescient as the Patriots used another, just two yards from the goal line.

Dion Lewis had been the one practicing the play all week, but he was hurt in the third quarter and wasn't available, so the offense substituted White, who was having a career night.

"This is what you dream about," he would say. "You want to go out there and give it your best shot. You don't want to have any regrets."[2]

On the final play, White was ready for his moment of glory.

Brady took the snap with White five yards behind him in the backfield. Tom pitched the ball to the young back and he plowed forward until he was face-to-face with three Falcons defenders. "It was a toss play to me," he remembers. "We ran through it in practice a bunch of times. The offensive line did a good job, the receivers did a good job and opened up a lane. There was just one guy there. I just had to put my pads down and find a way to get the ball in the end zone."

He lowered his shoulders and bulled his way through Atlanta's wall, stretching the ball forward and across the goal line just before his knees hit the turf.

"A touchdown and a title for the Patriots!" cried Joe Buck.

"It's what you dream about as a kid, to have the ball in your hands to win a championship," White said. "I just wanted to find a way in there. It's just an unreal feeling."

Chaos erupted on the field as a blizzard of red, white, and blue confetti rained down on the players.

Tom Brady took a knee in a moment of silent contemplation. The 199th pick–turned GOAT–turned suspended NFL icon let his actions speak for himself, and those actions spoke volumes for the man's career and his character.

The confetti storm continued as the media rushed the field, but the referees still needed to review the play. They were checking to make sure White had scored and that his knee didn't hit the turf first.

"They gotta review it," Edelman said as he hugged his quarterback, looking up at the wide screen.

"Is he in?" Edelman asked as reporters swarmed around him.

"Get out of the way. Get off the field!" Edelman yelled. "Is he in?"

The receiver was still ready to play. He wouldn't celebrate until he found his coach.

"Is it over? Are they going to review it?" he asked Belichick in a panic.

"Yes. They reviewed it," the coach confirmed, smiling. They hugged.

Belichick then found White, the game's unlikely hero.

"Oh man, that's some football," the coach said, hugging his running back.

"Yes it was, Coach," White replied with joy.

"Way to go, buddy. I'm so proud of you."

Edelman and the coach embraced again.

"It's going to be one hell of a story," Edelman said.

"They counted us out twenty times," Belichick pointed out.

"You gotta believe, Coach."

"Hell yeah," Belichick said.

Julian's focus turned to his quarterback and what he'd endured to get to this moment.

"He had such a tough year, and it just shows you the kind of guy he is to be able to compartmentalize so many things, and when you see one of your leaders do that, it's a contagious kind of thing, and I was just extremely happy that my buddy played with the cards we was dealt and played them well."

The entire Patriots team had played its cards well to complete this historic comeback.

"Look what we just did," McCourty said, embracing Josh McDaniels and LeGarrette Blount.

Belichick and Brady spotted each other. The two men were the architects of the Patriots dynasty. Both were now unequivocally considered the best of all time.

Coach and quarterback wrapped their arms around each other for their fifth time as world champions.

"I love you!" Brady said into his coach's ear. "We did it!"

Blount, standing nearby, shouted to Tom: "You're the greatest, bro! The greatest!"

It was jubilation. This team—a collection of afterthoughts, players who were undrafted or cast away by other teams and now given an opportunity to believe in themselves and one another—followed behind their aging underdog quarterback, who seemed to be gaining strength and regaining his youth on every play as the Falcons defenders grew tired and ultimately helpless.

"I knew we still had a chance to come back and find a way back in the game. We have a great group of leaders, a great team," White said. "There was no pouting or anything. Guys were actually kind of fired up to get back out there. Duron Harmon was saying, 'This is going to be the greatest comeback. We're going to tell everyone about it.' Guys were just excited to get back out there and just have that one more half to make things right."

White got some comeuppance on his winning score as well. Back in the first half, when Tom threw the crushing pick-six interception, White was walking back to the sideline when a Falcon turned to him and screamed in his face.

"I was just like, 'You better be careful,'" the running back said.

That player was Ricardo Allen, the very player that White ran over as he scored the winning touchdown.

"He was actually the person I ran through to get in the end zone, so that was kind of fitting," White said.

Robert and Jonathan Kraft hugged, cheered, and high-fived. They walked out of the owner's box flanked by security and headed down toward the field. They passed DeMaurice Smith on their way down, and he stopped to congratulate them on the victory.

Smith and Heather McPhee were Brady's other teammates.

Smith had watched history unfold in Houston while McPhee viewed the game at home. As player representatives, it was their job to be impartial when it came to rooting for one team over another. But this was different. The lawyers had gone to war with Brady. They saw the fire that burned inside him up close. Now that fire was blazing once more, lighting up the entire sports world. Smith and McPhee felt a sweet satisfaction in the game's outcome.

Once the Krafts made their way down to the tunnel, they were surprisingly stopped by security and denied entry onto the field until stadium officials could clear them. It was an absurd moment but one Robert and Jonathan could only laugh about later.

Gisele Bündchen, meanwhile, sent out a celebratory Instagram video of herself flailing her long brown hair and going wild with the confetti raining from the NRG stadium roof. Her excitement was infectious. She then dropped her phone in the chaos. Eventually she, too, headed down to the field to greet her husband.

Later, she would recall that Falcons fans around her were "really intense" and telling her and other Patriots fans that the game was over and that her husband was all done. As the comeback developed, she called and texted her family. When she couldn't calm herself down, she began meditating. Right there, surrounded by 70,807 screaming fans.

"I started meditating 'cause it was the only thing that could calm me down.... It was very stressful," she later revealed on *The Tonight Show Starring Jimmy Fallon*.

She joked that she was partly responsible for the turning of the game's momentum in her husband's favor.

"I channeled some great energy and, really, I feel a little responsible," she said with a laugh. "I brought love and peace and clarity and calmness into the game. And it shifted after that."

Arriving at the staging on the field, Robert and Jonathan spotted Brady with his family by the stairs. At that moment,

Tom's mother approached her son with her delicate arms open and they embraced. She was fighting for her survival, and her strength had given him the will and determination to overcome the greatest challenges of his own life. He dedicated the Super Bowl win to her.

While Brady hugged Galynn, his son Benjamin jumped up into Robert Kraft's arms.

"We were an extended family dealing with difficult family moments," Kraft recalled. "We had the whole world against us. You have a finish like that. It's almost anticlimactic. It's so invigorating. You just stay in the moment and you don't have to say anything. It's just a look and an embrace."

Kraft's hug of Brady's son gave Tom a moment to turn to his wife for a soft kiss. Their daughter, Vivian, and Tom's eldest son, Jack, held their hands.

"We did it!" Brady shouted as he hugged and kissed Gisele.

"It's the best ever. It's the best ever," Tom Sr. told CBS Boston sports reporter Steve Burton on the field. "I'm speechless...it was so spectacular and so fun and so nerve-racking and so awesome."

"I think he did it for his mom. He did it for the Patriots. He did it for all of New England," the elder Brady said.

Galynn arrived on the field wearing a white and silver "Brady's Ladies" jersey and a blue bandana on her head.

"Oh my god. I'm overwhelmed," she told Burton. "I was just praying. All I did was pray. The whole game. I'm so happy."

Tom Sr. later reflected on the emotional impact of the game and his son's decision to dedicate the game to Galynn.

"That one jerks the tear ducts big-time," he told SI.com. "She lives and dies with every one of her children, whether it's in a football game or anything else. And she was very thankful. Very thankful, yeah, just very thankful that this played out.

"Winning five Super Bowls, and coming back from all the stuff that he was accused of, that was a very difficult thing for the whole family, to be impugned," he continued. "It just meant a lot because anybody who's watched him play football for 15 years, in cold weather, in heat, on the road or at home, knows what he's been.

"It just meant redemption, frankly. It meant redemption. It meant that all of these people that questioned his authenticity are non-entities from this point on."[3]

The twenty-two-inch, seven-pound sterling-silver Lombardi Trophy was brought down to the staging area, removed from its sheath, and handed to TV analyst Willie McGinest, a three-time champion with the Patriots. McGinest walked the NFL's most treasured prize slowly through the crowd of Patriots as they took turns touching it and kissing it.

"Kiss this motherfucking trophy," McGinest told them with glee.

Hightower, Long, Patricia. They all kissed the silver statue. McCourty kissed it, too. McGinest then handed it to NFL Hall of Famer Michael Strahan, a Houston native and daytime TV host. Trumpets played, the confetti continued to swirl.

Brady took the podium with Robert and Jonathan Kraft and Coach Belichick.

Roger Goodell was standing by.

The team owners hugged their coach as the commissioner made his way over toward them. Brady stood on the podium and pumped his fist in the air, beaming with an ear-to-ear billion-dollar smile. He had tears in his eyes and was close to being overcome by the emotion of the moment as Strahan jogged up the stairs and handed the trophy to the commissioner.

"That was awesome," Roger Goodell said to Tom Brady, grabbing the quarterback's right hand and shaking it for several seconds. "Congratulations. Great football game." It was a brief and awkward concession speech.

The commissioner was then handed the microphone.

The moment Patriots fans had dreamed about was finally here.

"What a wonderful football game tonight," Goodell attempted to say.

Patriots fans stood up at their seats in the stadium and formed a massive chorus.

They booed the commissioner like few had been booed on live national television before.

"That's what NFL football is all about," Goodell continued.

Brady and Belichick stood behind the commissioner, watching the reaction and smiling. The Krafts stood to Goodell's right, unable to hear him over the deafening boos.

The commissioner looked at Robert Kraft and said, "Robert, you know how hard these are to get.... What an unbelievable achievement for your organization."

His voice was barely audible over the negative fan chorus.

"Congratulations...we're so proud of you...take this trophy home to New England," he concluded and handed the trophy to Robert Kraft.

The team owner, who had been targeted by Goodell and his Park Avenue operatives during Spygate and Deflategate, took the glistening hardware, shook the commissioner's hand, and looked away. He hoisted the trophy high into the air and the crowd changed its tune from deafening boos to rapturous cheers.

"Two years ago, we won our fourth Super Bowl down in Arizona," Kraft began. "And I told our fans that was the sweetest one of all. But a lot has transpired during the last two years."

Again the crowd cheered wildly.

"And I don't think that needs any explanation. But I want to say to our fans, our brilliant coaching staff, our amazing players who are so spectacular, this is unequivocally the sweetest. And I'm proud to say, for the fifth time, that we are all Patriots. And tonight, for the fifth time, the Patriots are world champions."

Terry Bradshaw, the ceremony's grand marshal, introduced Belichick and told him that he was the greatest coach ever, but the coach gave his players all the credit.

"We got great players and they're tough and they compete. We were down 28 to 3 and they never looked back," the coach said.

Bradshaw then turned to Brady and handed him the trophy.

"I've got the greatest coach of all time, might as well have the greatest quarterback of all time, too," Bradshaw said. It was high praise coming from the Steelers quarterbacking legend who had won four Super Bowls of his own.

Tom took the trophy and hoisted it high in the air, pumping it.

"Let's go!" he shouted. "Let's go!"

His son Jack stood in front of him.

Bradshaw asked what turned the game around.

"There were a lot of plays that Coach talks about...you never know which play it's going to be in the Super Bowl. There were about thirty of them tonight. If any of them turned out different, the game could have turned out different," Brady said.

Bradshaw asked about his family, and noted that he had dedicated the game to his ailing mother.

"They're all happy. It's nice to have everyone here," Tom said. "It's going to be a great celebration tonight. Thank you to all our fans. Thank you to everyone back in Boston. You've been with us all year."

More cheers. Brady's voice was building toward a crescendo.

"We're bringing this sucker home!" the legend declared in a thunderous climax.

The tweets poured down like the confetti, hailing Tom as the GOAT—greatest of all time.

Five-time NBA champion Kobe Bryant of the Lakers tweeted, Five rings can't be deflated #Brady.

At five minutes before midnight—less than a couple of hours after the world had Tom Brady dead and buried—Boston mayor

Marty Walsh, a season-ticket holder and former union laborer from Dorchester, sent out a tweet announcing the victory parade that Tuesday.

Congratulations to the greatest team, the greatest coach and the greatest quarterback of all time for winning their fifth Super Bowl victory in Houston. The Patriots have made Boston and all of New England proud—fire up the duck boats!

Brady and his teammates were presented with their championship rings during another glamorous event at Robert Kraft's home in June 2017. The rings were encased in lockboxes, each with the same three-digit code: 8, 3 (as in 28–3, the score the Patriots had to fight back from), and 1 (the final ranking of the 2016 New England Patriots). The rings were also bedecked with 283 diamonds in a gesture that angered Falcons owner Arthur Blank. Robert Kraft also had another surprise. Number 12 would not be the only member of the Brady family to receive a Super Bowl ring. The team owner had an extra one made for Galynn Brady, who completed her cancer treatments two months after the Super Bowl and had served as the inspiration behind her son's magical season.

What really mattered was that, when the stakes were at their highest, Tom Brady had delivered again. In victory, there would be no more discussion about who the greatest quarterback in NFL history was. Number 12 had now separated himself by a quantum leap from his peers. German philosopher Friedrich Nietzsche once wrote, "One has to pay dearly for immortality; one has to die several times while one is still alive." Ultimate triumph could not be attained without desperate struggle. In his painful saga of Deflategate and the bitter war against Roger Goodell and the NFL, Tom Brady had overcome one of the greatest personal challenges in sports history. While the commissioner had grown into a minor historical figure, it was Brady who was now the immortal, his image carved into the rock of the virtual Mount Rushmore of sports legends alongside fellow eternal athletes Babe Ruth, Michael Jordan, and Muhammad Ali. But when asked by the authors of this book about his lasting memory of the greatest comeback in sports history, number 12 brought the conversation back to his teammates once again.

"Mental toughness is a big thing in football and we found ways to be mentally tough in the biggest moments when a lot of people wouldn't really survive under pressure," Tom Brady said proudly. "All of our teammates, our entire team did, and that's what really stands out."

Chapter Thirty

THE COACH IS KING

Nearly one year after Brady's ultimate redemption, he had yet another opportunity to add to his legacy. Number 12 was now forty years old, and he had just been named the 2017 NFL MVP, making him the oldest player to ever receive the honor. He was also about to step onto the field in Minneapolis, becoming the oldest quarterback ever to play in a Super Bowl, in a showdown against the Philadelphia Eagles led by backup quarterback Nick Foles.

Fans and analysts alike had expected Brady and the Patriots to be here competing for their sixth Lombardi Trophy, but the road to Super Bowl LII was as difficult as the year before, though for different reasons. The team was not grappling with an external challenge like the one posed by "Deflategate." Instead, the Patriots were threatened by disagreements and egotism involving the franchise's three pillars of success. Brady, Belichick, and Kraft had maintained a near-impenetrable fortress for eighteen years, but the foundation was showing signs of erosion. The public got its first glimpse of internal dysfunction at midseason, when Belichick surprised everyone by trading backup quarterback Jimmy Garoppolo to the San Francisco 49ers for a second-round draft pick. At the time, however, no one outside the organization knew that the coach had tried in vain to move Brady instead of Garoppolo.

Questions about the team's stability were amplified in December when it was reported that Brady's trainer and business partner Alex Guerrero had had his special privileges revoked. This decision was made by Belichick, further fanning the flames of a deteriorating relationship between the head coach and his star quarterback, and by extension the owner. Brady and Guerrero had recently opened a TB12 Sports Therapy Center at Patriot Place, the high-end retail complex just steps away from the stadium. The two partners had been funneling Tom's teammates over to the small facility for pliability- and resistance-focused training. Belichick viewed this as a slap in the face to the Patriots' training staff and looked to undermine Guerrero's influence on his players, most notably Gronkowski, who had gone down with back and ankle injuries, missing three games. When Belichick discovered that his All-World tight end had fallen under Guerrero's spell, the coach blasted him in front of the entire team for being a TB12 client. The normally fun-loving Gronk felt particularly persecuted by his head coach, but not to the degree that Brady was.

To flex his own muscles and tighten his control over his superstar quarterback, Belichick cut off Guerrero's access to the locker room, forbade him to fly on the team plane, and refused to allow the trainer on the field during games.

"He's not a member of the organization," Belichick said about Brady's training guru. "He works at TB12. I think we're all aware of that."[1]

There were other simmering issues behind the walls of Fortress Foxboro as well, including the controversial way the team distributed its seemingly annual lot of Super Bowl tickets. Every Super Bowl player is issued four tickets to the game, and they are premium seats. The Patriots, however, routinely took those premium tickets and sold them to ticket brokers, and instead issued lower-quality seats to players for their families and friends. Although this seems like a petty issue, it was a source of contention that players' loved ones were forced to watch the big game from the cheap seats while corporate fat cats soaked up the action close to the field while further lining the owner's pockets.

An exclamation point was added in early January 2019, when ESPN reporter Seth Wickersham wrote that the relationship between Belichick and Brady and Kraft was broken beyond repair. The reporter portrayed Brady as angry and irritable in his dealings with members of the coaching staff, most notably offensive coordinator Josh McDaniels, who felt the quarterback's wrath during a game against the Buffalo Bills when the coach pointed out to Brady that he had missed a wide-open receiver. "Fuck you!" Brady shouted back for the television cameras to see.

The quarterback later apologized for the outburst and insisted that it was merely an "in the heat of the moment" reaction on his part.

The one player according to the article who had not been welcome at the TB12 Therapy Center on the Gillette Stadium campus was Garoppolo, who Wickersham claimed had been locked out of the facility in part because Brady wanted his protégé gone. Number 12 did not fare well in the ESPN piece, and once again, the palace intrigue at 1 Patriot Place in Foxboro gave sports radio hosts plenty of raw meat to chew on. Armchair-quarterbacks-turned-amateur-sleuths collectively deduced that Belichick was the mastermind behind the hit piece on Brady.

The Patriots managed once again to block out the noise and responded by blowing out the Tennessee Titans in their first playoff game and then pulling out another dramatic come-from-behind win in the AFC championship game against the Jacksonville Jaguars, which was highlighted by another heroic performance by Tom Brady. In that game, he threw two fourth-quarter touchdowns, with an injured throwing hand that required twelve stitches to sew up a bloody gash he had suffered in practice from a collision with a Patriots fullback.

Still wounded by the deep bruise to his own ego in the Jimmy G. trade debacle, Bill Belichick could not help himself when asked about his quarterback's gutsy performance afterward in a postgame press conference.

"We're not talking about open-heart surgery," the coach scoffed.

The slight against his quarterback fit a disturbing pattern. Belichick was notorious in team meetings for hammering Brady over any small mistake he'd made in practice or during a game.

To Belichick, the constant needling of his legendary QB showed the rest of the players that no one, not even Brady, was above the team. For years, number 12 had acted like the consummate company guy. But Belichick's act had grown old, if it was an act at all.

For Brady the digs had become personal.

"He's out there and he's throwing a damn near perfect game, but Bill would always find one thing to scream at him about and embarrass him about," one key Brady insider told the authors. "It's never enough. Bill is looking for the one thing you do wrong. He understands it's shallow, but he knows that if you can tear Tom down, that sends a message to the team. But at a certain point, it gets tiring. He's won six Super Bowls, and he's being yelled at like he's a fourteen-year-old. You just get worn down."

The Brady insider also revealed that Belichick's emotionless leadership style had been wearing thin for Tom for many years and had finally hit a breaking point. Despite their strong professional relationship and two decades of success together, a true personal bond between the coach and quarterback had never formed.

Brady and Belichick had never once, in nearly twenty years, had a personal dinner together to celebrate their success. They never went out fishing together on Belichick's boat. They'd never decompressed and shared a couple of cold beers together to unwind from a season.

"You should have a private dinner and say, 'What a season! Cheers!'" the insider said. "That never happened with Tom. Never once."

The Brady insider said the relationship was always one like in the military, in which Belichick—who hails from a military family—was the general, and Tom was the private. Socializing between privates and generals is not allowed, and the same has always been the case inside Fortress Foxboro.

"It's very much rank and protocol—a private should never be able to walk into a general's office. The general gives the orders and the private follows them. And it doesn't matter if you've won six Super Bowls. You don't become a buddy at all," the insider said.

Yet Belichick would routinely text Jimmy Garoppolo with words of encouragement after 49ers games.

Following the win against Jacksonville, New England had secured its eighth trip to the Super Bowl in the Brady–Belichick era and the franchise would have another opportunity to rewrite NFL history. But by this time, Brady was already working on his own narrative. He had published a successful self-help book earlier in the season and was now in the process of releasing a series of short documentaries on Facebook Live called *Tom vs Time*, which peeled back the curtain on Brady's intense training practices and his relationship with his wife and children. This rare behind-the-scenes look at his personal life was devoured by fans, the first episode receiving 11 million views alone. But just like everything else in Brady's life, critical praise was peppered with controversy. Some called the series nothing more than a glorified infomercial for Brady-sponsored health and wellness products. He was even criticized for including his family in the campaign. One part-time talk show host at WEEI radio in Boston, desperate to make a name for himself, went too far with his manufactured outrage by calling Brady's five-year-old daughter, Vivian, "an annoying little pissant." The quarterback justifiably took offense at the remark and threatened to cancel his weekly in-season interviews with the station. The story dominated Super Bowl week but did not impact Brady's preparation for the game. He appeared relaxed and confident throughout the week, and the narrative soon switched back to the quarterback's pursuit of excellence at an advancing age.

Brady proved that he was ready for a fight against the Philadelphia Eagles in Super Bowl LII, producing the greatest championship performance of his storied career. The forty-year-old legend shredded the Eagles' defense, passing for a record 505 yards and three touchdowns without an interception.

Brady and his offense, which featured a productive Rob Gronkowski fresh off concussion protocol, scored thirty-three points against a tough Philadelphia defense and propelled the Patriots into the lead late in the fourth quarter.

But the New England defense struggled throughout the game without starting cornerback Malcolm Butler, whom Belichick had curiously benched before kickoff. Butler, the hero of Super Bowl XLIX against the Seahawks, was left weeping on the sideline in Super Bowl LII while the defense was getting gouged by backup Eagles QB Nick Foles, playing in place of injured starter Carson Wentz. Foles showed the poise of a young Brady and brought the Eagles screaming back with a late touchdown pass of his own (he'd also caught one on a trick play earlier in the game) and put the Super Bowl out of reach, denying Brady his sixth championship ring with the final score of 41–33.

For his efforts, Foles was awarded game MVP honors and Philadelphia earned its first Super Bowl win in franchise history.

As Eagle green confetti rained down on the field at U.S. Bank Stadium in Minneapolis, former Patriot and first-year Eagle Chris Long sought out his dejected former quarterback. "I just came right up to him and said, I never told you how much I appreciate you," Long said. "He's given so many people rings."[2]

After the Super Bowl, Brady went underground for several days as he processed the bitter loss.

Bill Belichick offered no reason to the media or to the players for Malcolm Butler's benching. The coach never even explained the shocking move to Butler himself.

While the coach seemed to enjoy pointing out Brady's perceived flaws, the quarterback had no power to question why Belichick had allowed a Super Bowl win to slip through his fingers. The coach was king.

Later, Brady began to lift the veil from his personal feelings during an interview with sports reporter Jim Gray. When asked if he felt appreciated by the team and the coach, Brady responded, "I plead the fifth. That's a tough question. I think everyone, in general, wants to be appreciated more at work in their professional life."

Gray also pressed Brady about the mysterious benching of Malcolm Butler.

"I don't make decisions," he replied. "I wish he would have played. But the coach decided not to play him, and we still had a chance to win. How do I look at that? No, I haven't gone [to Belichick] to discuss those things."[3]

Chapter Thirty-one

THE LAST HURRAH

In the 2018 off-season, many fans began to question the Patriots' coach. The adage "In Bill We Trust" no longer carried the same weight among the Foxboro faithful.

Brady was also losing confidence in Belichick. The relationship was so strained that Tom's father, Tom Brady Sr., had been telling friends for years that there was "zero" chance his son would finish his career with the Patriots.

Tom was also frustrated because he had left money on the table with every contract. He did that not to help the Kraft family or Belichick, but to help himself by ensuring the team could afford to put talent around him. But when his sacrifices weren't respected contract after contract, Brady had had enough.

"Bill believes this is a business and everyone is expendable," a Brady confidant said. "If Bill thought that cutting Tom was better for the team, he'd do it without thinking."

In the days leading up to the 2018 NFL draft, Belichick explored trading Gronkowski, Brady's top weapon, to the lowly Detroit Lions.

The Lions had reportedly agreed to give up their first- and

second-round picks to seal the deal. But the trade was nixed after the brash All-Pro blocked the move by threatening to retire. Unlike Belichick, Gronk could not see himself working with another quarterback.

"Tom Brady's my quarterback," Gronkowski explained. "[I] wasn't going anywhere without Brady."[1]

The quarterback felt the same way and expressed outrage to his closest confidants.

By now, though, Gronkowski's body was breaking down due to excruciating back pain and frightening concussions. Brady had admittedly suffered head trauma also, which put pressure on his marriage to supermodel Gisele Bündchen, who pleaded with him to give up the game.

To make matters worse, Julian Edelman was ensnared by scandal after getting caught using performance-enhancing drugs while recovering from a torn ACL and was suspended for the first four games of the 2018 regular season. This was a major embarrassment for the receiver, and it also cast doubts on the training methods of Alex Guerrero. Like Gronkowski, Edelman had become a devotee of the fitness guru, whom he called "Mr. Miyagi."

Under media scrutiny, Guerrero did his best to protect the TB12 brand.

"It's disappointing to hear today's news," the trainer told NBC Boston sports reporter and TB12 client Tom E. Curran when the Edelman story broke. "Here at our facility, we take a natural, holistic...and above all, legal approach to training. Anyone who would suggest otherwise is irresponsible and just plain wrong."[2]

With Edelman now locked out of the facility for the beginning of the 2018 season, Brady returned to the field with an aging Gronk in tow, and together they ground their way through another winning campaign as the quarterback threw twenty-nine touchdowns against an uncharacteristic eleven interceptions.

Belichick's team was an afterthought to NFL pundits for much of the year as they lost to backwater teams like Jacksonville and Detroit. The coach grunted and snorted his way through each postgame press conference, and fans' expectations began to wane, especially when they compared the Patriots' chances against their high-flying AFC rival Kansas City Chiefs and their wunderkind quarterback Patrick Mahomes.

In overtime of the AFC championship against the favored Chiefs at Arrowhead Stadium in late January 2019, Brady proved once again that raw talent was still no match for experience and clutch play when the game was on the line.

On the first play of the game-winning drive, Brady connected with receiver Chris Hogan for a quick first down.

A few plays later, during a crucial third and nine, Brady fought his way through a collapsing pocket and threw a strike to Julian Edelman downfield. Edelman would make another third-down catch to keep the drive alive. Brady also hit Gronk a few plays later for a big gain. For Patriots fans and haters alike, it was déjà vu. All knew at that moment that the Patriots would not be denied the end zone and the victory. Kansas City's defense was exhausted, but Brady's offense refused to let up. Near the goal line during a drive that lasted just over five minutes, Patriots running back Rex Burkhead punched it in for the winning score.

"Hello, Super Bowl!" television announcer Jim Nantz wailed. "New England is heading back for the third straight year!"

The classic win launched the Patriots to their ninth Super Bowl in the Brady–Belichick era.

While most of the media focused on Brady's preparations for Super Bowl LIII against the Los Angeles Rams, Belichick had a plan of his own. The coach had been blasted by hosts and callers on sports talk radio after the poor defensive effort against the Eagles the year before. Belichick was driven to leave no room for doubt about his defensive genius this time around.

Against Coach Sean McVay and the Rams, Bill Belichick let the dogs loose. The Patriots' defense was relentless for four quarters of play while Brady's offense stalled on every series.

Belichick was in the heads of both McVay and his young quarterback Jared Goff. The Patriots had an answer for everything the Rams threw their way. The LA offense was trapped in an escape room and could not think or play their way out.

"We kept telling each other at some point our offense is going to make a play," All-Pro safety Devin McCourty recalled. "We kind of thought it was going to bust wide open and they would score a ton of points. But it didn't turn that way.[3]

Each time Brady and the offense came off the field, McCourty gave his fellow captain encouragement.

"Come on, TB, it's gonna hit. It's gonna hit," McCourty told him.

"Keep doing what you're doing, D. We're gonna break through," Brady replied.

While the offense couldn't put the ball in the end zone, they put together some solid drives that gave the defense time to rest and go over game plans, which McCourty thought was key to the win.

"One of the things that was big in that game was our offense being able, even if it wasn't to score points, just have the ball, have some drives, even if they didn't equal points," McCourty said. "We were able to get to the bench and talk about some things that we thought the Rams might do. We had time to really go over that stuff and that allowed us to keep the foot on the gas defensively and not to let up."

With the clock winding down, Brady showed a glimpse of his old magic, connecting with Gronkowski on the biggest play of the game.

"Hey, Gronk, I need you," Edelman told the big tight end on the sidelines as they stepped onto the field in the fourth quarter.

On second and three with just 7:43 left, the score knotted at 3, Brady took the snap at the 31-yard line, stepped back three steps, and floated a perfect pass toward Gronkowski, who was in the middle of triple coverage. The tight end found one more moment of magic, stretched out and hauled in the twenty-nine-yard bomb to put the Pats on the 2-yard line and in position to win it all.

"I knew the ball was coming to me," said Gronkowski. "I have a seam route and boom, I made that motion right at the right time where only I could go out there and make a play and Tom put the ball up right where I could do it.... It was one of the biggest plays of my career."[4]

Moments later, rookie running back Sony Michel pounded his way into the end zone for the go-ahead score.

The Rams got the ball back, and that's when Pats safety Duron Harmon—the locker room hero from the Falcons Super Bowl—stepped into the spotlight.

Although he'd seldom been used in the game up to this point, he was tasked with covering Rams receiver Brandin Cooks, another ex-Patriot. As he lined up opposite Cooks, Harmon could hear the voice of Belichick in his head.

"Bill always tells us, 'The journey's going to be long, it's going to be tough,'" Harmon told the authors. "'It's going to be hard and sometimes you're going to feel like you just want to stop, but that's when you've got to push through and push even harder.'"[5]

Harmon pushed harder. With 4:28 remaining, Goff took the snap at the New England 27-yard line. He threw a perfect pass to Cooks, who was hampered by Harmon and cornerback Stephon Gilmore. As Cooks tried to haul in the bomb at the goal line for the game-tying score, Harmon leveled the receiver, knocking the ball loose.

On the next play, Harmon and McCourty blitzed Goff, forcing him to make an ill-timed throw which was easily intercepted by Gilmore to secure the win—and an incredible sixth ring for Brady and Belichick, and a third for several players in the second half of the Patriots' twenty-year dynasty, including Harmon.

"It was magical. It was surreal," said Harmon. "It was a feeling of just, of awe, because everybody sees the Super Bowl, but not everybody sees the work you put in, the sacrifices you make as a team, the sacrifices Bill had to make as a coach, the time, the effort, the long days, the long nights."

Like Harmon, Devin McCourty also credits the team's greatness to Bill Belichick.

"He doesn't think he's this supernatural person," explained McCourty. "But you see his preparation, his work ethic, he's making sure he goes over everything. If you ever walk into his office to talk to him, he's in the back watching film. He's always doing something to get better. We're on a plane on a Saturday, he's watching film. He's always trying to get ahead. He's always thinking of things. He's always trying to reinvent himself."

Coming off the stellar defensive effort against Los Angeles, the Patriots' head coach was ready to reinvent the team's personality and makeup for the next championship run. He would load up on defense. But to do that, he'd have to take resources away from Brady and the offense.

The quarterback could see the writing on the wall, especially after Belichick made little effort to replenish his weapons in free agency.

Gronkowski was now retired. He had suffered a near-crippling thigh bruise from a devastating hit early in the Super Bowl against Los Angeles. He could barely walk after the game, and while his teammates were celebrating their victory together later that night, Gronkowski was laid up in bed, crying because the pain was so intense and because he knew it was his last game for the Patriots. The All-Pro, whom many consider the greatest ever to play the tight end position, would be forced to undergo several procedures to stop significant internal bleeding caused by the injury.

Brady's other favorite target, slot receiver Julian Edelman, was limping back from injury after being voted Super Bowl MVP.

Belichick now wanted the game's greatest quarterback to return to the days at the beginning of his career when he had been asked to manage the game while the defense led them to victory.

This was not how Tom Brady wanted to finish his career. There were still records to be broken at the quarterback position and he wanted them all. That summer, Belichick dented the quarterback's ego once more by shortchanging him with a paltry $23 million contract, making him the sixth-highest-paid QB in the NFL. The coach was also unwilling to extend the contract, while Brady had long expressed a desire to play until he was forty-five years old.

At that moment, the Patriots legend and NFL GOAT knew that his time in Foxboro was just about over. Brady's agent Don Yee demanded that the contract "automatically void" on the last day of the 2019 league year in March 2020 and that he not be franchised but be allowed to test free agency for the first time in his storied career.

Brady had expected this kind of treatment from Belichick, but not from owner Bob Kraft. The quarterback had helped Kraft in trying to repair his image after it was all but destroyed when, in February 2019, he got caught allegedly paying for sex in a human trafficking sting operation at a massage parlor in Florida.

While Kraft became a national embarrassment and the subject of constant ridicule on sports radio and late-night TV, Brady showed his support for the embattled billionaire by offering him a very public hug when Kraft's private plane touched down at Boston's Logan Airport during his first trip home after the scandal broke.

But that loyalty was ancient history now, and Kraft had a business decision to make. Which man would be of more value to the Patriots franchise over the next five to ten years? Brady was now two years older than he'd been during the turmoil over Jimmy G. In this case of Sophie's Choice, Kraft would have to stick with Belichick.

Chapter Thirty-two

BITTER ENDS
AND NEW BEGINNINGS

As the 2019 NFL season kicked off, many experts from around the league could read the tea leaves regarding Tom Brady's future in Foxboro.

"It just felt so obvious to everyone in the business nationally—coaches, players, agents, front office guys—that it would have been stunning if he had stayed," former *Monday Night Football* host Joe Tessitore told the authors.[1] "In the circles that I'm in, by the time it got to covering the Pro Bowl and the Super Bowl, through February [2020], that did not come as a shock at all that he was leaving. It was more: Where will he land? It was more shocking that he landed in Tampa. The fact that it was Tampa was the shock. It was not stunning that he left. Leaving, to me, was expected."

Tessitore has spent a good deal of time with Brady and Belichick prepping for broadcasts as well as at other league events, and occasionally in social settings.

"These are very distinct and opposing personalities," he said. "But it's great the way everyone is wired there. And it's a proven track record. Great personalities win."

Early on in 2019, the Patriots did just that. Belichick's defense dominated their opponents right out of the gate, leaving many NFL insiders to wonder if they were watching the greatest defense ever assembled.

At the same time, Brady wondered if his sputtering offense would ever get going. There was a sliver of hope when All-Pro wide receiver Antonio Brown was cut from the silver and black Oakland Raiders and joined the Patriots. Brady was so excited that he invited Brown to live with him at his mansion in Chestnut Hill, Massachusetts. The experiment lasted only eleven days and just one game, however, because Brown, a player with a long history of bad behavior and emotional problems, was alleged to have sexually assaulted his former trainer and had sent intimidating messages to another accuser and her children.

Even so, Belichick's Patriots continued to win on defense as the unit came up with its own nickname, "The Boogeymen." But for Tom Brady, the season had become a nightmare filled with visions of dropped passes by inexperienced receivers and a collapsing offensive line.

The coach had even pulled his quarterback out of the offensive game preparation.

"I'm just an employee here like everyone else," a frustrated Brady told reporter Jim Gray.

When he sat down with NBC *Sunday Night Football* analyst Chris Collinsworth before the team's first loss of the season, to Baltimore, the quarterback legend sounded even more morose.

"I have to be the most miserable 8–0 quarterback in the history of the league," Brady told Collinsworth.[2]

Patriots fans were overwrought with worry, especially after news broke that Brady and his trainer Alex Guerrero had both put their houses up for sale.

But Brady wouldn't mail it in, even if it was going to be his last season with the Patriots.

"From a teammate standpoint, if I knew one thing, I knew Tom Brady was going to be all in every day," Duron Harmon observed. "Whether it was working out, whether it was OTAs, training camp, week eight, Thursday practice, Friday practice. He was going to be the same. He was going to be the most prepared out there. He was going to have his body ready and he was going to do everything he could to lead our team to victory."

But Harmon's unit started to break down over time and the vaunted "Boogeymen" turned out to be a pack of paper tigers in disguise. The celebrated defense began to give up big plays to subpar teams, and soon the Patriots relinquished home field advantage in the playoffs.

After the stunning Titans loss eliminating New England from the postseason and an opportunity to defend their championship, the Patriots' locker room was stoic. Players were down about the abrupt and unceremonious end to the season, but they had even more on their minds: the looming departures to free agency of several core players from the team's most recent five-year Super Bowl run, led by Tom Brady, the face of the organization and the league.

"It was different—just because, obviously, with Tom as a free agent," Patriots team captain Devin McCourty told the authors. "We had a good stretch with a good group of guys that played together for a long time, and a good chunk of those guys were free agents....Everyone left [Gillette Stadium] with uncertainty and the unknown that was a little different than years past. You just felt like a lot could be different."

After the game, Belichick told his players, including Brady, that now was not the time to discuss the team's future.

"Everybody's season once you get in the playoffs ends one of two ways: you win the last game and you're ecstatic, or it's kind of like a crash landing, where everything is high and it just comes to a screeching end," the coach stoically told his team. The next day, the team gathered at Gillette for the annual exit meeting. It was a somber affair, as many in the group had won multiple Super Bowls with Brady at the helm and were now looking at an unclear future without the security of their legendary quarterback.

"There's not much to talk about, guys," Belichick told the team. "The future is coming up, next season, free agents, all that. That time will come.

"This year didn't end the way we wanted," he added. "Guys, hold your heads up. You should be proud of the progress and what we did as a team."

Brady cleaned out his locker, leaving no trace of his past twenty years behind. Just like that—he was gone.

Patriots fans who'd had a hard time swallowing the bitter pill of an uncharacteristically early exit from the playoffs now turned all their collective focus on Tom Brady's future.

The TB12 watch was on.

Less than a week after the defeat by Tennessee, the importance of wins and losses on the football field was put into proper perspective with the tragic helicopter crash that claimed the lives of Los Angeles Lakers legend Kobe Bryant, his teenage daughter Gianna, and seven others as they were on their way to a youth basketball game in Bryant's luxury chopper. Their deaths shocked the nation and hit home within the Patriots organization. Bill Belichick had invited Bryant to address the team in May 2018. The retired superstar talked about his family and stressed the importance of leading a balanced life.

Brady was deeply affected by the tragedy and shared his feelings in an essay that he posted on social media.

"Who is going to carry the load and be the superhero that he was?" Brady wrote. "The answer is simple to me, ALL OF US. Decide to make the change in yourself. . . . SEIZE THE DAY."

It was a rallying cry for everyone to be like Kobe. But it was also motivation for Brady himself to gain greater control over his own life and his future.

The quarterback and his head coach shared the same field a few weeks later at Super Bowl LIV in Miami when both were introduced before the game as members of the NFL 100 All-Time Team. When the television camera zoomed in on Belichick, the coach grinned and flashed three of his eight Super Bowl rings, which included two he had won as an assistant coach with the New York Giants.

The evening was doubly satisfying for Belichick as his former prize pupil Jimmy Garoppolo led the charge for the 49ers against the Chiefs. The Patriots coach looked prescient at the start of the game as Jimmy G. appeared to be handling the bright lights on the game's biggest stage like a Super Bowl veteran. His former coach flashed another rare smile while watching the game from a luxury box with his longtime girlfriend, Linda Holliday. Belichick was seeing what he had wanted his own team to be under Jimmy G., one that was efficient and methodical.

However, the chasm between Garoppolo and Brady revealed itself later in the game when the 49ers quarterback began to crumble under the pressure. With the game on the line, Jimmy G. threw two interceptions and suffered a costly nine-yard sack. While Brady had always performed with ice water in his veins, his former understudy flopped in the big moment and virtually handed the Lombardi Trophy to Kansas City and Patrick Mahomes.

As weeks went by, speculation continued to grow that Tom would not return to the Patriots. There were even reports that Brady had purchased a home in Greenwich, Connecticut.

"Could he be headed to the New York Giants?" asked some sports radio hosts.

NFL insiders believed that Brady would head west to Los Angeles or Las Vegas, where he could continue to build TB12, his health and wellness brand.

Fans around New England began playing their own version of *Clue* and *Where's Waldo?*

Brady was spotted with Mark Davis, the owner of the Raiders, at a UFC fight in Vegas before the Super Bowl.

There was also talk that he would be wearing lightning bolts on his helmet with the Chargers, who had just dropped longtime quarterback Philip Rivers. The Chargers were preparing for the opening of their much-anticipated new L.A. stadium, and what better way to fill the gleaming new seats than signing Tom Brady?

Virtually no one was talking about the lowly Tampa Bay Buccaneers.

Speculation soon shifted to Tennessee, where Brady's friend and former teammate Mike Vrabel was head coach. Vrabel had built a solid team in Nashville and the team appeared to be one superstar quarterback away from competing for a Super Bowl title.

Brady then added fuel to the fire by appearing at a college basketball game in Syracuse with Edelman. They were caught on social media FaceTiming with Vrabel while sitting courtside. Was this an indication that Brady would sign with the Titans?

Edelman smiled for the video cameras and announced that Brady was coming back to New England. Brady looked uncomfortable. In fact, he looked pissed off.

The video sent a mixed message to fans in Patriots Nation. Speculation continued to swirl.

Meanwhile, Patriots owner Robert Kraft leaked the news that there was a $35 million offer on the table for the legend to return. The team appeared to be painting Brady into a corner.

Brady and Belichick began to negotiate by phone, but the coach refused to budge on terms. He offered the quarterback only a one-year deal.

It was take-it-or-leave-it time.

Belichick and Kraft both believed that Brady would back down and take what was on the table.

But the Buccaneers had other ideas. Coach Bruce Arians was

ready to move on from the talented but troubled Jameis Winston and go all in on Tom Brady.

But would the GOAT reciprocate? The Bucs had a uniquely special way into the discussion. Tampa's director of player personnel, John Spytek, had been Tom's teammate for one season at the University of Michigan. Also, another former U-Michigan teammate of Brady and Spytek, Larry Foote, was the Bucs' linebackers coach. The Bucs' pursuit of Brady reportedly had its own code name: "Operation Shoeless Joe," as in *Field of Dreams.*

Nearly the minute Tom became a free agent, Bruce Arians placed the call.

The coach promised the quarterback a chance for continued success and the opportunity to have some fun while they were at it.

The word "fun" had been removed from Brady's mental dictionary over the past few years in New England, where he had felt stifled, detached, and disrespected by the organization.

Inside his barren home in Chestnut Hill, Brady took out a notepad and made a list of all the teams that had expressed interest in him. When he was finished, he found that the Bucs checked all his boxes. The most important thing for Brady was to remain on the East Coast and close to his twelve-year-old son, Jack, who lived with his mother, actress Bridget Moynahan, in New York City.

He then called Bob Kraft at home and asked if he could visit. It was 9:30 at night when Brady's truck appeared in the owner's long driveway.

It was time for Tom to show that he was in control of his own destiny.

He remembered how his owner and coach had turned their backs on him during Deflategate. He remembered the sting he felt each time Belichick tried to embarrass him in team meetings.

Brady was the greatest quarterback in NFL history and was treated like a football god everywhere but inside the corporate offices of Gillette Stadium.

Brady's insecure self-image, the one he'd carried throughout his career, had to be shattered on this night once and for all.

Kraft offered a fatherly smile and was genuinely happy to see him. The owner believed that Brady was there to agree to terms on a new contract.

Instead, the football legend announced that he was ready for a divorce. Brady wept as he thanked Kraft for the opportunity to realize his dreams. Despite all the turmoil, the quarterback loved Kraft.

The owner was stunned. Kraft had planned for this moment, but the news was almost too difficult to bear. In an interview with Peter King, the owner had recently spoken about his adoration for Brady. "I love the young man like he's part of my family. Blood family.... [M]y hope and prayer is [that] number one, he plays for the Patriots. Or number two, he retires."[3]

But Brady had no desire to retire. While at Kraft's home, the quarterback called his coach. The men kept the conversation civil as Brady told his coach he was leaving Foxboro.

The news came as a surprise. Belichick also believed that Brady would capitulate to his lowball offer. In fact, the coach had no backup plan at the quarterback position. Brady's likely successor was a former fourth-round pick out of Auburn named Jarrett Stidham, whose only regular season experience lasted just one series, four plays in all, and ended when he threw a pick six in a rout of the Jets in 2019. Few believed that he was ready to take the reins of the Patriots' offense.

The Machiavellian Belichick had just been outmaneuvered by his player turned rival.

After the meeting, Brady walked out of Kraft's front door feeling a sense of freedom and career control he'd never had in Foxboro.

The next day, Brady announced on social media that he was leaving New England. It was Saint Patrick's week in Boston, and all the Irish pubs were closed due to the coronavirus pandemic. A depression had begun spreading through cities and towns across the Northeast—and now this.

Fans were outraged—not at Brady but at the Patriots ownership. Children wearing their #12 jerseys cried in their parents' arms. A generation of fans, who had known only winning through Tom Brady, was now in mourning. ESPN ran Brady coverage nonstop, and sports-radio shows weighed in like they were discussing President Trump's impeachment trial.

Feeling the heat, both Kraft and Belichick released joint statements praising the man they'd just let walk out the door after two decades of exemplary service.

"How do I possibly sum up the depth of my gratitude to Tom Brady for what he's given us these past 20 years, or the sadness I feel knowing it's ending? I love Tom like a son and I always will. He has brought so much happiness to me personally and to all of our fans," Kraft said. "I had hoped this day would never come, but rather that Tom would end his remarkable career in a Patriots uniform after yet another Super Bowl championship. Unfortunately, the two sides were unable to reach an agreement to allow that dream to become a reality. While sad today, the overwhelming feeling I have is appreciation for his countless contributions to our team and community."[4]

Belichick offered equally flowery praise. "Tom and I will always have a great relationship built on love, admiration, respect and appreciation. Tom's success as a player and his character as a person are exceptional. Nothing about the end of Tom's Patriots career changes how unfathomably spectacular it was. With his relentless competitiveness and longevity, he earned everyone's adoration and will be celebrated forever. It has been a privilege to coach Tom Brady for 20 years."

Unfortunately for all involved, the coach never shared those sentiments with Brady while he was still on the team. The coach's words were seen as hollow and too little, too late.

Devin McCourty learned about his longtime teammate's defection from the Patriots on Twitter. He was sad, but not surprised, as he'd seen many great teammates leave suddenly over the years.

"He's one of the greatest guys to ever play the game of football," said McCourty, who was reminded of the time when offensive lineman Logan Mankins got traded by the Patriots in 2014. "Logan Mankins was a guy that, when I got there [in 2010]…everyone was like, [they] said he's the definition of a Patriot. He's played with a torn ACL before. He's never missed a practice. And then he's gone, and I remember being like, 'Wow, that's so weird.' So now you just take it up a notch. Tom Brady is the greatest to ever play. But now he'll be playing for someone else. For us as players, it's gotta be one of those things: it is what it is."

Duron Harmon spoke to Brady after he announced on social media that he was leaving and wished his longtime teammate well. "I just wanted to wish him luck and let him know how much I'm going to miss him as a teammate, miss being around him, miss learning the lessons from him," Harmon said. "He was the perfect example of the true professional. How he went about his business, not only as a football player, but as a husband, a father, a businessman. And how much he gave to the game. You see how people perceived him coming out of the draft in the sixth round and how he just kept working and how he gained more and more respect."

Soon Harmon himself would join the ranks of the ex-Patriots as he was shipped off to the Detroit Lions in a salary-cap savings move by Belichick.

But where would Tom Brady go next? Bucs coach Bruce Arians knew.

The sleepy football town that is Tampa Bay had been lulled into a state of apathy during recent losing seasons, and the coach wanted to shake up the city in a seismic way.

The story quickly broke that Brady was headed to the Buccaneers after accepting a two-year, fully guaranteed $50 million contract, and within hours, Florida fans were ordering Brady–Tampa Bay jerseys at such a breakneck pace that sales almost broke the Internet.

"Excited, humble and hungry," Brady wrote on Instagram. Normally a signing of this magnitude would come with a big news conference, no doubt carried live by ESPN and television news stations in Tampa and Boston. But America and much of the world was in the throes of the coronavirus pandemic, so instead, Brady had his son Jack snap a photo of his dad signing the multipage contract in the kitchen of their home. "I have always believed that well done is better than well said, so I'm not gonna say much more—I'm just gonna get to work!"

Back in Foxboro, Bill Belichick was still smarting from Brady's rebuff, but he also got what he had long wanted—the opportunity to win his way.

A month after the biggest breakup since the Beatles, Tom Brady emerged ready to take advantage of his new found freedom. Appearing for the first time on *The Howard Stern Show,* the greatest of all time expressed that he still had one more mountain to climb and that was beating Belichick in the Super Bowl. He also revealed for the first time that he had tried marijuana in high school and admitted to some earlier tensions in his marriage to Gisele that he'd had to correct. For fans, this was a new Tom Brady. He was less guarded and more real than he'd ever appeared before.

Meanwhile, it was the same old, same old from his former coach, who was grilled by the media about Brady's startling exodus.

"It would be of course impossible to sum up everything that Tom did in twenty years into a comment, then or now," Belichick said in a conference call with reporters. "But I meant everything I have said about him, and I'm sure we'll be talking about him for years and decades to come. For right now, we're moving forward."

And that was the final word the coach would say to the press about his quarterback of twenty years, a player who led the team to nine Super Bowls and six rings.

Brady was also moving forward and he had one more major card to play. The quarterback was looking to reunite with his retired friend and former teammate Rob Gronkowski.

Gronk had been out of football for over a year dabbling in everything from big beach parties to color commentary for Fox Sports and even professional wrestling in the WWE. But he was still young at thirty years old, and his success with Brady was otherworldly. Together they had won three Super Bowls and had broken just about every Patriots passing record, connecting for ninety touchdowns over nine seasons. Gronkowski also had his own payback in store for Belichick, who had tried to trade him years before.

The Patriots were in an uncommonly difficult position because of the salary cap and had no wiggle room to pay Gronkowski his $10 million salary for 2020 if they were to add him to the active roster. The future Hall of Fame tight end was able to call his own shots and force the coach's hand to trade him to Tampa for two low draft picks. Savvy NFL insiders saw the deal for what it was— a kick in the teeth to Belichick—while media apologists for the coaching legend marveled at his ability to squeeze out compensation for a player that was retired. What cannot be lost on anyone was the fact that Gronk could have returned to the Patriots if Brady were still with the team. The one thing holding him back was his disdain for playing under Belichick.

When the NFL draft arrived in late April 2020, Pats fans expected their coach to invest in a quarterback, but Belichick once again did things his way. He predictably traded out of the first round and in the second round grabbed safety Kyle Dugger out of Division 2 Lenoir-Rhyne University—the first player drafted from the tiny North Carolina campus in twenty years. It was the most Belichickian draft pick one could envision. He drafted two tight ends in the third round—marking the first time the team had selected two TEs since drafting Gronk and Aaron Hernandez in 2010—and in the fifth round, the coach took an unknown kicker from Marshall University with allegedly racist tattoos. He later signed two undrafted free agent quarterbacks from Michigan State and Louisiana Tech, presumably to turn up the heat on Stidham and old friend Brian Hoyer, a journeyman and former Brady backup who was signed in March, marking his third stint with the Patriots.

Meanwhile, the only controversy facing Brady—after the uproars over Spygate, Deflategate, Alex Guerrero, the Aaron Hernandez debacle, and all the contract drama with his former team—was getting caught working out in a park in Tampa that was closed due to the coronavirus pandemic. Mayor Jane Castor quickly apologized to the GOAT for what she called a "misunderstanding." Tom, already a local folk hero who trademarked the slogan "Tompa Bay," made a donation to a local charity and all was forgiven.

Tampa Bay and the Patriots are not scheduled to face off until the 2021 regular season, when Brady will be forty-four years old. But you can bet that the legendary quarterback and his equally legendary former coach have each marked the same day on their calendars—February 7, 2021—which is when Super Bowl LV is slated to be played in Brady's new home, Raymond James Stadium in Tampa, Florida.

ACKNOWLEDGMENTS

We were committed to writing this book fairly and accurately. *12* is as much a story about institutional power and corruption as it is about the game of football. All quotes that appear in this book are real and from published sources or sourced interviews. I am very thankful for the cooperation of Tom Brady, Robert and Jonathan Kraft, Stacey James, and DeMaurice Smith and Heather McPhee of the National Football League Players Association. Without their support, this book could not have been written. I feel the same about all the others who contributed to this work. A big thanks to Julian Edelman, James White, Malcolm Mitchell, and Devin McCourty for sharing your Super Bowl stories with us. I personally reached out to the NFL with a request to interview Roger Goodell and was ignored for weeks before I was eventually denied the opportunity during a call with an NFL executive. However, the commissioner's thoughts on the matter are presented in the Wells Report and his public comments. Goodell had the chance to present his case more fully but declined our request.

I also want to acknowledge my coauthor, Dave Wedge. His dedication was invaluable here. I'd like to thank our Hollywood partners, Paul Tamasy and Eric Johnson, who nudged us toward this project, as well as our manager, Ellen Goldsmith-Vein, and our attorney, Barry Littman. On the literary side, I offer a big thank-you to our agent, Peter Steinberg at Foundry Literary & Media in Brooklyn, New York, Alex Rice at the same address, and our editor, Phil Marino, and all the great folks at Little, Brown. On the home front, I'd like to thank once again Kristin York for her unwavering love and support; my studious and talented daughters, Isabella and Mia; my parenting partner and rock, Laura Sherman; my dedicated brother Todd and his son, Jack; my uncle Jimmy; my cousins Mark Sullivan and Paul Rapoza; my stepfather Ken Dodd; and my mother, Diane F. Dodd, who was herself battling cancer while I wrote this book. Your strength inspires me. Finally, I'd like to thank my dear friends Corly Cunningham, Tom Cunningham (no relation), Frank Capolino, Marc Lidsky, Kip Diggs, Huffa Eaton, Jeannie McNown, Ross Peterson, Michael Jermyn, Jason Lucas, Rick Meade, Tim Lus, Jonathan Thompson, George Regan, Pete Barry, and Bobby and Ellen Bandera.

—Casey Sherman

As I am a lifelong Patriots season-ticket holder and a born-and-bred Bostonian, it's been an honor to write this book about one of the most sensational roller-coaster rides in Boston sports history. I have had the pleasure of covering the Patriots at Super Bowls, victory parades, and charitable events over the years at the *Boston Herald,* as well as covering a variety of news stories involving the team, including the Aaron Hernandez murders, the passing of Myra Kraft, and the construction of Patriot Place at Gillette Stadium, among others.

Always, the team has been accommodating and professional, and that is a quality that continued with the writing of this book, so I'd like to thank Robert Kraft and Patriots director of communications Stacey James for their assistance and cooperation. I'd also like to thank Mr. Kraft for keeping the team in Foxborough. My dad and I sat in those same metal benches at Schaefer/Sullivan/ Foxboro Stadium watching some pretty dreadful teams over the years. But we loved those games, and those early Patriots days are some of the best memories that my dad and I have together. So to the whole Patriots organization, especially all the players past and present, thank you.

I'd also like to thank the Patriots players and staff, the NFLPA, DeMaurice Smith and Heather McPhee, Luke O'Neil, and the Hogan Patriots Facebook group for making my Sundays hilarious, even when the Patriots lose. Perhaps especially then. I'd also like to thank my colleagues at VICE; my former colleagues at the *Herald;* my team at State6; the whole Wedge, Cornelius, and Heslam families; all my friends and family from Brockton and Boston College; our editor, Phil Marino, and all at Little, Brown; our agent, Peter Steinberg, and all at Foundry Literary in New York City; our attorney, Barry Littman; my friend Keith Davidson; our entertainment agents at The Gotham Group in Beverly Hills; Phil Gilpin and all at the ITV Fest in Vermont; Kris Meyer; Dick Haley; and especially Casey Sherman for the hard work and collaboration in putting this book together with me. Thank you most of all to my smart, talented, and beautiful wife, Jessica, and my amazing children, Danielle and Jackson. You guys make me so happy.

—Dave Wedge

NOTES

Prologue: San Francisco, California, May 19, 2015

1   Author interview with DeMaurice Smith, 2017.

Chapter One: A Cold Rain

1   Author interview with Bob Kravitz, 2017.

Chapter Two: Storm Fronts

1   Author interview with Bob Kravitz, 2017.
2   Author interview with Kirk Minihane, 2017.
3   The Wells Report.

Chapter Three: Pressure

1   Mike Reiss, "Jim Nantz, Phil Simms Discussion Adds Context to Deflated Football Talk," ESPN.com, January 20, 2015.
2   Will Brinson, "Brad Johnson Paid $7,500 for Altered Balls in Bucs-Raiders Super Bowl," CBS Sports.com, January 21, 2015.
3   Bill Belichick conference call, WEEI Radio, January 19, 2015.
4   Letter of T. David Gardi to Robert Kraft, January 19, 2015.
5   Bryan Curtis, "Mr. Goodell Goes to Washington," Grantland.com, February 4, 2013.
6   Ibid.
7   Roger Goodell alumni profile, Washington & Jefferson College.
8   Glenn Davis, "This Is How the Roger Goodell Era Began," Sportsgrid.com, October 24, 2012.
9   Tex Maule, "The NFL Suspends Its Golden Boy," *Sports Illustrated*, April 29, 1963.
10 Mark Maske, "Owners Pick Goodell as NFL Commissioner," *Washington Post*, August 9, 2006.

Chapter Four: The Ultimate Fan

1   Thomas George, "Kraft a Fan First, Foremost and Forever," *New York Times*, January 31, 2002.
2   Ibid.

3   Mark Pazniokis and Greg Garber, "The Art of Kraft," *Hartford Courant*, December 13, 1998.

4   "Bob Kraft's Prequel to the Patriots," *NFL Films Presents*, December 21, 2016.

5   Peter King, "Kraftwork," *Sports Illustrated*, February 6, 2012.

6   Robert Thomas, "Sold! Time to Call Them the New England Permanents," *New York Times*, January 22, 1994.

7   Dan Shaughnessy, "Bill Parcells Reflects on His Patriots Years," *Boston Globe*, August 2, 2013.

8   *30 for 30: The Two Bills*, dir. Ken Rodgers, ESPN, February 1, 2018.

9   Ibid.

10 Ibid.

Chapter Five: The Underdog

1   Sanjay Kirpalany, "The College Recruitment of Tom Brady," *Bleacher Report*, September 24, 2015.

2   Mitch Stephens, "Brady Was No Goody Two Shoes at Serra High School," MaxPreps.com, January 30, 2015.

3   Dennis O'Donnell, "Former KPIX Producer Looks Back on Dan Fouts Feature on Tom Brady While in High School," KPIX, February 6, 2017.

4   "Tom Brady's High School Posts Local News Interview from 1994," CBS Boston, July 14, 2017.

5   Kirpalany, "The College Recruitment of Tom Brady."

6   "Year of the Quarterback: The Brady Six," prod. Mark Durand and James Weiner, ESPN, April 12, 2011.

7   Michael Rosenberg, "Tom Brady as You Forgot Him," *Sports Illustrated*, January 9, 2012.

8   "Year of the Quarterback: The Brady Six."

9   Stephen J. Nesbitt, "Flashback: Teammates Reflect on Tom Brady–Drew Henson Battle," *Michigan Daily*, August 31, 2012.

10 Dave Caldwell, "Tom Brady's Michigan Days: The Kid Had the Sangfroid to Succeed," *The Guardian*, January 26, 2017.

11 "Illinois Stuns No. 9 Michigan," CBSnews.com, October 23, 1999.

12 "2000 Orange Bowl Postgame," WXYZ-TV, January 1, 2000.

Chapter Six: Game Changers

1   *30 for 30: The Two Bills*, dir. Ken Rodgers, ESPN, February 1, 2018.

2   Ian O'Connor, "Meet Tom Brady's First Believer," ESPN.com, January 16, 2015.

3   "Tom Brady's Pre-Draft Scouting Report," IGN.com, January 24, 2005.

4   O'Connor, "Meet Tom Brady's First Believer."

5   "Year of the Quarterback: The Brady Six," prod. Mark Durand and James

Weiner, ESPN, April 12, 2011.

6   Ibid.

7   O'Connor, "Meet Tom Brady's First Believer."

Chapter Seven: Learning Curve

1   Author interview with Robert Kraft, 2017.

2   "Brady Told Kraft 'I'm the Best Decision This Organization Has Ever Made,'"
     CBS Boston, January 20, 2012.

3   Author interview with Jack Mula, 2017.

4   Mike Freeman, "Belichick Has Patriots' Ears: Now the Hard Part," *New York
     Times,* July 26, 2000.

5   Author interview with Chris Eitzmann, 2017.

6   Author interview with Dave Nugent, 2017.

7   John Dennis, "Flashback Friday—Interview with Rookie Tom Brady," *Patriots To-
     day,* Patriots.com.

8   Author interview with Damon Huard, 2017.

9   Dennis, "Flashback Friday—Interview with Rookie Tom Brady."

Chapter Eight: Taking Hits

1   Author interview with Jermaine Wiggins, 2017.

2   Author interview with Patrick Pass, 2017.

3   Jeremiah Delgado, "Tom Brady and Drew Bledsoe Reflect on Mo Lewis Hit 15
     Years Later," CBS Boston, September 23, 2016.

4   Bill Belichick news conference, Foxboro Stadium, September 25, 2001.

5   Jim Corbett, "Remembering Tom Brady's First-Ever NFL Start against Peyton
     Manning," *USA Today,* January 17, 2014.

6   "Bledsoe Cleared for Return," Patriots.com, November 13, 2001.

Chapter Nine: It's Good!

1   "The Tuck Rule 10 Year Anniversary," ESPN, January 2012.

2   *Tom Brady's First Super Bowl Victory,* NFL Films.

3   Mark Farinella, "Coach's Widow Gets Ring," *Sun Chronicle* (North Attleboro,
     Mass.), March 20, 2002.

Chapter Ten: Legendary Status

1   Author interview with Kerry Byrne, 2017.

2   D'Qwell Jackson interview, Barstool Sports Radio, February 1, 2018.

3   Author interview with DeMaurice Smith, 2017.

4   Ibid.

5   Author interview with Michael Curley, 2017.

Chapter Eleven: "It's About Honor. It's About Respect."

1   Henry McKenna, "Behind Tom Brady's Preparation for Super Bowl LI," *Patriots Wire*, February 2, 2017.
2   Robert Kraft news conference, Indianapolis, January 16, 2015.
3   "Brady Bashing Reaches All-Time High as Ex-Players Slam Tom's Take on Deflategate," Boston.com, January 23, 2015.
4   *Do Your Job: Bill Belichick and the 2014 New England Patriots,* NFL Films, 2015.

Chapter Twelve: Brady's New Team

1   Greg A. Bedard, "Pats Sources: Strong Statements by NFL Officials Left Out of Wells Report," *Sports Illustrated*, May 11, 2015.
2   Gabriel Sherman, "The Season from Hell: Inside Roger Goodell's Ruthless Football Machine," *GQ*, January 19, 2015.
3   Tyler Lauletta, "Roger Goodell's Contract Demands Reportedly Include $50 Million Per Year and a Private Jet," BusinessInsider.com, November 13, 2017.

Chapter Thirteen: Power Play

1   Author interview with DeMaurice Smith, 2017.
2   Author interview with Heather McPhee, 2017.
3   Wells Report Executive Summary, 5.
4   John Branch, "The Deflategate Scientists Unlock Their Lab," *New York Times*, September 21, 2016.
5   Wells Report Executive Summary, 9.
6   "Reaction to Wells Report: Colts' LB Says Brady Cheated," NFL.com, May 6, 2015.
7   Austin Ngaruiya, "Tom Brady's Father Accuses NFL of Framing His Son," *USA Today*, May 7, 2015.
8   Tom Brady interview with Jim Gray, Salem State College, May 7, 2015.
9   "NFL Suspends Tom Brady for 4 Games," ESPN.com, May 12, 2015.

Chapter Fourteen: Kraft's Counterattack

1   D'Qwell Jackson interview, Barstool Sports Radio, February 1, 2018.
2   "League Failure to Correct Misinformation," *The Wells Report in Context*.
3   Gerry Boyle, "Deal Maker: Robyn Glaser Makes It Happen for the Kraft Group and New England Patriots," *Colby Magazine*, 2017.
4   *The Wells Report in Context*.
5   Extra Mustard staff, "Patriots Fans Arrested at NFL Headquarters Now Celebrate Super Bowl Victory," SI.com, February 6, 2017.
6   President Obama's speech welcoming NE Patriots to the White House, April 23, 2015.

Chapter Fifteen: Tom Brady vs. the NFL

1 National Football League Management Council & National Football League v. NFLPA & Tom Brady, United States Court of Appeals for the Second Circuit, Nos. 15-2801 (L), 15-2805 (Con), May 31, 2016.
2 DeMaurice Smith interview, "Outside the Lines," ESPN, May 22, 2015.
3 Don Van Natta Jr. and Seth Wickersham, "Roger Goodell Has a Jerry Jones Problem and Nobody Knows How It Will End," ESPN.com, November 17, 2017.
4 *The 2014 Patriots Super Bowl Ring Ceremony*, NFL Films Presents.
5 Pat Bradley, "Tom Brady Takes Jabs at Peyton Manning in Private, Unsealed Emails," NESN.com, August 25, 2015.
6 NFLPA, "National Football League in the Matter of Thomas Brady, Appeal Hearing, Tuesday, June 23, 2015," transcript.
7 Ibid.

Chapter Sixteen: Highs and Lows

1 "Judge Richard M. Berman's Decision on Tom Brady DeflateGate Suspension," *Washington Post*, September 3, 2015.
2 Author interview with Tom Brady, 2017.
3 *Tom vs Time*, episode 1, *The Physical Game*, HBO Watch, January 25, 2018.

Chapter Seventeen: Isolation

1 Zack Cox, "Patriots Officially Jimmy Garoppolo's Team as Tom Brady's Suspension Begins," NESN.com, September 4, 2016.
2 Author interview with Ryan McManus, 2017.
3 "Brady Strong," *NFL 360*, prod. Andrea Kremer, NFL Network, October 20, 2017.
4 Adam Kurkjian, "Tom Brady Honors Late QB Coach Tom Martinez in Facebook Post," *Boston Herald*, February 22, 2016.
5 Daniel Mano, "Tom Brady Visits Michigan for First Time Since 1999, Plays Catch with Jim Harbaugh," *Mercury News* (San Jose, Calif.), September 21, 2016.

Chapter Eighteen: The Return

1 Author interview with Robert Kraft, 2017.
2 Jim McBride, "Tom Brady's Return Creates a Buzz at Patriots Practice," *Boston Globe*, October 5, 2016.
3 Author interview with Devin McCourty, 2017.
4 Ian O'Connor, "Now You've Pissed Off the GOAT: Tom Brady Returns," ESPN.com, October 7, 2016.
5 Author interview with Ted Karras, 2017.
6 Author interview with Julian Edelman, 2017.
7 Erik Scalavino, "Brady's Back and Almost All Is Well," Patriots.com, October 9, 2016.

Chapter Nineteen: Rolling

1   "Dressed for Success," *Boston Globe*, November 21, 2007.
2   Ibid.
3   "Brady Shows No Ruts in Return as Pats Romp," Reuters, October 10, 2016.
4   "Don't Buy the Coachspeak: QB's Return a Big Deal," *Boston Globe*, October 9, 2016.
5   "Tom Brady: Tough Day with Jamie Collins Traded," ESPN.com, October 16, 2016.
6   "It's Time to Start Worrying About the Patriots Defense," *Washington Post*, November 14, 2016.

Chapter Twenty: Freight Train

1   Patriots.com, February 1, 2017.
2   Patriots.com, February 2, 2017.

Chapter Twenty-one: The Ties That Bind

1   "Brady Strong," *NFL 360,* prod. Andrea Kremer, NFL Network, October 20, 2017.
2   *Do Your Job Part 2: Bill Belichick and the New England Patriots,* NFL Network, 2017.
3   Roger Goodell news conference Super Bowl LI, February 1, 2017.
4   Matt Bonesteel, "Roger Goodell Says It Would Be an Honor to Hand the Super Bowl Trophy to Tom Brady," *Washington Post,* January 25, 2017.

Chapter Twenty-two: The Locker Room

1   Author interview with James White, 2017.
2   Ibid.
3   *Do Your Job Part 2: Bill Belichick and the New England Patriots,* NFL Network, 2017.
4   Ibid.
5   Ibid.

Chapter Twenty-three: Fire and Ice

1   Author interview with Jonathan Kraft, 2017.
2   *Do Your Job Part 2: Bill Belichick and the New England Patriots,* NFL Network, 2017.

Chapter Twenty-four: They Will Fight Their Asses Off!

1   *Do Your Job Part 2: Bill Belichick and the New England Patriots,* NFL Network, 2017.
2   Peter King, "Super Bowl 51: Patriots Take the 5th in Epic Comeback," MMQB, February 6, 2017.
3   Author interview with Tom Brady, 2017.
4   *Do Your Job Part 2.*
5   Author interview with Julian Edelman, 2017.
6   Steve Politi, "How a Former Rutgers Player's Speech Reminded the Patriots of Their Strongest Trait," NJ.com, February 6, 2017.

7   Author interview with Tom Brady, 2017.
8   Author interview with Malcolm Mitchell, 2017.
9   *Do Your Job Part 2*.

Chapter Twenty-five: No Room for Error

1   Albert Breer, "For the Brady Family: Redemption," *Sports Illustrated*, February 6,
     2017.
2   Author interview with Robert and Jonathan Kraft, 2017.
3   Daniel S. Levine, "Watch: Mark Wahlberg Leaves Super Bowl Before Patriots'
     Comeback," Heavy.com, February 6, 2017.
4   *Do Your Job Part 2: Bill Belichick and the New England Patriots*, NFL Network, 2017.
5   Ibid.

Chapter Twenty-six: Unsung Heroes

1   Author interview with Malcolm Mitchell, 2017.
2   *Do Your Job Part 2: Bill Belichick and the New England Patriots*, NFL Network, 2017.

Chapter Twenty-seven: The Steep Climb

1   Author interview with Devin McCourty, 2017.

Chapter Twenty-eight: You Gotta Believe

1   Author interview with Malcolm Mitchell, 2017.
2   *Do Your Job Part 2: Bill Belichick and the New England Patriots*, NFL Network, 2017.

Chapter Twenty-nine: Redemption

1   Author interview with Julian Edelman, 2017.
2   Author interview with James White, 2017.
3   Albert Breer, "For the Brady Family: Redemption," *Sports Illustrated*, February 6,
     2017.

Chapter Thirty: The Coach Is King

1   Nicole Yang, "What You Need to Know about Alex Guerrero's Involvement with
     the Patriots," Boston.com, August 29, 2018.
2   Chris Long interview, *NFL GameDay*, February 5, 2018.
3   Jim Gray interview with Tom Brady, Milken Institute Global Conference, May 1, 2018.

Chapter Thirty-one: The Last Hurrah

1   Justin Rogers, "Patriots TE Rob Gronkowski Confirms He Nixed Trade to Li-
     ons," *Detroit News*, September 23, 2018.
2   Tom E. Curran, "Guerrero Statement on Edelman Stresses 'Legal Approach to
     Training,'" NBC Sports Boston, June 7, 2018.

3   Author interview with Devin McCourty, 2020.

4   *America's Game: 2018 New England Patriots,* NFL Network.

5   Author interview with Duron Harmon, 2020.

Chapter Thirty-two: Bitter Ends and New Beginnings

1   Author interview with Joe Tessitore, 2020.

2   John Breech, "Is Tom Brady Getting Frustrated? QB Apparently Said He Was 'Miserable' during Recent Interview," CBSsports.com, November 22, 2019.

3   Peter King, "FMIA Wild Card: Tom Brady the Pragmatist Controls His NFL Future," ProFootballTalk, January 22, 2020.

4   Statements from Patriots chairman and CEO Robert Kraft and head coach Bill Belichick on quarterback Tom Brady, March 17, 2020.

SELECT BIBLIOGRAPHY

Author Interviews

Tom Brady, quarterback, New England Patriots
Robert Kraft, owner, New England Patriots
Jonathan Kraft, president, New England Patriots
Stacey James, vice president of media relations, New England Patriots
DeMaurice Smith, executive director, NFLPA
Heather McPhee, attorney, NFLPA
James White, running back, New England Patriots
Malcolm Mitchell, receiver, New England Patriots
Julian Edelman, receiver, New England Patriots
Devin McCourty, safety, New England Patriots
Ted Karras, offensive lineman, New England Patriots
Jermaine Wiggins, former New England Patriot
Joe Andruzzi, former New England Patriot
Damon Huard, former New England Patriot
Patrick Pass, Former New England Patriot
Chris Eitzmann, former New England Patriot
Dave Nugent, former New England Patriot
Jack Mula, former New England Patriot executive
Ryan McManus, former Dartmouth College receiver
Kerry Byrne, Cold Hard Football Facts
Kirk Minihane, WEEI Radio
Luke O'Neil, *Esquire*
Bob Kravitz, columnist, WTHR, Indianapolis, Indiana
Michael Curley, Cape Cod resident

Documents and Books

Gardi, T. David. Letter to Robert Kraft, January 19, 2015.
Halberstam, David. *The Education of a Coach.* Boston: Hachette Book Group, 2005.
Holley, Michael. *Belichick and Brady.* Boston: Hachette Book Group, 2016.
National Football League Management Council & National Football League v. NFLPA

& Tom Brady, United States Court of Appeals for the Second Circuit, Nos. 15-2801 (L), 15-2805 (Con), May 31, 2016.

Price, Christopher. *Drive for Five: The Remarkable Run of the 2016 Patriots.* New York: St. Martin's Press, 2017.

Weiss, Paul. *The Wells Report: Investigative Report Concerning Footballs Used During the AFC Championship Game on January 18, 2015.* Rifkind, Wharton & Garrison, LLP.

The Wells Report in Context. Patriots.com.

INDEX

ABOUT THE AUTHORS

Casey Sherman is a *New York Times* bestselling author of *The Finest Hours* (now a major motion picture) and nine other books, including *Above and Beyond; Boston Strong,* inspiration for the feature film *Patriots Day,* and *The Ice Bucket Challenge,* now in development for a major motion picture (both coauthored by Dave Wedge); and *A Rose for Mary: The Hunt for the Real Boston Strangler.* He is also an award-winning journalist and recipient of the Edward R. Murrow Award for Journalistic Excellence and the prestigious Truth & Justice Award given by the Cold Case Research Institute, and has been nominated for an Emmy Award. He is also a contributing writer for *Esquire,* the *Huffington Post,* and FoxNews.com. He has appeared on more than one hundred television programs and outlets, including CNN, Fox News, the *Today* show, C-SPAN, *Unsolved Mysteries,* the History Channel, *ABC World News Tonight, The CBS Evening News,* Discovery, the Travel Channel, and even *The View.* He is the founding partner of Whydah Productions. He is also a sought-after public speaker and is represented by APB Speakers Bureau. He can be reached on Facebook and on Twitter at caseysherman123. He lives in Massachusetts.

Dave Wedge is a writer based in Boston. He writes for *Vice* and was an investigative journalist for the *Boston Herald* for fourteen years. His first book, *Boston Strong: A City's Triumph over Tragedy,* written with *New York Times* bestselling author Casey Sherman, was adapted into the film *Patriots Day,* starring Mark Wahlberg. Wedge and Sherman teamed up again for *The Ice Bucket Challenge: Pete Frates and the Fight Against ALS,* which is in development as a feature film. *12* is their third collaboration. They are also partners in Whydah Productions, an entertainment content development company. Wedge is a graduate of Boston College and has also written for *Esquire, Newsweek, DigBoston, Boston,* and *Noisey.* He has hosted a radio show on WRKO 680-AM in Boston and is a regular radio and TV commentator who has appeared on CNN, MSNBC, CBC (Canada), CNBC, Fox, E!, and CBS.